Global Technology and Corporate Crisis

Accelerating change, the 24 hour news cycle, and an increasingly complex web of attitudes, opinions, perceptions and misperceptions are generating a volatile, shifting and potent array of risks and threats for business and corporate management. The challenging environment now taking shape is moving at internet speed, the message constantly changing direction and content, distorted and altered by individuals and groups exploiting the power of technology to pursue agendas that may have little to do with the risk itself.

How can tomorrow's managers react and respond? *Global Technology and Corporate Crisis* explores the collision of emerging technology, corporate vulnerabilities and new flows and counter-flows of information and communications. It argues for radical and urgent changes to business practice and planning which demand an innovative approach to analysing and managing the interaction of communication and management under crisis conditions, with serious implications for sudden disaster as well as latent, long running risks.

If business is to survive and recover, a major shift is needed that embraces corporate culture, operational planning and the key role of communication in the information revolution. This innovative and readable text meets the challenge head on and will be invaluable reading for all those involved in the strategic management of technology, reputation and corporate communications.

Simon Moore specialises in international corporate communication, public affairs, issues management, risk communication and crisis preparedness. He is Associate Professor in Information Design and Corporate Communication, Bentley College, Waltham, Massachusetts, USA.

Mike Seymour is International Director of Crisis and Issues Management at the global PR firm Edelman, and is based in London. An internationally experienced crisis manager and planner, Mike Seymour provides strategic and communications counsel to senior management teams as they face major issues and emergencies. Drawing upon his experience of leading multi-disciplined teams, he is a regular lecturer and media commentator in the crisis management and planning fields.

Global Technology and Corporate Crisis

Strategies, planning and communication in the information age

Simon Moore and
Mike Seymour

Routledge
Taylor & Francis Group

LONDON AND NEW YORK

First published 2005
by Routledge
2 Park Square, Milton Park, Abingdon, Oxon OX14 4RN

Simultaneously published in the USA and Canada
by Routledge
270 Madison Ave, New York, NY 10016

Routledge is an imprint of the Taylor & Francis Group

© 2005 Simon Moore and Mike Seymour

Typeset in Perpetua and Bell Gothic by
Book Now Ltd
Printed and bound in Great Britain by
MPG Books Ltd, Bodmin

British Library Cataloguing in Publication Data
A catalogue record for this book is available from the British Library

Library of Congress Cataloging in Publication Data
A catalog record for this book has been requested

ISBN 0–415–36596–1 (hbk)
ISBN 0–415–36597–X (pbk)

The structure of the multiverse is defined by information flow.
David Deutsch. *The Structure of the Multiverse* (2001: 1, 2)

Nothing annihilates an inhibition as irresistibly as anger does it.
William James. *Varieties of Religious Experience* (1901–2: 290)

Contents

Acknowledgements

We want to acknowledge advice, support and friendship from students, colleagues, friends, families and organisations. They include the Bobiash family; Jon Boroshok; everyone in Bentley College's Information Design and Corporate Communication Department: particularly Bill Buchholz, Linda Gallant, Bill Gribbons, Roland Hubscher, Mary Marcel, Terry Skelton and Gail Wessel; Don Chand; Jacqueline Curthoys; Gary David; Emma Joyes; Mildred Kelley; Martin Langford; Byron Lew; Mildred Lundstrom; Bruce MacNaughton; Mike Michielin; Daniele M. Morgan; Adam, Anna, Terry and Tessa Moore; Sandra den Otter; Cliff Putney; Maureen Robusto; Stuart Smith; Javed Siddiqi; Sri Vasudevan.

We are grateful to those who gave permission to quote their work and wish to apologise to anyone we have been unable to reach or whose material we may unwittingly have made use of. If any such person contacts us, we will gladly give due acknowledgement.

The names of people and organisations used in the 'Labaddia' case are fictitious and not intended to resemble any person or organisation.

Introduction

As answers become devalued, questions become more valued. We have lived for a very long time in an answer-based society.

Roger C. Schank. *The Next Fifty Years* (2002: 209)

PROBLEMS

'How can a man in a cave outcommunicate the world's leading communications society?' The question was asked by former US special envoy Richard Holbrooke, who was reflecting on Osama Bin Laden's appeal to many Muslims. The answers, recorded in the 9/11 Commission's Final Report on the terrorist attacks upon the USA (9/11 Commission 2004: 377), should reverberate through leaders and organisations everywhere in the world, businesses not least among them.

Al-Qaeda has a 'media group', according to operative testimony (Bergen 2002: 31). Bin Laden understands how much now hinges on the manipulation of communication, more than even a mere decade ago. This manipulation, he and all of us know, is made possible by globally available technology. Our book explores how technology has shaped the corporate crisis environment. It argues that communication is accruing unprecedented power to itself both in times of disaster and over active but not yet erupting risks or threatening issues. We try to look forward, review what little has been said so far and make recommendations for the new century, believing that future-watching is a shared academic and managerial responsibility. We have tried to picture the new crisis-topography for business around the world; and risked what might conservatively be called 'informed projections' – but not predictions. At any rate, chances must be taken when considering the future, and in writing this book we are accepting the risks associated with them and welcome all comment.

Our research risks breadth as well, for corporate threats are pouring from a crucible heated by society, politics and technology quite as much as by corporate activities and operational decisions. Crisis and the way that threats are starting to express themselves to business means leaders, managers and interested scholars must now try to understand much more about once irrelevant corners of that larger world. This broad effort should not be seen as negating the drama and uniqueness of a specific disaster whether looming or breaking. Business disaster is always very harsh but because of planet-wide changes its face is changing and so is the damage it can do. Global business, warns the head of the multinational public relations (PR) firm Edelman, 'cannot cede public dialogue on big issues to regulators, governments, or NGOs [Non-Government Organisations]' (Edelman Worldwide 2004: 5).

It is also plain that finding convincing, threat-reducing answers to stakeholder demands is getting harder. Schank's introductory comment reminds us that inaccurate and accurate answers alike can be objects of suspicion. It is getting easier to ask questions and ask them rapidly. The belief (and a belief or perception in crisis and risk communications can become more powerful than a fact), voiced at least since the start of the industrial revolution, that the world is getting 'faster'. The latest acceleration of questions, decision and actions owes everything to globally distributed communication technology and in the field of crisis it is fair to say that because of this humans have reached an historic point. Technology is pushing rates of information provision and exchange to astonishing speeds and volumes. We find it inconceivable that this still-embryonic development, already affecting so much business activity, will leave untouched the way sudden crises and latent threats to corporate stability will rise and unfold. It is consequently inconceivable that this does not change the way business must respond.

We therefore suggest, unoriginally, that the information revolution creates urgent issues for the task of crisis management. We believe, more specifically, that the size, nature and breadth of these changes now developing – especially the threats – demand new approaches to corporate vulnerabilities, and that technology's opening up of the planet for business, and the ways in which businesses are learning to pursue the new opportunities, require revolutionary change inside corporations that accepts the essence of the information revolution – the communication of information itself, especially in volatile conditions. These and other changes technology is triggering in the crisis arena cannot all be controlled, and might not be admitted, but they are certainly occurring.

Maybe denying there is a problem is a natural reaction. One of the authors of this book has written elsewhere: 'At times when serious issues, problems or emergencies are catapulting organisations under a relentless spotlight, this discouraging trend leads corporate managers to conclude that communicating is too difficult or even positively dangerous' (Seymour 2004: 25). The premise of *Global Technology and Corporate Crisis* is that communication is more important than ever before. It is forging a highly volatile crisis structure, a prism concentrating then scattering powerful change agents across the traditional spectrum of corporate activities:

- Globally available technology rearranges the way groups, individuals and societies communicate. In the process it reshapes global attitudes to the organisations that affect those groups, individuals and societies.
- This rearrangement does not leave communication technology content to be the conduit for information exchange about vulnerabilities or disasters; it must also be the cause, participant, and agent of resolution. Communication is the arbiter of corporate fates.
- All this activity is fuelled by a confused, constantly fragmenting but always onrushing stream of emotion.
- These changes do not simply require a reform of existing crisis strategies; they force corporate leaders to radically re-examine internal and external cultures, to reinvent their approach to communication, in the new communication order.
- This re-examination depends upon senior management grasping what communication is becoming, and what it can do.
- A complex communication strategy must now be a top corporate responsibility.

Certainly, there is nothing new in this conflation of technology, threat and radical social change; nothing new, either, in the denial of critical change by some, or the exploitation of it by others. Nor is there anything unprecedented about overlooking communication's true influence in all this. Other volatile epochs in history repay study. In the mid-nineteenth century, for example, the technology of war had essentially not changed since Bonaparte but by the 1860s several drastic changes appeared at once. Mass-produced rifled and breech loaded firearms were capable of projecting bullets and shells further, faster and more accurately than their smooth-bore, muzzle loaded predecessors. The expansion of rail networks allowed armies to be carried in large numbers and rapidly concentrated at carefully chosen destinations. Like the current information revolution, these technological leaps had large organisational consequences and Michael Howard's seminal history of the 1870–1 Franco-Prussian War records some of them. Rifled, breech loading weaponry made useless the basic military strategy of the previous 150 years, founded on less accurate weaponry, massed lines of defenders and attackers firing at close range, and ensured the rise of individuals acting on their own initiative in accordance with a general plan. Railroads meant that, instead of smaller armies of tough, fit professionals, massive massed armies of less well trained civilian conscripts – useless in former times when marching armies covered long distances and survived off the land – could be carried swiftly with their provisions to planned 'jumping off' points (Howard 1962: 1).

The organisational consequences had a social impact. Mass armies convinced far-sighted leaders that major continental European powers – including France and

Prussia – must urgently reorganise their societies to incorporate the training and service of millions of young men, and induct them into a new social system revolving around long service in a conscript army and reserve. A reorganisation of society in turn meant reorganising public perceptions of that society, which meant influencing the public communication process. Prussia achieved the necessary changes more fully, less imperfectly and much faster than its rival France.

In common with the railroads, technology was forcing, as it is today, a massive acceleration in the carriage of information and opinion from its origin into the public domain. Telegraph wires sent instantaneous communication across countries and continents; a large popular press fought for readers by seeking out and striking veins of powerful public emotion. That all these changes and ferments would perilously widen existing emotionally sensitive fault lines at a certain place and time in Europe was probably unavoidable and came about in July 1870 at the German spa town of Ems. A local telegraph office transmitted a message from a Prussian official about a brusque encounter between the Prussian King and the French Ambassador over the inflammable issue of the Royal Succession in Spain. The 'Ems Telegram', as it was later known, reached the Prussian Minister-President, later her 'Iron Chancellor', Otto von Bismarck, at dinner in Berlin. Bismarck grasped the full emotive potential of the message at a time when French and Prussian relations were approaching rupture and public emotions were running high. He edited it, not to insert untruths, but to give radical emphasis to useful points of tension, and then released it to the media. Bismarck's exploitation of new communication technology unleashed a storm of public emotion in both France and Germany that produced the expected war at a time of his own choosing, and the defeat and humiliation of France six months later at the hands of a mass army, concentrated at the French border by rail, with the enthusiastic consent of the civilian population from whose ranks the army had been drawn.

Threats and exploding crises, whether military or corporate, will always be with us, but themes similar to those that produced intense volatility in 1870 are at work again. Technology, much of it technology for the transmission of information and opinion, is forcing organisational change; organisations are shaping and driving social changes, which in turn are creating instability, energy and uncertainty, all of which may be harnessed and directed by those who know how to communicate. In these conditions, corporate officers must reappraise communication's dilemmas as much as they hasten to exploit its opportunities.

The new dilemmas are grave indeed. At the furthest and darkest end of Threat's sombre spectrum, Sir Martin Rees, Astronomer Royal and Professor of Cosmology and Astrophysics at Cambridge University, is deeply worried about the prospects for this new century. In *Our Final Hour* (2004) he assesses the fatal perils that science presents to our planet – nuclear, genetic, computer generated, biochemical, nanotechnological. One of Sir Martin's central ideas is that, with the end of the two-bloc cold war and the incredible expansion in human access to knowledge and technology, myriad rogue individuals and lunatic groups can now gather earth-shattering technology into their hands and use it – 'there are', he warns, 'alarmingly many ways in which individuals will be able to trigger a catastrophe' (Rees 2003: 3). One of his supporting points is global emotional instability created by 'ever more persuasive communication media' (65): 'Instant communications mean that the psychological impact of even a local disaster has worldwide repercussions on attitudes and behaviour' (62).

Of course, if planetary Armageddon, or at least a mighty series of civilisation-wrecking calamities, is truly and irresistibly nigh, there is nothing more to say even in a book about crisis, so we prefer for now to concentrate on the two latter points of Rees's thesis: how individuals will use technology and particularly communication technology to trigger and exploit threats and crises; and the impact of the new conditions on stakeholder attitudes and behaviour. What do they mean for a business confronted by the possibility of its own Armageddon, in the form of a twenty-first-century corporate crisis? For business too, can hardly evade the consequences of what could be termed the 'democratisation of destruction', and the catalyst to our interactions presented by the information revolution, which has scarcely started and which, barring a conclusive global cataclysm, does not seem set to decelerate.

It is our contention that the world is more threatening for company officers than it was just a few years ago. Technology's new powers to punish businesses, and to communicate about their actions, are indeed interlinked – more profoundly and seriously than is usually grasped. Many companies must urgently reassess what communication strategy means to them, their stakeholders, their subcontractors and employees. They must learn to talk differently, because technology can fuse information, perception, opinion, strong emotion and the impulse to punish. For some threats, this is the work of moments. Is the power of communication in this new century actually vindicating, most visibly in the shape of corporate disaster, the Scottish Enlightenment philosopher David Hume (1711–76) and his dispiriting theory that humans are mere bundles of perception: open to the force and violence of received impressions and ideas?

We have said that companies, countries or international organisations fighting future crises, or containing damaging issues, must learn to adjust their methods and their culture. This is not an impossible task, any more than its causes need scare us into immobility. Like opportunities, crises are the inevitable offspring of whatever the prevailing environment happens to be. Changes to that environment bring changes to existing crises, along with the introduction of new forms of disaster. This is certainly the case with the Information Technology (IT). But something can be done about it. We are adaptable organisms after all. It is not yet the case that business leaders are readying their organisations for the new threat. They are largely overlooking the stronger role of communication.

There is naturally far more understanding among executives of the information age's commercial potential. IT gives customers around the world the gift of ecommerce, more product choices and more information about those choices. With technology, managers free themselves from expensive and now 'non-core' functions by turning to increased outsourcing. The coordination of global operations is improved, including marketing international brands or corporate identities (Moore 2004: 29).

Public, media and corporations alike – whenever they do consider the part technology plays in crisis – usually focus on technology's ability to trigger disaster by accidental or malicious systems failure. Attention is paid to hackers, worms, viruses or accidental breaches of privacy and security. But technology's role in a crisis is bigger and subtler than that. IT is profoundly affecting all causes of crises and generating many new threats; from terrorism to corruption, health scares to product recall. Fighting these crises in the information age must continue to address how information is managed, crafted and used, but information will not be used properly in future unless Business understands the changing communication environment (Moore 2004: 29).

This understanding comes in two parts, and the danger is that the understanding will be incomplete; that the importance of communication will be belatedly perceived, but the full nature of the information revolution will not. Even entities usually alert to communication – namely political and governmental organisations – are flirting with this danger.

In the corporate world, it often takes a violent shock for companies to change their communication relationship with stakeholders. That change does occasionally include the necessary revision of corporate culture – the culture that created the communication that helped decide the intensity of the crisis experience, and much of the damage sustained. In relations between America and the Middle East, for example, violent shocks have certainly occurred, and some revision is underway. The United States Government operates in the conditions arising from the terrorist murders of September 11, 2001. 'The United States', a US Muslim scholar of international relations recently remarked 'is suffering from a crisis of legitimacy in the Muslim world and overcoming it must be the first priority' (Khan 2003: 87). It is inconceivable that communication has no part to play in that process: but what should that part be?

Without doubt, the need for public communication to play a more sophisticated part in the Middle East is agreed by many influential politicians and diplomats. The first steps were taken almost at once by the United States Government in the wake of September 11 (9/11). An Under-Secretary of Public Diplomacy and Public Affairs was appointed at the State Department, charged with 'engaging, informing and influencing key international audiences' to help 'to advance US interests and security and to provide the moral basis for US leadership in the world' (State Department 2003). Over 15 private and Governmental groups reported on the communication challenge after 9/11, among them the Djerejian Committee, which was asked by Congress to investigate US public diplomacy in the Arab and Muslim world. The Committee ended its 2003 report with words which must resonate among leaders of many multinational corporations, American or otherwise:

> A process of unilateral disarmament in the weapons of advocacy over the last decade has contributed to widespread hostility toward Americans which has left us vulnerable to lethal threats to our interests and our safety.
>
> (Djerejian Committee 2003: 14)

At the same time, former House Speaker Newt Gingrich warned in the July/August edition of *Foreign Policy*:

> To lead the world, the United States needs to communicate effectively. This crucial capability must receive adequate resources, and the State Department must learn to fulfill this role. . . . A country this large and powerful must work every day to communicate what it is doing. The world does not have to love us, but it must be able to predict us.
>
> (Gingrich 2003: 46)

The United States Advisory Committee on Public Diplomacy has responded to this charge with several recommendations: more resources for American Presence Posts – in the shape of information officers charged with communication responsibilities in American embassies and consulates; the expansion of 'American Corners' – a library, or other information forum organised by local residents; deploying the resources of the internet to widen the concept of virtual consulates by funnelling consular services through locally branded web addresses (Advisory Commission on Public Diplomacy 2003).

'We frequently hear that the Americans are sort of one-way communicators', the coordinator for the United States State Department's International Information Programs conceded at a briefing. 'We are also exploring new ways of using the Internet – not new to the world but new to the State Department – but using moderated discussions' (State Department Briefing 2003a). He later remarked: 'The important thing is that we need to apply all of our resources to figuring out what the most effective way of communicating is. That is a very critical priority' (State Department Briefing 2003). Nevertheless, in February 2004, another one-way communication platform was launched. United States-funded TV channel Al Hurrah ('The Free One' in Arabic) began broadcasting in the Middle East, joining other efforts such as *Hi* magazine and radio Sawa. 'Where do they get this stuff from?' complained one Lebanese journalist, 'Why do they keep insulting us like this?' ('Unhip' 2004)

While the response to US communication efforts from its target audiences has not been unanimously favourable, there are other signs that the United States Government has understood the first part of the change, perceiving the importance of communication, but is wrestling with the second – the need to satisfy twenty-first-century audience communication expectations. Heavy public emphasis is placed on:

- *One-way communication from source to audience, with audience opinion sought only in order to better refine an existing message.* The recently-established White House Office of Global Communication, was apparently formed because 'President Bush understands the importance of conveying America's message to the world' (Office of Global Communication 2003). Whether State Department or White House, a view exists that public diplomacy equals an effective explanation of American policy and actions. This rather rigid view is not softened by the 'Innovative Communication Concepts' recommended by the Advisory Commission and outlined above, where the proposals are largely methods of distributing information and gauging public opinion without engaging it.
- *Apparent marginalisation of the senior strategic expertise of professional communicators.* Of the seven-person State Department Advisory Committee on Public Diplomacy in 2004, one only is a professional international communicator.
- *Focus on the news media.* The 'one-way' view of the communication process also finds expression in a heavy focus on using news media to get America's message across. Attempts are also made to moderate or control the metastasizing media environment which in any case, despite the launch of US backed magazines and TV stations, runs beyond the writ of America and her allies. 'The global marketplace of news and information is no longer dominated by the United States', warned a US legal scholar in a critique of Al-Jazeera, the controversial satellite news station ('Mass media' 2002).

As this book was nearing completion, a report on 'Strategic Communication' by the Pentagon's advisers on the Defense Science Board built substantially on the Djerejian Committee's earlier work, candidly and in 111 pages of penetrating detail:

> Information saturation means attention, not information, becomes a scarce resource. Power flows to credible messengers. Asymmetrical credibility matters. What's around information is critical. Reputations count. Brands are important. Editors, filters and cue givers are essential. *Fifty years ago political struggles were about the ability to control and transmit scarce information. Today, political struggles are about the creation and destruction of credibility.*
>
> (Office of the Under Secretary of State for Defense 2004: 20;
> emphasis in original)

Institutionally-generated, marketing-dominated, one-way, campaign-based approaches to achieving understanding, agreement and acceptance certainly cannot engage with a feeling, expressed by British economic historian Lord Robert Skidelsky, that:

'The world history of the future cannot be written according to an exclusive American script' (Skidelsky 2003: 50). In an intense geopolitical setting: 'Strategic communication is not *the* problem, but it is *a* problem' (Office of the Under Secretary of State for Defense 2004: 2).

Business worldwide grapples with precisely the same themes, and must also find communication solutions for the times. New scripts are being written for global commerce by international audiences, freely-operating and uncontrollable influencers driving opinion by forging a powerful relationship with technology. This book gauges their especial impact on business. In a world characterised as one of latent disaster, preventive communication must become a central corporate strategy. In this new corporate world, the world of global technology and corporate crisis, strategic communication may well not be *a* problem, but *the* problem.

Technology will force threatened businesses to understand that communicating about crisis or vulnerable issues is not subsidiary to the more familiar communications like marketing, human resources or public relations. The nexus of global technology and corporate crisis means that communication as a coordinated whole is becoming *the* function, perhaps the only function that everyone concerned with a business has in common, from within or without. This function cannot be left to operate independently, or be conducted on behalf of a business according to the tastes or prejudices of particular executives in particular jobs. Communication changes things, and is of itself changing.

THE BOOK

The first part of *Global Technology and Corporate Crisis* investigates the communication environment's shift, and how it is changing the conditions and strategy of crisis, risks and issues.

In Part One, it is asked how emerging technology will cause corporate crises, participate in them, and affect our thinking about them: our perceptions of events, our decisions, our view of the main actors, and the people whose opinions we trust. We assess the changing nature of the 'general public', the threats to 'rational' communication in a high-speed society and its impact on the crisis lifecycle, equipped with the technology to take instant, painless decisions about a company, and examine the rise of new opinion-leaders, who owe their influence solely to their ability to understand the online world. We ask why companies are growing more exposed to crises, discuss the stresses placed on information storage and retrieval, and longer-term tensions presented by recurrent risks and issues.

We say in Part One that these developments call for a new perspective on crisis management, and the management of information, and for a new relationship between communication, perception, reputation and brands, to safeguard trust and credibility in the coming decade.

Part Two lays out practical proposals for preparing and managing information age crises. We suggest a crisis response that better reflects the unstable, faster, dispersed transparent society in which business is starting to operate, and enables communication at even greater speed than at present. A reform of risk and issues communication strategies is also investigated, which recognises the new balance being struck between likeability, emotion and objectivity. Steps for identifying and building continuous relationships with new audiences are suggested. All these subjects are then consolidated in a wider examination of communication strategy, and a positive reappraisal of its proper place in any organisation concerned about its reputation.

We have also prepared a fictional disaster, which appears throughout the book. It tries to demonstrate, in a vivid, immediate way, how drastically the nature of crisis, risks and issues is changing, and growing more critical to the existence of companies big and small, regional or multinational. Like the rest of the book, it asks today's leaders, managers and business students to consider the consequences of interacting with a widening technological world moved by fears and hopes that go far beyond their customary professional responsibilities. By reappraising communication they will master the threats – and discover the opportunities – of the information age. This book is both an inquiry, and an exercise in assistance.

Part One

Shocks and the system: the coming crisis environment

LABADDIA I

How long have I been on your buddy list?

Does it bother you Etsuko?

I suppose not but I'd like to know how you got hold of me.

Google scholar.

I didn't even know I was on it. We're just civil servants who met online. We're not powerful or anything.

But you will be.

*

Jennifer Stone, at that moment, was badly missing her old job in the healthcare technology sector. This really was too much. But it was also too late. She involuntarily squinted, trying to reduce to a blur the rows of men hacking at pigs' heads.

'It's the last butchery operation we've got left in Europe', Roger Thomas was telling her. 'End of the year we're switching to machines. There may be one other in Argentina but I'm not sure.'

The trouble is, Jennifer reflected as they made their way down the reassuringly wide aisle, industry just isn't nice to look at. Especially the food industry. Today, it was the realisation that food actually was an industry that struck her; passing between the men in protective chain mail vests and arm guards, and their thudding knives.

'They're all properly qualified butchers, you know', Thomas said. 'On good money. We can't play games here.'

'What's going on here?'

'Cheeks and foreheads. For our Wychwood & Stevenson Gold Medal pâté range.' He watched Stone grimace involuntarily, and moved in with his favourite line to new executives since Corporate's relocation. 'Welcome to your company. Don't get to see what it's all about down in London, do you? Living the high life in nice offices – the dolce bloody vita. No smells. Well this is the food industry this is – after today, you can forget all about it and stick to Powerpoint presentations and strategic planning: whatever that is. Excuse me one second – must check something.' He walked over to a nearby foreman.

Yes, it was a basically fair if slightly childish, defensive, obvious and exaggerated point. Stone accepted that. And yes, technology was so spick and span, so twenty-first century, at least when it wasn't processing meat. When Stone decided to switch from hi tech to food manufacturing, it was the food part that had attracted her, not the manufacturing. But the fact was – and there was no other way of looking at it – that feeding millions of people processed meat inevitably involved smells and sights that would revolt the average person. Yes, she realised the average person knows that, understands that this is what has to happen, and is prepared to look the other way, so it's not *exactly* a PR issue *per se*.

It's the things people don't know that do the damage, the momentum bestowed by shock, and powerlessness; and in any case clean, safe technology had its messy revelations. She stopped to check her emails, remembering as she fished for the mobile the activists and celebs who 'helped' the mobile phone industry 'accept' that their product contained Congolese coltan – a highly conductive mineral torn from a national park in the heart of Africa by desperate men, women and children; funnelled through a wrecked ecosystem by warlords and finally put into the bright shiny gadgets displayed at electrical goods stores. Of course the telecommunications industry reacted – found another source of supply almost instantly – supply chains did incredible things nowadays. Mind you, that decision destroyed the precarious livelihoods of many desperate people in the Congo, but how far down the economic chain can companies think? Yes, it was helpful just now, watching the butchers at work, to recall that tech too has – literally – dirty secrets. Next year, what's more, it would provide Labaddia with machines to butcher pigs faster and cheaper.

And in any case, food manufacturing wasn't so bad. In fact it was interesting: a complex blend of law, industry, politics, product safety, marketing and plain honest consumption. Her new employer, Labaddia, supplied superior meat products across Europe, South America and Asia.

Thomas returned and pushed open a set of doors, leading to a small tiled chamber. 'Don't worry – we all get used to it', he said over his shoulder. 'It's much nicer at the other end. Mainly smoked foods and pâtés here, nicely wrapped. Some of it's processed on the other side of the site, pie filling for that new baked goods line in Salford. We'll see it in a bit.'

Stone already knew what they made here. She had been soaking up information all week and still felt as if she'd scratched the surface. Labaddia, before that Atkinson Quality Meats, before that Atkinson and Son Family Butchers of Durham, UK, established 1901, now operated facilities in twenty-three countries, either under its own name or local affiliates. Revenue down 4 per cent this year to €900 million.

They splashed through a shallow bath of disinfectant. 'Here's another little surprise for you', Thomas grinned maliciously and started off again. 'Don't see much of this back at Corporate eh? Well, take a good look – it's why you're living it up in London – going to all those PR lunches.'

'Corporate communication, actually.' Jennifer Stone sighed to herself, thinking of Thomas's no doubt inexpensive and large house compared to her small and extremely expensive flat. Some clichés about her chosen profession never seemed to go away.

'Did this pâté really win a Gold Medal?' She asked – maybe there was something there to work with.

'It did. Seoul Expo 2003. Global Chefs Association. I'll say this', Thomas's eyes were serious and unblinking, staring into the mirror at her as he washed his hands, 'it is quite true about this company. I've been here five years and they really do pick the best meat. I've been amazed at what they've turned down. They don't lie. No corners are cut. The label says "finest and best" and it really is true in my opinion and I've been fifteen years in the industry. There's a real commitment to quality here. Now then, let's see the pâté vats. Word of warning: the, uh, environment may surprise you.'

They walked through another set of heavy doors into a wide and high space. A salty, slightly decaying odour hung in the air. Not too bad to begin with.

'We break down the meat and then reform it, in layman's terms.'

'Er – pâté shaped you mean?' Stone climbed some steps and peered into a pinkish-grey liquid.

'Basically, yes. It's in the documentation I gave you. Can't imagine what you're going to do with all that stuff. Means nothing to your average punter.'

'I don't want it for marketing purposes – but if I find anything good we'll use it.'

*

Stone had been hurt before: six years ago, in another place. She knew that food was always a crisis waiting to happen and she wanted to be ready for it. Of course, Roger Thomas couldn't be allowed to know about that just yet, at least not the details. When they were ready with the crisis training plan, then he'd be included. He'd have to be, she realised. This was Labaddia's first and oldest facility – the place where things were most likely to go wrong; one of the places likely to attract attention. It would be the same as it had been with her last company, Bluepage, which made personal alarm systems for the elderly.[†] The day things went wrong there – a customer falling, a failed alarm, an activist group and a well-known brand – the media had gone to the gates: or at least the front door. Cameras, reporters, bad news, company name all mixed up – and unfairly too as it turned out. They had recovered, but it had taken a few quarters to get back on the road again.

Stone had indeed – as the tiresome management cliché put it – learned from that experience. She'd been forced to realise that communications was a discipline much larger and wider-ranging than supporting the next sales effort with a few releases. She'd learned the need for a wider vision – making sure that any communication activity blended with corporate reputation needs.

That was a reason why she'd been hired as Corporate Communication manager at one of the world's biggest food firms. She knew nothing about food, but she'd learned

---

[†] See Mike Seymour and Simon Moore (1999) *Effective Crisis Management: Worldwide Principles and Practice*. London: Thomson Learning.

all about reputation management the hard way which was, as it happened, exactly what Labaddia's CEO, David Corio, wanted. Corio was also an outsider, but with a global vision and an acute belief in the overall communication function. A few months before Stone joined, he'd led the charge to change the company name and relocate from Durham to London. Labaddia meant nothing in any language, but it sounded inoffensive (unlike poor old Atkinson's Quality Meats), it sounded multinational, it sounded multi-capable and therefore a serious sell to big institutional investors.

Yes, she had mainly marcomm people in her small department (running a whole department: another learning curve), but Stone led on the rest of it: issues management, financial relations, employee communications. This was the attraction for her along with the attractive salary and promotion, the fact Corio had moved their head office from Durham to London, and the chance to gain expertise in a whole new industry with many more opportunities than those offered by medical alarm systems.

A crisis plan was top on Stone's list, and the main reason for her trips around Labaddia's Empire, starting in the UK, then Europe, then Asia and Latin America.

'We need to update the plan we do have', Corio had told her two weeks ago, on her first day. 'The last one was done after the mad cow scare and a lot has gone on since then. Like', he smiled, 'going global and growing our product range by 400 per cent'.

*

'What keeps you awake at night?' Stone asked Thomas. They were at the end of the tour, in a room filled with shelves containing the finished products: wrapped chicken, goose and beef pâtés, actually hand-wrapped with a traditional look, branded with the names of long-gone farms, family butchers, and trademarked English or Scottish surnames. The smoky, savoury smell should have been much more pleasant here, but there was far too much of it.

'Nothing you haven't thought of already – I hope.' Thomas was thinking about lunch. 'A good health scare. We're obsessive here but who can be certain? We boil some products which immediately exposes us to the risk of salmonella as well our old friend listeria.'

'Ever had that before?'

'A scare? We had a big one with BSE – mad cow disease as the bloody press loved to call it. Apparently we've got a recall plan in place, but I don't know anything about it. Before my time but it was the same where I was working back then. Sales dropped like a stone. It was out of our control though. We just had to sit tight and hang on and wait for the suppliers to be changed. They went overseas for them. That's really what started Atki- – I mean Labaddia's – overseas growth. Can't get used to that name', he admitted.

'What else?'

'Well, suppose there's the animal rights and all that. Hardly worth picking on us though is it? Bit after the fact, in a way. That's more the farmers and abattoirs.'

They waded through a last puddle bath of disinfectant, and pulled their boots off.

16

'Funny when you think of it', Roger Thomas reflected, removing the regulatory and – to Stone – odd-looking 'snood' protective covering from his head, then the even odder one from his beard. 'Phenomenal international expansion because of a national disaster. One person's poison is another person's meat, I suppose. National panic sent Atkinson's Meats into Asia, and now it's doing so well it even changes its name to avoid sounding too British. Yes, hard to get used to, that new name.' Thomas privately hated it. 'Is it Italian like our new CEO?'

'He's Canadian.'

'Right. Forgot. He's been in Italy though hasn't he?' Thomas, overalls off and in his suit, strode for the exit. 'Right, let's have lunch.'

*

So is it worth it?

For sure.

I agree.

But who knows that name.

They know the brand names of the products yeah?

Enough people?

In my country, yes.

And mine. People here do not like being poisoned.

Are they being poisoned?

That's not what I said.

Is this the right place on the chain to get involved?

That material is great, Etsuko. Where did you get it from? It's a good trigger. Pull it and see what happens.

*

Surprisingly few offices in Tokyo have air conditioning, so Yuzo Yamada was uncertain whether his discomfort was due to the searing humidity or the stress he was currently experiencing.

17

Tatsuo Fujimori felt the same, although he was trying not to show it. His interest in temperature was rather more urgent. An email was up on his computer. Both men were looking at it uncertainly.

'Tell me then about this – inconsistency – as you call it.'

Yamada cleared his throat. 'It is difficult. I can't say for certain what happened, but I think . . . I'm not sure.'

Cars blocked the late afternoon streets, sending off yet more waves of metal heat that seemed to come right through the glass in company with the burning sun.

'Well – is it possible to find out?'

'We're looking into it.'

The two men waited. Nothing happening seemed preferable at the moment.

'And', Fujimori eventually asked, 'is there anything we can say at the moment?'

The email seemed to radiate a silent warning.

'We have it under control now. I would like to suggest waiting until further testing is completed.'

*

Stone was on the London train, enjoying the countryside, when her phone rang.

'Sarah.' Sarah Collins. Her immediate superior, and a senior Board Member. They liked each other.

'Hello – question for you. How was Durham?'

'Bit of a culture shock, to be fair. In healthcare technology it's easy to forget there are people who still have to make real things for the rest of us. Including pâté.'

'Pâté – that's a nice link to my real question. We've just had a call – or rather I have – from Tokyo. The head person there is Tatsuo Fujimori. Hard to understand at first. I think he said they've had an email from an ex food safety official of some description – I've got the contact details.'

'I see.' Jennifer waited. 'And is it important?'

'And . . . I'm not sure. She's now an analyst with the . . .' Stone heard paper being pushed about. 'Worldwide Nutritionists Alliance . . . WNA . . . know anything about them?'

I've only been in the industry a fortnight, she thought, but all she said out loud was: 'Not yet. Do you?'

'Not this one. We keep an eye on food regulations, Brussels and so on. Nonprofits aren't on our radar screen. It's physically impossible anyway – do you know how many groups are into food? Food safety? Try an internet search.'

She had. 138,000 on google with the keywords 'food safety nonprofits'. Not much of that was about actual non-profit groups of course – and in any case we only needed to target a few of them. On the other hand, a lot of those hits were comments about nonprofits and food safety: which at least displayed their communication power. 'We only need to target a few of those groups', Stone said out loud.

'A few? How many is that?' Stone didn't know. 'If we choose that road we've got to think', Sarah informed her, 'about groups in twenty countries, about international groups, plus other nonprofits like consumers' associations or cookery clubs. Chuck in all the local regulators and you're just flushing money and time down the toilet.'

She stopped abruptly, catching Jennifer in the middle of sipping her tea. She put it down hastily.

'Why are you calling me then, Sarah?' she asked light-heartedly. 'Just to tell me about someone who doesn't matter calling someone who called you?'

Sarah Collins laughed. 'No – you see it seems this man has talked to someone at ITYO, our subcontractor in mainland China, which as you know –'

'Sorry. I have to admit that I don't.'

'– supplies the Japanese market with speciality European style meat products. Mainly convenience stores and department store food halls.'

'I see. And is there something you need me to do, Sarah?' Stone felt a small, premonitory frisson of tension.

'Says there's something we need to see – right now, on their website. I don't know what it is but I do know the stock market is already reacting.'

'Fine, but I'm afraid I'm not sure how exactly I'm meant to do that at the moment. I'm stuck on this train. It's already running late. Really late.'

'Train?' Collins was the perennial Londoner. 'What's wrong with City Airport?'

'I'm in Leeds tonight – visiting the regional distribution centre.'

'Well you may not be in Leeds tonight. Don't they do wifi on board?'

A minute later, Stone was at WNA's homepage, reading.

*

Six hours earlier, when Stone was navigating the butchery section of Labaddia's Durham facility, four separate websites inserted the same piece of information and four separate nonprofits in London, Hong Kong, Buenos Aires and Brussels, emailed their media, academic and regulatory contacts with information about how to access a joint webcast on whistleblowing and one of the world's biggest food multinationals, etc. etc., with some added background on Labaddia. The fact that it was hosted by four activist groups – two of them household names – had helped attract a small but influential group of visitors.

Back on the train, her mobile was ringing. As one or two of the other passengers were starting to get impatient, Stone took it between the carriages. 'Meg – what did you find out?'

Meg, Stone's deputy, sounded preoccupied. Her voice was accompanied by the continuous tap of a keyboard. 'An awful lot of speculation. I checked some blogs. Someone else has got there first though – full of stuff about us – we knew about problems and so did regulators – cameraphone pictures of workers slaughtering animals – blood and guts. Also something about undercooked meat at low tempera-tures. Some of the investment blogs have picked up on it.'

'But surely these sites are all inspected by us and the authorities?' Stone insisted.

'Don't ask me. Maybe the pictures aren't real – or they're from somewhere else. They look real enough: you know the grainy handheld effect. No one's questioning their authenticity yet.'

'We need to get a crisis team together', Jennifer decided. Of course it would happen now, when Labaddia was reinventing itself.

'Well if we do it's got to happen right now and we'll need to react right now.'

'Okay so you're telling me there's no time. Okay. We've got to do what we can with what we've got. Meg – go to David Corio's office. Check he's on for the webcast and –'

'He's not in. He's at the Frankfurt office. Meeting analysts in a couple of hours.'

'Excellent.' Stone shook her head. 'Sarah Collins needs to call him about what to expect when he gets a question.'

'What should David be saying?'

'He needs to say that we take health and safety *extremely* seriously, that consumer safety comes before *everything* – including sales – and that we've launched an internal investigation.'

'Have we?'

'Yes – starting now. You're in charge of it for the moment. You talk to Sarah Collins and find out what else she knows. Talk to Tokyo, talk to China, talk to anyone and everyone. Oh, and make a note of the more active blogs – we may have to get back to them. We'll need a statement fast.'

'Very fast.'

It suddenly struck Stone that she hadn't a clue what the actual problem was. And she realised that it didn't totally matter. It was the talk that would contain or spread the damage.

'Contaminated food, bribery and corruption in Shanghai.' Meg filled in the gaps. 'With those pictures and whistleblowers thrown in plus rumours of massive prosecutions. I think they're government whistleblowers. All pretty vague at the moment.'

Stone hoped, as she waited, and the train entered the outskirts of Darlington, fifteen minutes late – well, she hoped for two things actually: first, that investors and analysts weren't in the audience and second, that her internet connection wouldn't freeze at 3.45 GMT, when the webcast would start.

Half an hour later. She tapped the guard's elbow.

'Excuse me – I need to go straight through. Can I change my ticket?'

And as she did so, the train slowed. Then it stopped. Muttering angrily, Stone went to Labaddia's intranet to get onto email but as she did so, the screen went black, then red, then black again.

Chapter 1

The change

Everyone is too prone to keep their mouths open. There's too much talking, too much publicity, too much hype, too much spinning.

> Peter Drucker. 'Peter Drucker takes the long view' (1998: 162)

The challenge for tomorrow's leaders is to manage an organization that is not there in any sense which we are used to.

> Charles Handy. *The Empty Raincoat* (1994: 39)

INTRODUCTION

If competing businesses agree on anything, it is that they live in a time of astonishing change. Many make a virtue of it; others a necessity. Not a few believe it is noisy, overrated and deeply damaging. Perhaps most feel the truth of all these views at different times. The world is constantly confronted by rapid changes to society, and especially to the world of business. Most of us probably agree – with varying degrees of enthusiasm – that investing habits, consumer behaviour, the workplace, employment patterns, global commerce, social responsibility, corporate culture, identity, language and structure have all altered drastically in the last decade and will continue to do so in the decade ahead.

Feeling the pace of change is nothing new, and neither is reacting against it. Marx and Engels used the flux of industrialisation – 'constant revolutionizing of production, uninterrupted disturbance of all social conditions, everlasting uncertainty and agitation' (Marx and Engels 1848: 38) – to support their manifesto for Communism, the self-described 'spectre haunting Europe' (33). In respect of *perceiving* change perhaps little has changed since 1848, except that now, in what some call a post-industrial age, Information Technology (IT) is the main agent for revolutionising production, disturbing social conditions and creating uncertainty and agitation. Managers are challenged indeed to live up to the energetic online 'TomObservation' of business cheerleader Tom Peters: 'Run the whole damn company and relations with all outsiders on the internet at Internet speed. No halfway! [Be] reluctant to work with partners who don't share their view on this' (Peters 2002).

We are beginning the information revolution. Can companies succeed in it without radically changing their approach to information – their communication strategy and therefore their culture, for 'culture and communication are inextricably intertwined. . . . All culture, including corporate culture, is a social product; it is constituted and maintained by the ongoing communicative interaction of the corporation's members. Culture is therefore a product of communication' (Phillips and Brown 1993: 1549–50).

In the flux, din and excitement, one element released by the collision of information revolution, culture and communication is in danger of being overlooked: Crisis. What is going to happen during the next ten years to companies that find themselves in trouble? Will a corporate crisis and the issues and risks that ignite it behave differently in the information age, or will it be possible to fight it by existing rules?

The stakes are high in the search for answers. A crisis is a 'Big Bang': a volatile, high-density mix of events, persons, speed and actions, shot through with vivid streams of communication. The initial detonation sends the components flying outwards, overwhelming everything in their path, until – either sooner or much later, depending on the company's response – they slow, and drift, and finally come to a stop. By then, every part of the company may be marked by the event. Whether managers are aware of the fact or not, their universe has changed.

Understanding the shape and frequency of crises in the coming decade, the damage it will do, the changes it will make, and how to cope with it, are the subjects of this book. *Global Technology and Corporate Crisis* takes the view that because much of the environment surrounding a crisis is changing, and in complex ways, change can hardly fail to affect Crisis itself. There is sporadic understanding of this. The Kansas Bankers Association, for instance, was advised at its 2002 meeting on Technology to 'conduct a comprehensive risk assessment that includes identifying threats and evaluating existing policies and controls' ('Kansas conference' 2002). Nevertheless, there is scant evidence that businesses, governments or non-profit organisations understand the nature of the threat facing them. A survey of 1,350 executives at large European and US companies, conducted in 2001 for insurers The St Paul, 'revealed that most businesses do not adequately understand the risks posed by technology, have difficulty identifying potential risk and lack formal processes to both monitor and manage them effectively' (The St Paul 2001). Further, 'Employees – the people who employ technology daily in their jobs – are described as the least knowledgeable about technology risk and its potential impact on their companies' ('The St Paul Survey' 2001: 1).

'Cyber risk' is largely viewed as a technical issue of compromised software or hardware that is best left for IT specialists to manage. This view is short sighted and dangerous. Information age Crisis is the spectre haunting modern organisations all over the world, and it cannot be exorcised unless we try to learn what it can do and what to do about it.

Global Technology and Corporate Crisis describes:

- The changing crisis environment, and the effect on the existing crisis management model.
- The new threats and their capacity for doing damage.
- How crisis-hit companies, and their opponents will use technology.
- How 'traditional' crises will also be changed.
- The changing pattern of public opinion, and changing relations between interest groups, activists and other key publics.
- The new online audiences and influencers who will help drive crises, risks and issues.
- The impact crises will in future have on the present corporate model, and proposals for a more resilient crisis-management structure for 2010 and beyond.
- Internal crisis coordination: crisis communication proposals for outsourced workers and management, and skilled and deskilled employees.
- External crisis management: the new ways corporations must interact with their external audiences to contain threats and crises.
- Why crisis/issues strategy must take a more central place in twenty-first-century corporate planning.
- Why companies must reinvent their identities to anticipate changes global technology and crisis management will bring.

We shall start by considering how changes to the business environment are dangerously altering the shape and frequency of crises. Chief among these are the multiple impacts of IT. The point may be developed a little further here by introducing three examples of technology's most significant impacts, to be investigated in detail later.

THE IMPACT OF INTERNET DIVERSITY

Perhaps ironically for such an overpowering, scrutinising and invasive technology, the business of calculating the number of people actually using the internet is notably inexact. Nevertheless, and allowing for some 'give' in the estimates that follow, several large trends are apparent. Spreading internet use offers commercial potential, a chance for the world's citizens to get to know each other better and a chance for many of them to find a voice. It has been estimated that only 35.6 per cent of the world's online population is English-speaking. The rest mainly speak European (34.9 per cent) and Asian (29.4 per cent) languages (Global Reach 2004).

23

For the moment, though, this linguistic diversity is muscled aside by persistent geographical monopoly. The International Labour Organisation's (ILO) 2001 *World Employment Report*, unlike its more recent 2004–5 report, examined the 'impact of the new information and communication technologies'. It found: 'Barely 6 per cent of the world's people have ever logged onto the Internet and 85 to 90 per cent of them are in the industrialized countries' (ILO 2001). The respective percentages are changing, but are still only 12.7 per cent globally, with between 65 and 70 per cent in industrial nations, according to a recent estimate from Internet World Stats, a non-profit US site synthesising data from Nielsen/Net ratings, the International Telecommunications Union and monitoring network internet card use (Internet World Stats 2004).

The dominance of North America, Japan and Western Europe: two perhaps predictable facts, amounting to a 'safe', commercially acceptable form of diversity on territory familiar to all the participants. Venture forward a few years, and it is possible to glimpse a very different situation developing. The inexact science of internet research has at least agreed on a continued rise in online users, beginning with Gartner's forecasts of 604.7 million and eMarketer's 709.1 million in 2002 (eMarketer 2002) to the Internet World Stats 2004 estimate of over 812 million (Internet World Stats 2004) and Global Reach's revised estimate of 940 million for 2004 (Global Reach 2004). Good news for sales, but it must be asked if this changes anything in future years for issues, risks and ultimately crises. One sign that it will – there are others – is the knowledge that online population growth will no longer be concentrated in North America and Western Europe. By the end of the decade geographic diversity will catch up with linguistic diversity. The number of net users from outside both North America and Western Europe are indeed already rising, with increases from 2000 to 2004 put as high as 125.6 per cent in Asia (114 million to nearly 258 million); and 347.8 per cent in Central America, 173.6 per cent in South America according to Internet World Stats. Afghanistan now has its first 1,000 internet users, China 87 million (Internet World Stats 2004).

WorldPay is a UK firm providing online purchasing and payment services to 12,000 businesses (most readers of this book will have used its services). It is also representative of the companies now driving this global internet realignment. As early as August 2001, for example, residents in Bhutan, Benin, Cape Verde and Micronesia were joining WorldPay customers from Uzbekistan, the Falklands and Cambodia (WorldPay 2001). In October 2001 the same company monitored the habits of consumers in 35 countries who now used its services, finding that 68 per cent were making one purchase online every two months, with 16 per cent shopping at least once a week ('Online shoppers 2001'). By 2004 the company was providing services to clients in 75 countries and territories (WorldPay 'About us' 2004). In the world economy, online commerce has been projected to rise from $1 trillion in 2001 to around $12.6 trillion (or 18 per cent of global sales) by 2006 (Forrester Research 2001).

What is the cumulative impact of the statistics and forecasts, and what are they telling governments, corporations and nonprofits about crisis, risk and issues management? One firm conclusion can be drawn from the worldwide internet movement that all estimates and guesstimates are attempting to track. 'North America's share of ecommerce will inevitably fall as this boom echoes across other regions of the world', Forrester, an internet research firm, has pointed out (Temkin 2002). There is no reason why e-commerce should uniquely buck the geopolitical rule that a greater share of trade means greater political influence. New customers in Asia-Pacific, the Middle East, Africa and elsewhere, accessing the services of energetic companies like WorldPay, will weaken western domination of the web in lock-step with its declining share of e-commerce. If online diversity changes these conditions, it is going to change the world of crises and issues. Consumers enjoying total access to information about the products or cultures presented to them cannot escape having feelings and forming viewpoints, and points of view cannot escape activists and opinion leaders. It has often been declared that modern corporations, 'only wield their power in active collaboration with localities and regions, organizations and communities, and groups and individuals' (Slevin 2000: 205). The importance of the internet as a platform for collaboration on issues will therefore increase because of a rise in online diversity, and crucially – as we shall see – new kinds of activism and messages made possible by new kinds of technology.

How will that collaboration occur, and who will do the collaborating? Large and scattered groups will converge online, drawn together by the issue or crisis situation, perhaps aided by experienced intermediaries. Companies with worldwide operations are already exposed to the impact of global issues management, particularly highly visible symbols like McDonalds or Nike. Expanding e-commerce will pull many others into the process. They too will face the wider consequences of doing more of their business on a bigger and enhanced internet that, we shall argue, possesses more power to foment crisis and harm a company's commercial *and* non-commercial IT operations. Since approximately 6.7 per cent of the Middle East population is currently online, (Internet World Stats 2004) it may not much matter to American companies using the internet that 'the US is viewed unfavorably by overwhelming majorities in Egypt (98 percent), Saudi Arabia (94 percent), Morocco (88 percent) and Jordan (78 percent)' or that: 'In a State Department (INR) survey of editorials and op-eds in 72 countries, 82.5% of commentaries were negative, 17.5% positive' (Zogby, in Office of the Under Secretary of State for Defense 2004: 15). Will it matter more as tens of millions more Asian Muslims come online to engage in e-commerce, and users in the Arab nations of the Middle East, as is predicted, continue to rise rapidly every year, from an August 2001 estimate of 2.75 million (Nua 2001, 2002) to Internet World Stats 17 million in 2004? (Internet World Stats 2004). Will it matter more still by 2010, when that audience includes many more online consumers and opinion leaders talking among themselves, perhaps rejecting or shutting out other contributors, and taking direct action online? What are the implications for issues management and the creation of credible dialogue?

THE IMPACT OF INTERNET CULTURE

Everywhere, always-on, super-fast, super-capable. Such traits in IT have consequences for issues, risks and crises. They exert a collective impact, which we have barely started to grasp in our regular business activities, let alone when facing disaster. Tom Peters exhorts executives to 'work with a changing portfolio of state-of-the-art partners throughout the supply chain. This includes vendors and consultants and, especially, pioneering customers who "will pull us into the future"' (Peters 2002). Unfortunately, the future remains a step ahead, as technology accelerates. 'There's no immediate limit in sight for the next five to ten years. Bandwidth, storage and computer power will all increase', predicts IBM's Research director ('Fast-forward' 1999). Gordon E. Moore's now-famous 1965 forecast that the number of transistors per integrated circuit would double every 18 months continues to hold true, well beyond its predicted expiration date of 1975, and has become a guiding principle for the semiconductor industry (Moore 1965).

Much of this is baffling to the layperson. 'By 2010,' says one enthusiast typical of many, 'computers are expected to match the computational capabilities of the human brain' (Molitor 2001). It is easy to get the impression that much of this imminent technology – everywhere, always-on, super-fast – is less of a boon to actual users and more a pet enthusiasm of tech specialists. Once access becomes more or less instantaneous, does it really matter whether information technology has the ability to go any faster? Our cars may theoretically be capable of 180 miles per hour, but that is of little use to the everyday motorist. Realistically, how many people need to go online from their refrigerator, or store the Library of Congress in a portable, miniaturised device or process trillions of bits of information in a second? Such bemusement is not new. In 1965 few people, including the author of 'Moore's Law', foresaw the size of the revolution they were launching. Moore, who three years later was to co-found Intel, wrote in his original paper that while it was becoming possible 'to build such component-crammed equipment', 'we ask under what circumstances we should do it' (Moore 1965), and hedged this final part of his article with 'perhaps', 'may' and other caveats. When Moore speculated, it was the informed speculation of a specialist. He did not fantasise about the social effect of his Law, but spoke about better differential amplifiers, oscillators and radar, and the economies of being able to manufacture large systems out of smaller functions.

Nearly forty years later we are clearer about the social impacts of the information age and can forecast carefully and more accurately, at least in the medium term.

One Computer Scientist has commented: 'As the user's response time and ease of use continue to improve, people will start to use the internet for more diverse applications' (Cordes 2001: 14). They will naturally include people who, for whatever reason, exploit the net's applications because they are unhappy about something and use the arena for expressing their opinions and ideas without risk of criticism or overt opposition. Convenient technology and the rise of e-commerce, offers activists, victims, consumers, investors, employees and other audiences the chance to translate outrage into easy and convenient action – perhaps to comprehensively boycott a country or company's products, a prospect raised by BT's 'futurologist', Ian Pearson, or to invade its systems (Pearson 2000).

Audiences may not be inclined to reflect for long on their decisions. If 'everywhere, always-on' technology offers instant gratification to happy shoppers, it also provides less space for taking a deep breath and counting to ten. There will be more capacity for that first, overwhelming surge of indignation to take deeply damaging and all-too concrete forms.

It is a problem that begs many questions. Who will be responsible for provoking or containing those surges of emotion? How can the turbulence be managed? How will the communication challenges be tackled by players who not only use newspapers, digital TV or a website for information; but who merge information and action via a host of cutting edge tools. How for instance will computers that respond to spoken language change the way messages about risks and issues are exchanged? What implications are raised by personalised personal computers 'that will recognize users visually and present customized interfaces' ('Fast-forward' 1999).

One breakthrough is followed swiftly by another. The gap between inception and obsolescence is small. But questions persist: will the tidal wave of information carried by technology make busy, harried, audiences and those influencing them patient, calmer and more reasonable, or less rational, more demanding and more impulsive? How complex and multidirectional must crisis and issues messages become to navigate new technology and strike their targets?

This book arises out of a search for answers. It also considers the pressures on strategy and tactics, and asks how the next decade will affect familiar methods of risk, issues and crisis communication. A troubled company seeking to control its message might at present prepare a carefully crafted position paper and branded statements for reproduction in the traditional media or posting on their corporate website. But polished announcements in corporate-speak may not have a future in the rough and tumble new environment, inhabited by people who see the net as a space for free interchange and expression and access to unlimited, unvarnished and thus 'authentic' information. In their world, information is not one-way or controlled but fluid, confused and tumbled within a stream of continuous information exchange and dialogue.

THE IMPACT OF IT OUTSOURCING

Outsourcing is rampaging across many organisations, be they in the public, private, service or manufacturing sectors. Market research firm Forrester is reported as estimating that by 2015 'some 3.3 million US jobs and $136 billion in wages will transfer offshore to countries including India, Russia, China, and the Philippines' (Anderson 2004). McKinsey Consulting predicts that IT outsourcing expenditures dominated by America, Europe and Japan will reach $346 billion by 2008 (Daruvala 2003). Some commentators originally saw outsourcing as a harbinger of a new corporate order, where intelligence is the only corporate asset and companies are 'more like a collection of project groups, some fairly permanent, some temporary, some in alliance with other parties' (Handy 1994). The offloading movement has certainly carried manufacturing, IT and many other functions offsite, driven by familiar economic rules. In Australia as elsewhere, internal IT departments are being outsourced because they have not shown quantifiable returns or kept within budget ('Back to basics' 2001). In Britain, the pharmaceutical company AstraZeneca outsourced IT operations across 45 countries to IBM in a $1.7 billion seven-year contract; the British airline BMI outsourced its reservation system to Lufthansa and other systems to ICL ('Business – IT costs' 2002).

Companies and countries are hunting outsourcing business across the planet. IBM has a subsidiary providing IT outsourcing services to regional banks in Japan ('In Brief' 2000: 20). IBM Malaysia targets financial institutions, the communication and distribution sector, public services and small and medium industries, advising local companies to expect savings of up to 15–20 per cent of the costs of running their own IT departments ('Outsourcing can save' 2001: 2). InfoSys, the Indian outsourcing titan, saw revenue rise 611 per cent between 1998 and 2003 (Infosys 2004).

Meanwhile, developing countries have seized the chance presented by their western counterparts. In India tech company activity reflects a local outsourcing entrepreneur's comment that 'at least 50 to 60 percent of the business we do is in services that we did not operate in six or seven years ago' ('Why India' 2002). In the Philippines, the Department of Trade and Industry promotes the country as a major centre for IT outsourcing companies worldwide, offering call centre services, software development, animation, medical transcription and business process outsourcing ('Government Promotes' 2002).

IT outsourcing, then, is part of a movement enveloping many functions including human resources, customer relations and manufacturing. CEOs have not hesitated to shed such tasks in order to focus on 'core' activities such as brand management. Outsourcing, the head of IBM Malaysia explained to local journalists, 'will be like taking the IT department of a company and transferring it to IBM where the people and the assets will both belong to IBM' (Outsourcing can save 2001: 2).

During this decade then, many of the personnel responsible for handling a company's information systems will be transferred, along with their assets, to companies like IBM, or downsized in favour of new staff and facilities working cheaply for distant subcontractors in India, China or the Philippines. It is dispersal with considerable consequences for crisis and issues management. The main ones can be summarised here (they are examined more closely in Chapter 4):

- Business is exposed to the vulnerabilities of the companies and regions where their services are outsourced.
- Outsourcing complicates the process of managing instantaneous crises – the most common feature of a crisis in the information age – across time zones.
- Outsourcing makes the task of internal message coordination more challenging.
- It creates problems of loyalty and commitment from subcontracted employers and part-timers with, at best, divided allegiances or, at worst, resentment about their relocation if it is accompanied by lower pay and worse conditions.
- Outsourcing makes oversight of the full array of IT activities required in the midst of crisis much harder to achieve.
- Information gathering, collation and analysis become more complicated.

It is also worth noting in parenthesis that IT outsourcing, along with increased data entry and information dispersal from Government to contractors, places other responsibilities on the private sector, not the least of which relates to security: personal, corporate, and even national. Large amounts of national security are bound up with Information Technology. As a result, security too is seen as a valid outsourcing opportunity. 'The responsibilities for our nation's security no longer rest solely at the Federal level', the head of EDS's 'Homeland Security initiatives' has pointed out ('EDS appoints' 2002).

The tasks of a CEO include seeking growth and savings, and planning against threats. The first is occurring but not the second. We have rejoined Charles Handy and Peter Drucker who opened this chapter, and the problem of how corporations no longer all 'there' should manage vulnerabilities in a noisy, hyped, diverse, transparent, information-overloaded world. In 1848 Marx and Engels understood that through globalisation 'the intellectual creations of individual nations become common property' (Marx and Engels 1848: 39). As we start a new century, millions more people use technology to access that common property, wrap it into opinion and turn it to action. They are forging a culture that melts any remaining boundaries between 'neutral' commercial transactions and high-voltage opinions on social issues.

In such a world, being publicly surprised by one's vulnerabilities – or more precisely, failing to develop a culture that faces up to its weaknesses in advance – will be less of an option for companies. This is partly because of the three impacts described above, and because of others described in the pages that follow. We explore options for companies facing crises, issues and risks in a world where reputation and perception are continuously shifting, more complicated, depending on outsourced operations, part-time workers, distant subcontractors, and the opinions and actions of customers and influencers the corporation has never met or needed to understand.

Crisis management is entering a new world. We must briefly understand where it stands now before exploring where it might be going, and why.

THE CRISIS DISCIPLINE

In the last twenty years, crisis management has become an established corporate discipline. The lessons of now-infamous events, some well handled, like the Tylenol Scare in 1982 and Pepsi Cola's 'needles in the bottle' incident in 1993; others less so such as the 1984 Bhopal tragedy, the Exxon/Valdez spill in 1989 and the Dalkon Shield litigation in the 1970s and 1980s, helped develop a distinct practice supported by consultants, scholarship and specially tasked managers inside vulnerable organisations. In that period, communication also became central to the crisis management discipline, with many public relations firms offering services as 'crisis planning, development of contingencies, risk identification and crisis avoidance . . . Through communication, the various resources necessary for crisis response are systematically organized in relation to one another' (Sellnow and Seeger 2001: 153).

While an experienced crisis manager (Pines 2000: 15) agrees that 'most real crises have an important and central communications challenge', he cautions that it is not the only factor in resolving a crisis. Nevertheless, the growth of communication's role in crisis management could scarcely be avoided. The dramatic expansion of media outlets, the advent of perpetual global news cycles, and citizens' activism and consumer power, enabled in differing degrees by new technologies, has already created a communication-charged crisis lifecycle and as a result, a communication-dominant model of crisis management which, allowing for slight variations, is generally accepted and used to help companies through turbulent times.

Now however, there is evidence that the crisis model and lifecycle will come under strain from emerging information technology and new social conditions made by that technology. This process is being changed by the increasing ability of technology to communicate, act and influence perceptions during a crisis, as well as its more-recognised potential to cause a crisis.

THE CORPORATE CRISIS: DEFINITION, LIFECYCLE, OPERATIONAL MODEL

It is equally helpful to glance at the existing lifecycle and management model, about which there is general agreement, and to offer some definition of a crisis.

A crisis has been defined as an intrusive event such as an accident, scare, damaged product or scandal that sparks widespread and critical public attention, radically disrupts a company's regular operations, shakes its culture and reputation, at the very least retards its future prospects, and at the most destroys the company. According to Sellnow and Seeger 'crisis creates an immediate set of novel conditions, including high uncertainty about cause, blame and consequences, stress and fear regarding the future, and usually intense media scrutiny' (2001: 153). It has been pointed out by practitioners and academics (Benoit 1997; Lukaszweski 1997; Seymour and Moore 1999) that crises will damage several or many areas central to the success of the company and its operations: image, sales, stakeholder confidence, profits, share price, product lines, brand names, quality procedures, litigation, profits, employee morale. Some of the consequent damage – including product recall and pickup, stock replacement and transportation – can be directly assessed in financial terms. But other kinds of damage – such as stakeholder confidence, employee morale and company reputation – are harder to quantify but are shown to have a significant impact on the company's fortunes and especially in the speed and strength of its recovery.

Despite inherently high and sustained levels of shock, disorganisation and even chaos, crises have cradle–grave lifecycles. Practitioners and researchers hold that the lifecycle passes through distinct phases of emergence, escalation and de-escalation. The phases may overlap in places, and vary in length and severity according to the specifics of each crisis, but are identifiable nevertheless. Seeger (1986) for example tabled a three-step process of pre-crisis – when the underlying causes are not remedied; crisis – the eruption of an event that forces the stakeholders to intensively respond; post-crisis – when the dominating pace slackens and more regular operations recommence. In a previous book (Seymour and Moore 1999) we explored the actual crisis period in more detail, identifying within it three stages:

- The first is the breaking of the crisis – a time defined by shock, information shortages and loss of perspective.
- The second stage is the spread of the crisis, a time of stakeholder and media speculation, rumours, distracting coverage of related issues and exposure to opinions or actions by influential third parties such as regulators, independent experts and politicians.
- Finally, the most intense period of the crisis eases, there is more time for explanation, for internal rebuilding, for facts to emerge, and for a more realistic perspective to develop.

31

Pauchant and Mitroff (1992) charted the process that converts a 'pre-crisis' into a crisis and identified a flow of events that starts with an incident, is given impetus by an accident that leads to conflict, and thus escalates into Crisis.

Prudent companies attempt to control the volatility and ensure their own messages are credibly delivered to stakeholders over the noise and confusion. As Penrose points out, 'reviews of crises and crisis plans typically include four common elements: the plan, the management team, communication, and post-crisis evaluation' (2000: 155). These are accepted as pillars of crisis management, deployed in actual crises and used as a foundation for crisis research.

The plan is either drawn up in anticipation of a crisis or hastily assembled in the stress of an emergency, and identifies threats, key messages, spokespeople, stake-holders, locations for handling the crisis, other likely crisis participants including media, and the facilities for communicating with them, and strategies for recovery. This 'hot planning' technique as the crisis breaks has been shown to be less effective and more prone to short-term decision-making which is often subsequently proved to be flawed.

The planning and preparedness process often includes training sessions ideally repeated on an annual basis – in which a crisis is simulated and the plan tested. Fink (1986: 24) contends that companies without a crisis plan suffer the effects of a crisis up to two and half times longer than companies with a plan in place. Kamer, a crisis consultant, offered an emergency plan for unready crisis managers denoted by the numerical milestones of 60, three and one. An initial communication from the company must be distributed within *60 minutes* of the crisis event, a basic crisis communication organisation should be in place within *three hours*, and 'by the end of day one, a short-term communication plan needs to be in place – one that specifies key messages, key facts, identifies spokespersons and indicates the next day's needs' (1997: 27–8).

The ideal crisis team traditionally consists of a small group of senior managers drawn from key corporate and operational disciplines and will include key man-agers responsible for external communications/corporate affairs, legal, investor relations, sales and customer relations, *inter alia* (Hickman and Crandall 1997; Silva and McGann 1995; Sklarewitz 1991). This team meets periodically through the crisis event to take integrated management, operational and communication decisions, assess information, keep track of stakeholder opinions, and so far as possible, separate the business of handling the crisis from the regular activities of the company.

Given the potential for rumour and speculation to distort and escalate these complex situations, communication becomes one of the crisis team's most important responsibilities (Fishman 1999; Hickman and Crandall 1997). The tasks include communicating information and key messages to investors, customers, employees, regulators and other stakeholders, and particularly the media in the opening phase. This work involves careful consideration of the company's position as well as expressing it, close assessment of the impact of operational actions on stakeholder perception, sensitivity to the feelings of audiences who may know little about what the company does but whose opinions are important, the selection of a spokesperson and at least one deputy, and where necessary a lead role for a CEO skilled in public communication.

Besides the process of damage assessment, the post-crisis phase involves a focus on image repair which might include reconsideration of the company's internal culture, product strategy, a detailed and frank appraisal of public perceptions of its activities, and as a result, changes to its language and communication strategy (Seymour and Moore 1999; Benoit 1997; Brinson and Benoit 1996). A notable example resulted from Shell's failed attempt in 1995 to sink the decommissioned Brent Spar oil platform in the North Sea, which sparked a dangerous maritime game of cat and mouse, with Greenpeace protestors occupying the abandoned rig under tow in stormy conditions in the North Sea. This high profile action, played out through dramatic TV reports and pictures, was followed by demonstrations in Germany and the United Kingdom, boycotts of Shell products, attacks on employees and finally firebomb attacks of employee cars and even petrol stations in Germany. Subsequently Shell published a list of its acknowledged mistakes during the crisis (Hunt 1997:1), most of which turned on the need for better communications and can be summarised here:

- The Company should have consulted a wider range of stakeholder groups.
- It failed to appreciate the need for genuine two-way dialogue.
- It should have considered people's emotional reactions as well as operational issues.
- It should have realised that the general public would be interested in its activities.
- It needed to adjust its messages for different cultures without sacrificing the truth.
- It needed to educate its key audiences, particularly the media, *before* the crisis occurred.

It is significant to note that the resulting push within Shell to align internal culture more closely to corporate communication needs included a new project-planning procedure known as the 'Spar Test'. Shell's Hunt wrote: 'This is a check on how we FEEL about something as much as what we THINK about it' (Hunt 1997: 9). This approach underlined the corporation's attempt to minimise 'the conflict between internal feelings and rational, scientific solutions' (PR Week 1995).

As we shall see, Shell's approach to communicating its vulnerabilities is a fascinating example of work in progress. Many others have yet to follow in its footsteps. Follow they must: the familiar approach to crisis communication, it is proposed in the following chapters, can no longer absorb technology's shock.

33

Chapter 2

'Cobra technology'

It is questionable if all the mechanical inventions yet made have lightened the day's toil of any human being.

John Stuart Mill. *Principles of Political Economy* (1848: 129)

And who can think of the heroes of science without a thrill of admiration and of pride? What matters it that, despite the helps of steam and electricity, men work as unremittingly as ever? We live at least no longer in the outer darkness of a dense ignorance.

'1901 – a new century.' Editorial in *The Melbourne Age* (1901)

INTRODUCTION

The Cobra has a fast attack and a paralysing bite. It is a predator, shedding old skin and renewing itself for the hunt. In a previous book, we used the term 'cobra crises', to emphasise crises that strike fast and unexpectedly: an explosion, or crash. A 'python crisis' is one that, driven by a slower burning issue, gradually coils itself around unresponsive or paralysed companies and squeezes the reputation out of it over a period that may be measured in years. (Seymour and Moore 1999).

By 2010 this situation will have changed. Technology is not just machinery. Already it is recalibrating the balance of crises and issues. These will become defined less by a particular cause, and more by the communication technology that participates in them. 'Now', the United States Government's 9/11 Commission concluded in its report, 'threats can emerge quickly. An organization like al-Qaeda, headquartered in a country on the other side of the earth, in a region so poor that electricity or telephones were scarce, could nonetheless wield weapons of unprecedented destructive power in the largest cities of the United States' (9/11 Commission 2004: 362). Business is not isolated from that trend, with this difference – while the threats to them are hopefully less catastrophic, they will in future often be incubated, delivered and either contained or aggravated by communication via technology. If John Stuart Mill's celebrated remark applies anywhere, it is in the effort that these circumstances will demand from executive businessmen and women trapped by technology, often technology used by them and familiar to them, but directed by more hostile groups and individuals. In its 2004 report on Strategic Communication the Pentagon's Defense Science Board commented:

> A host of information technologies – in addition to Satellite TV – are creating greater global transparency: cell phones, wireless handhelds, videophones, camcorders, digital cameras, miniaturized fly away units used by TV crews in remote locations, high resolution commercial space imaging, blogs and email. Many are cheap; costs are declining.
>
> (Office of the Under Secretary of State for Defense 2004: 19)

Those technologies and their descendents may fairly be called cobra technology. Each and every tool that will emerge in this decade cannot be known, but their main characteristics can be anticipated. We know why these are predatory technologies – fast to strike, potentially paralysing and constantly strengthening themselves by shedding older versions for new. The existing model of effective crisis communication – a small team, a focus on particular locations, a spokesperson, a series of position statements, fast contact with other stakeholders, early concentration on media relations – will need adaptation.

Technology's enveloping impact on the various components of issues and crisis, and on communication strategy, is a part of every other chapter. In this chapter, its general effects on the crisis setting need separate attention.

In Chapter 1 we suggested that trends created by Information Technology – like internet diversity and culture, and IT outsourcing – raise communication problems for business. Professional communicators seem aware that difficulties lie ahead but this is not the same as knowing exactly what those difficulties will be, or what to do about them. Given this uncertainty, it is understandable that the communicators do not always welcome communication technology. A survey of one hundred US public relations practitioners for the New York based Council of Public Relations Firms (CPRF) at the start of this century found they viewed five of the net's nine biggest agreed impacts on PR as obstacles not benefits. Many respondents liked the prospect of targeting audiences more accurately, building value into websites and bypassing the media, but as the researchers pointed out: 'The few opportunities cited . . . were about automating what PR already does, not using the Net to do new things' ('The impact' 2000: 3). The biggest impact by far was also seen as an obstacle – increased speed, as was the proliferation of new media that PR practitioners were forced to deal with ('The impact' 2000: 3).

'Despite these tectonic changes', cautioned a White Paper on CPRF's website, 'many public relations agencies continue to run their businesses the way they have since the dawn of the mass market in the 1950s and the concurrent rise of national TV networks and magazines' ('Interactive PR' 2001: 3). If professional communicators have not fully focused on the information revolution today, it is unsurprising business in general is often ignorant of what communication will do to it tomorrow.

Perhaps for this reason business in general has still to fully connect technology with crisis resolution, on the evidence of a 2002 survey of Britain's biggest FTSE 250 companies by Edelman Worldwide Public Relations. The results point to a chasm between accepting the importance of IT, and knowing what can be done with it: 85 per cent of the respondents rated online communications as 'important or very important', and 50 per cent conducted 'some form' of news group and discussion forum monitoring, but 82 per cent do not use 'dark site technology' – websites ready and waiting to be lit up in response to a breaking issue or sudden crisis. 'While there is recognition of today's 24/7 world, the survey revealed that over 70 per cent of respondents had never successfully utilized their corporate web presence as an issues and crisis communication channel.' 'Role of technology acknowledged, but may not be fully understood', the survey tersely bulleted. 'Indications are that internet tools are utilized tactically, but lacking cohesive, strategic approach' (Edelman: 2002). Edelman's UK Chairman cautioned: 'Companies are unnecessarily leaving themselves open to risk despite the availability of traditional crisis management tools and leading edge on-line techniques' ('Ready to' 2002).

Technology can already help companies in a crisis, and it can help managers understand the future shocks that it will bring. Yet evidence indicates that technology – already so dominant a feature of a crisis – is significantly affecting the communication environment but not getting the necessary strategic attention. Given the speed of technological change, there is little time left for learning at leisure. Cobra technology challenges and changes many of the assumptions behind crises and issues.

This chapter explores:

- What cobra technology will look like.
- Why cobra technology changes crises, risks and issues.
- Cobra technology's threats.

WHAT COBRA TECHNOLOGY WILL LOOK LIKE

The ideal input device, probably just beyond our present technology and science, would be a non-invasive, direct mind-into-computer communication device to bypass the use of our muscles as input devices. We'd get speed, ease of use, and it would be a tremendous boon to many people who have physical disabilities that keep them from using computers efficiently.

Jef Raskin. 'Technology visionaries' (2001)

'Computers change from cutting-edge technology to junk to museum pieces within a couple of decades', cautions the *New Scientist* ('Shock of' 2001: 54). Nevertheless, it is possible to understand the shared characteristics of the IT that will mediate future crises. 'What must be remembered by anyone preparing for the future is that technology change isn't very important in itself. What matters is what this change enables or destroys', BT's resident futurologist Ian Pearson advises ('Technology timeline' 2001: 3). Even without knowing each and every tool that will appear on the scene, many critical characteristics of cobra technology can be anticipated by understanding the characteristics of a crisis.

The most popular notion of technological disasters, epitomised at the end of the last century by Millennium Bug overreactions, is the compromise of a piece of software or hardware leading to operational paralysis. Technology experts, regulators and lawyers working to protect 'privacy' and 'security' are the ones usually expected to fend off such disasters, but the role of technology in future crises is more interesting and subtle.

It is worth reiterating three points mentioned earlier:

- IT will create a crisis because of technical failure, caused by accidental, mischievous or malicious activity.
- IT will create an issue because it forces certain audiences to confront ethical or social difficulties.
- IT will influence a crisis or an issue by its use as a tool for shaping opinion before facilitating discussion.

The last point is arguably the most neglected. As Naomi Klein claims in *No Logo*, the internet is becoming a blueprint for organisation by protest groups, but of equal or greater importance will be how people access it. The fact that a computer will not be the only or even the main internet gateway is as significant for a future crisis as information exchanged during the event. The best-designed 'gateways' will be those created for specific audiences. Knowing the location and culture of those gateways lets crisis participants tailor messages and information. This challenge is already confronting marketers: 'Sophisticated 21st century consumers get information from so many sources that advertisers find it hard to target those who might be interested in their products' ('The ads' 2002).

A similar outlook confronts crisis managers. Cobra technology offers *all* audiences ease of use with an internet 'gateway' that together attract, inspire and motivate. Crisis managers must be able to harness the growing capabilities of the internet in order to better gratify users' knowledge and emotions, whether they are numbered in millions or mere dozens. To do these things, cobra technology must:

- Exploit new power relations between organisations and publics.
- Guide users deftly through the intricate 'web' of twenty-first-century public opinion to help them participate and draw conclusions.

37

- Since reaching understanding is unlikely to be subjective, the technology should be able to deliver convincing levels of *feeling*, on top of a convincing amount of detail.

It will need to possess:

- Speed. Traditionally, the first messages set the pattern of questions and responses and of attitudes in the opening phase of a crisis. There is nothing so far to suggest this principle will change during the information age.
- Convergence and reach – the ability to bring the right 'influencers' together for concerted action.
- Ease of access. Those who have the right IT tools to hand and can use them faster than other participants will have the fastest influence on a crisis.

One place to access this technology will be the workplace – or more accurately, the 'workspace', since cobra technology will be found in both the office and the telecommuter's own space, a situation that presents the crisis hit company with risks and benefits:

- The threat of losing control of the crisis immediately. This will occur if centrally coordinated messages are ignored, misunderstood and wilfully distorted by dispassionate part-time employees scattered across countries and continents, and by external audiences influencing events from their own workspaces.
- The opportunity to use the same technology to coordinate detailed plans and messages thoroughly, and to respond rapidly.

Whether the opportunity or the threat prevails will depend on the nature of the event, and also on the company's internal culture.

All these points may help us to understand the future for workplace technologies. Some forecasts will prove more accurate than others, the shiniest new technology tool ages rapidly, the cutting edge blunts rapidly. But insights can be gained from a brief survey of the actual shapes technology is expected to take, and how they meet the conditions already outlined. A decade ahead is perhaps the furthest we can venture. One IT columnist noted, 'each technological innovation starts out crudely, becomes refined and then is widely adopted, in about a 10-year timeframe' ('Is your' 1994: 84). Looking forward ten years, it seems clear that, whatever its precise shape, the IT we will use at work will easily meet the conditions for cobra technology, and give more individuals more ways to express themselves in a crisis.

There is a large amount of agreement about the kind of technology we can generally expect. Haworth is an American office furniture company with offices in 120 countries and a desire to be on the frontier of technology and design. The company has made a series of forecasts for the opening years of this century in a 2000 research paper on 'The technological explosion in the workplace'. The technology that Haworth believes will 'explode' into the workplace is not fantasy, since we are close enough to see the trends and 'join the dots' connecting us to the decade ahead. By then, Haworth believes, good office design will no longer depend on 'accommodating the PC with the primary focus on cable delivery and management' (Kruk and Lavenhar 2000: 3).

> Personal computers and related applications will support more mobile computing, voice recognition, incorporate intelligent agents to customize routines and data to personal needs, *and become more of a communications rather than a computational device.*
>
> (Kruk and Lavenhar 2000: 8; emphasis added)

A new array of access devices will replace traditional office features. Workers will be liberated from 'keyboarding' by a plethora of voice recognition features, web-enabled personal digital assistants (PDAs) and flat-panel monitors for face-to-face communication. 'Transpaque' dividing walls will become transparent or opaque for privacy' (Kruk and Lavenhar 2000: 8).

IBM worked to visualise similar themes with Steelcase, another US office furniture company specialising in 'harmoniously integrating architecture, furniture and technology' ('Overview' 2002). The two companies unveiled BlueSpace in January 2002, a prototype workspace of the future with the ability to 'turn just about any object into an interactive display', and 'wireless, touch-sensitive technology' allowing 'fingers to double as cursors' ('Steelcase and IBM' 2002: 22).

Similar ideas are reiterated and supplemented by other IT watchers contemplating likely advances over the first years of the new century. 'Mobile conferencing from a handheld computer', 'the role of games and simulations together is going to be very powerful . . . moving into other areas such as education and literature', 'spoken-language understanding and dialogue', or more daringly, 'head-mounted or eyeglass-mounted displays', and by 2020, 'the assent to meaning . . . computers making a small jump in their ability to comprehend what you're saying, first a little, then a lot better'. These are the forecasts of several experts gathered together by *Computerworld* in 2001 ('Technology visionaries' 2001: 54). Purdue University's Associate Dean of Engineering anticipates advances in videoconferencing this decade that will deliver greater realism, perhaps in three-dimensions. 'You won't need to fly to San Francisco for a meeting', he says. 'You'll just have to sit in a chair and push the right buttons' ('What lies ahead' 2000: 16). In the next fifty years, predicts a scholar of psychology and computer science: 'We will achieve a wristwatch-size worldwide communicator/videocam/computer/animator/global positioner/notepad, with a 3-D projection display' (Holland 2002: 176).

Such tools 'annihilate distance' (Johnson 1991: 165) by exploiting fast highways:

'broadband access, LAN [Local Area Network] technology, wireless access, multi-service networks and home networking' according to 3Com ('Networking new' 2000). 'Memory with access time of 1 ns' (one nanosecond, or one billionth of a second – that is, assuming US usage in which a billion is one thousand million), 'supercomputers as fast as human brain', 'integrated circuits on 1mm silicon spheres' according to BTexact, BT's future-probing division, which also forecasts a 'desktop computer as fast as human brain' by 2015 ('Technology timeline' 2002).

Whatever the literal shape of the future, threads common in all emerging Technology suggest important shared characteristics. IT will be:

- Lighter, more portable.
- Always on.
- Everywhere. Not restricted to computers.
- For all practical purposes, instantaneous.
- More appealing to more senses – making use of colour, voice, sound and touch.
- Available to more people.
- Able to find, store and present complex information according to the user's personal preference.
- Capable of semi-independent action as well as information exchange on your behalf.

Not every prediction will be realised. Early reports of the death of keyboards, for example, are probably premature. Without keyboards, it is hard to imagine intricate detail being entered, or lengthy reports being composed. Bob Thacker, a senior engineer at Microsoft, agrees speech recognition 'will be mostly used for dictation', while others argue it will 'be used primarily in coming years for "command and control", driving menus and opening files in conjunction with a mouse or other input device' ('New way' 2002: 48). Perhaps the question for crisis managers to ask though, is simply whether voice commands will be used more often. Will an employee, politician, activist, consumer, journalist or even regulator be more likely to employ voice command technology in the high pressure, high-velocity environment of a crisis? In the heat of the moment, will the voice – surging with anger, irritation, impatience or fear – be preferred over the slower, more reflective keyboard to execute far-reaching commands?

It is probable that the latest cobra technology will not be available to every audience at the same time. A relative 'digital divide' will persist, with more of the latest and best IT found more often in the West and parts of Asia. This need not handicap new, less well equipped and as we have suggested, growing, online populations elsewhere. At the very least, as described below, even they will have the means to collaborate with and influence better-equipped sympathisers overseas and at home. If not always at the forefront of action and communication, these technologies will have a larger and more powerful influence shaping public opinion.

Whether this or that particular tool arrives on the scene, the weight of these trends makes it futile to imagine that future crises can be contained by the old methods. The power of these tools to communicate means it is unwise to ignore a bigger role for communication in the activities of companies and their personnel.

WHY COBRA TECHNOLOGY CHANGES CRISES, RISKS AND ISSUES

> I now see McDonald's as just like a tiny insignificant little speck because I've seen their top executives, I've seen all their material and really it's just completely transparent.
>
> Dave Morris. 'McLibel' Defendant. ('Interview. Dave Morris' 1996)

Because of cobra technology, managers must rethink crisis strategy. To do that we must be clear about what happens when technology mediates our desire to communicate. Good communication is important to business, but does not confine itself to business. Effective public relations, one academic points out, must 'connect with specific society-wide economic, political and cultural trends' (Moloney 2002: 32). Crisis communication – at the sharp end of public relations practice – must make such connections if it is to do its job.

The balance of communication power

Even before e-commerce makes a decisive impact on the crisis and issues power balance, the web's value as a platform for opinion, argument and action is already well established. We learn how effectively guerrilla technology can sidestep its lumbering targets from groups like the hackers who 'domain-hijacked' Nike's corporate website for several hours by diverting it to the homepage of Melbourne's S11 Alliance. This is a self-styled 'anti-corporate', 'pro global justice' group opposed to the sports company's employment practices (S11 2001; 'I hate you' 2000: 84). We hear about environmental protestors entering Shell's London headquarters one Monday morning in January 1999, taking over three rooms and spending the day broadcasting their occupation live to the press with a palm top computer, digital camera and mobile phone, while Shell vainly cuts electricity and phone connections ('Modem warfare' 1999). We also see communities forming online on single issues: a virtual forum of Israeli residents opposed to a non-kosher McDonald's in their neighbourhood ('Beit Shemesh' 2001); the Afghani women who used US-based websites to describe oppression under the Taliban, and their supporters who printed out emails and circulated them among women 'offline' in refugee camps ('Afghan women' 2000).

41

On 3 December 2004 a BBC producer investigating the twentieth anniversary of one of the world's worst industrial accidents at Bhopal, India was directed to the website of Dow Chemicals, since 1999 owners of Union Carbide, the company responsible for the deadly leaks from the pesticide plant in 1984. There a Dow representative was contacted who offered an exclusive interview on a major announcement. The 9 am TV interview with Mr Jude Finisterra in Paris centred on an announcement that a $12 billion Trust was being established for the families and victims. By 10 am, the news was running on many BBC outlets. Dow shares fell 34 per cent in Frankfurt and 50 cents in New York and the hopes of the victims rose even as Dow emailed the BBC demanding a retraction ('Cruel $12 billion hoax' 2004). The interview, it was learned, was the internet creation of 'Mike and Andy' or The Yes Men, two anti-corporate pranksters with several other victims to their name. Andy himself had played Jude (Patron Saint of lost causes) Finisterra (earth's end). They had come across a BBC email of 29 November on Dowethics.com, a Dow lookalike site satirizing the multinational, seeking a Dow executive to discuss the Bhopal legacy. On their own website The Yes Men said:

> Knowing Dow's history of gross negligence on this matter, we think it unlikely they will send a representative themselves – and if they do, he or she will likely only reiterate the old nonsense yet again, which will be depressing for all concerned. Yes, we'd better just do their PR for them.
>
> (The Yes Men 2004)

These first, crude steps demonstrate that the shift in the power balance between an organisation and its publics is now well underway. Ian Angell, Professor of Computer Security at the London School of Economics, warns in one of several controversial publications that society is being sucked into an accelerated, tech-led version of Natural Selection, resulting in a world in which democracy matters less than the need for nations 'to behave as merely another form of commercial enterprise', by competing for talent and income against the 'virtual enterprises' established by global companies (Angell 1999). This echoes fears expressed during the Industrial Revolution, from late-nineteenth-century philosophers like the Scot, D. G. Ritchie.

These are sizeable ideas, and related to this subject so far as all participants in issues or crises should attempt in advance to understand the power balance that produces them. It is likely in this case that crisis communication strategy must address a different challenge than the idea of Natural Selection at warp speed.

Participants nevertheless must change their understanding of where the balance of power resides and how it will be defined in a more competitive and noisier world. Anyone involved in communication recognises that power and communication are intimately related. Long before our own information revolution, humans have been improving ways to input, store and transmit increasing quantities of information, to break the shackles of time and move messages rapidly across vast spaces. The true impact of all this is not widely appreciated, even by the power-centres exploiting those improvements.

Harold Innis is little known today, but his students included Marshal McLuhan, who absorbed his study of communication at the University of Toronto. This was a late project, grown in part from a more traditional investigation of Canada's fur trade routes, railroads and pulp and paper, which in the last decade of his life drew Innis away from economics and towards the idea that power in society really depended on the control of 'space-binding' or 'time-binding' communication.

In *Empire and Communications* (1950a) and *The Bias of Communication* (1950b) Innis set out his principle arguments. The earliest civilisations, he wrote, used 'time-binding' media: long-lasting stone, clay tablets or parchment that were hard to circulate and inscribe, and, because of that, confined power in two ways: first to special messages meant to withstand the test of time – such as legal questions or religious edicts; second, to limited areas, a combination leading to 'decentralization and hierarchical types of institutions' (Innis 1950a: 7). Later technology, such as paper or papyrus were 'space-binding': perishable but light, less able to survive over time but much easier to circulate over more space and open to the rapid, emotive expression of cursive script, better able to carry more fleeting, detailed, secular information and instruction into more areas of daily life and so able to extend the power of the sender. Materials 'which emphasize space favour central-ization and systems of government less hierarchical in character' (Innis 1950a: 7).

Innis disapproved of society's continuing thrust towards ever-more space-conquering media. By the twentieth century mass circulation newspapers made from Canadian pulp and paper were dominant, and soon joined by radio. At the end of Innis's life, the age of mass television was at hand. Innis's work on newspapers and radio led him to believe that the world was disproportionately concentrating cultural and political power, around an American model. He feared this movement destroyed the stability and regional diversity delivered by more 'time-binding' media.

Unlike his initially optimistic and more famous pupil McLuhan, Innis was consistently pessimistic about communication technology's influence on political power. He used his idea to plot the rise of kingdoms, empires and nations. His theories are equally applicable to corporate or activist power. Now, many stake-holders exploit 'space-binding' IT and interact with organisations whose power can reward and gratify, and disturb, inspire, threaten or anger.

Emerging technology is therefore changing power. The internet and the tools that supply it are re-calibrating the balance between communication and control. It is 'space-binding', but it is not yet centralised. There are simply too many ways to get onto the internet. It is also 'time-binding'. A permanent repository for messages, dialogue, action and information, delivered in space-conquering volume and intricate detail. It is potentially available to all, with no constraints to where it can go, or how fast it can go there, other than those defined by personal choice, by cost, or authorities vainly trying to control it.

The new tools – uniting the potentialities of space and time – take communication power, and therefore power itself, from governments and corporations, and redistribute it among smaller entities, and also the individual citizen who is no longer a mere receiver of carefully crafted messages, but has a voice in their creation.

The new, flatter, freer power-spaces are where corporations, governments, interest groups, Non-Government Organisations (NGOs) and citizens must meet. Important relationships will be built between stakeholders and new conditions created for the management of crises. Innis himself presciently sketched the tactics that work best in freer environments: 'elasticity of structure involves a persistent interest in the search for ability and persistent attacks on monopolies of knowledge' (Innis 1950a: 216).

Whatever new technology emerges in future, it will exert time- and space-conquering power by exploiting speed, reach, volume and interactivity. It will attract humans by stimulating their senses – sight, hearing, touch, and perhaps even taste and smell – in arresting ways. This stimulation will influence what we know, and how we *feel* about what we know. If power is the communication of knowledge, cobra technology will melt the boundaries between knowledge, information and feeling.

Whether in crisis or not, companies must learn to communicate differently, and to bind it tightly to their own 'centres' of authority.

Many of those changing power by communication are too busy communicating to grasp what they are doing. Tony Juniper of Friends of the Earth simply calls the internet 'the most potent weapon in the toolbox of resistance' ('Modem warfare' 1999). Naomi Klein reproduces this remark in her influential polemic *No Logo*, and in the next sentence offers a slightly better definition: 'But the net is more than an organizing tool – it has become an organizing model, a blueprint for decentralized but cooperative decision making' (Klein 2000: 396). Research for the US Council of Public Relations Firms made the full connection in 2000, when it noted that: 'Centralized information control will continue to decrease.'

> The ongoing demand for more information and simplicity of its dissemination means that traditional controls over access to information will become increasingly unmanageable.
>
> ('The impact' 2000: 3)

'The global marketplace of news and information is no longer dominated by the United States', warns a US academic attacking Al-Jazeera, the controversial Qatari satellite news station ('Mass media' 2002). Or, from a slightly different perspective, 'censorship is no longer effective for information', says an Al-Jazeera director. 'The government media is marginalized . . . Arab officials who used to refuse to participate in analytical news reports or debates on sensitive issues, now take the initiative and show interest in taking part in discussions of hot issues' ('Qatar: Al-Jazeera' 2002). One wonders what Innis would make of this situation: like the BBC or CNN – there is no reason why Al-Jazeera or lively competitors like Dubai-based Al-Arabiya or Lebanon's LBC-al Hayat should confine themselves to Arab regions, presenting dilemmas to western governments once broadcasts begin in their own countries. The BBC has, after all, greatly expanded its own service to Muslim countries to counter Al-Jazeera, while a French court banned Lebanon's Hezbollah supported al-Manar television from broadcasting via a local satellite company on the grounds it incited racial hatred ('France pulls plug' 2004).

From the new satellite channels and websites changing the Middle East to America and beyond, the organising model of communication is being swamped by new technology. This technology involves the mass media, and other tools that are erasing the 'mass' from 'media' and targeting smaller groups of people. Executives are being drawn into this torrent, and face a decentralised rearrangement of public power. This in turn requires a new relationship between a company and its audiences. That relationship hinges on transparency.

Technology and transparency

Transparent financial reporting, transparent supply chains: transparency is becoming a benchmark, and especially 'social transparency'. According to the United Kingdom Government and the poll company MORI, 'the proportion of people who regard an organisation's social responsibility as "very important" when selecting a product has risen from 28% in 1998, to 46% in 2001' (DTI 2002: 8). Transparency seems likely to have a sizeable influence on the future of corporate communication, particularly inside multinational companies:

> Transnational corporations evoke particular concern in relation to recent global trends because they are active in some of the most dynamic sectors of national economies, such as extractive industries, telecommunications, information technology, electronic consumer goods, footwear and apparel, transport, banking and finance, insurance and securities trading.
>
> (Weissbrodt and Kruger 2003: 901)

The same authors capture the charged moral environment now experienced by multinationals: 'With power should come responsibility, and international human rights law needs to focus adequately on these extremely potent international non-state actors' (Weissbrodt and Kruger 2003: 901).

Meanwhile, international law and national governments use transparency as a crucial measure of corporate responsibility. In August 2003 for example, the United Nations subcommission on the promotion and protection of human rights approved the 'Norms on the responsibilities of transnational corporations and other business enterprises with regards to human rights.' Article 16 tries to set global standards for corporate scrutiny:

> Transnational corporations and other business enterprises shall be subject to periodic monitoring and verification by United Nations, other international and national mechanisms already in existence or yet to be created, regarding application of the Norms. This monitoring shall be transparent and independent and take into account input from stakeholders (including non-governmental organizations) and as a result of complaints of violations of these Norms. Further, transnational corporations and other business enterprises shall conduct periodic evaluations concerning the impact of their own activities on human rights under these Norms.
>
> (United Nations 2003)

A year later, the United Nations itself felt transparency's authority when its officials were implicated in Iraq's food for oil scandal. Other corporations offer at least some degree of transparency about their non-commercial activities. The British Government found that 'around 80% of FTSE-100 companies now provide information on their social and environmental policies' (DTI 2001: 3). What information is provided? How does the communication work? Regardless of where they are based, transnational issues and expectations must influence the approach of large companies. Dutch grocer Ahold employs 450,000 people in 28 countries and is the largest grocer on the United States east coast. It is also a representative example of what multinationals currently feel transparency means. Ahold's website is replete with initiatives covering the environment, the community, social issues, health and food safety. The company is, for instance, working towards a 'Global Food Safety Initiative' – the creation of independently audited, certified and world-wide standards from farm to fork (Ahold 2002b). It is 'committed to embedding diversity throughout in our organizational culture', not just among employees, but also suppliers (Ahold 2002a).

In addition to 'social transparency', companies also seek 'operational transparency' because it makes them more nimble and profitable. In this area, technology is very welcome. United States Federal Reserve Chairman Alan Greenspan told Congress in February 2001: 'New technologies for supply-chain management and flexible manufacturing imply that businesses can perceive imbalances in inventories at a very early stage – virtually in real time – and can cut production promptly in response to the developing signs of unintended inventory building' ('Not ready' 2002: 32).

Transparency, then, is about achieving open evaluation and measurement of people and machines, of social responsibilities, and economic performance. It is often demanded by a company's external publics, or by its internal culture.

Transparency is also starting to de-fog global accounting and financial practices, a development which affects the other forms of transparency. An international survey of central bankers' views on the determinants of credibility in their field placed 'openness and transparency' midway in a list of seven, prompting the researcher to comment:

> Frankly, I was surprised to learn that central bankers view openness as such a fine way to build credibility. This may be a recent development. After all, the traditional view in central banking circles prizes secrecy and even a little mystery in monetary policy-making. Too much openness is sometimes portrayed as a threat to credibility.

> (Blinder 2000: 1429)

The shift has certainly been assisted by serial shocks to the west's finance sector, in the shape of large-scale corporate crises. The collapse of energy trader Enron and accounting giant Arthur Andersen, the undetected rogue trader at a subsidiary of Allied Irish Banks, the problems at Parmalat and its auditors Grant Thornton and Deloitte Touche would be unconnected corporate crises were it not for the extra fact that they collided with higher expectations of openness made possible by technology. 'The corporate scandals that have undermined investor confidence', British tech journal *vnunet* declared in March 2002, 'will make IT even more of a mission-critical asset in the next few years' ('Management Week' 2002: 34). The article's headline, 'Technology stops scandals', looks over-confident, but nevertheless tools are appearing designed to achieve this result. It will also confront audiences and organisations with choices that cut into conscience, ethics and habit.

Thanks to raised expectations in the money markets, globally communicated crises are forcing companies far from the epicentre to revamp ethical assumptions, and extend transparency to their finances as well as to so-called 'softer' issues. The change can be abrupt. In Ahold's 2001 Annual Report the CEO avowed: 'Our strategy is very transparent and consistent' (Ahold 2001). But shares fell 10 per cent when it was seen, in the wake of Enron, that Ahold's 2001 net income was €1 billion under Dutch accounting rules, but only €120 million under US rules. By the following week the company had radically reformed its accounting practices. 'We realize', admitted Ahold's CEO, 'that we have fallen short of the transparency requirements that the market demands today; a much higher level than just twelve months ago' ('Dutch grocer' 2002).

In developed markets companies must become fiscally transparent because the technology for delivering financial information is either expected or available. 'IT systems must deliver timely information in a manageable and useful way', *vnunet* comments, 'with easy access for shareholders, if firms are to promote trust and confidence in their stock' ('Management Week' 2002: 34). New rules for disclosure, financial reporting and corporate governance encourage technologies that offer faster and greater transparency. These include Extensible Business Reporting Language (XBRL), a freely licensed framework that automatically exchanges financial data regardless of borders, formats and technologies, and helps financial systems 'interoperate smoothly' ('XML to speed' 2000: 93).

There are more obstacles in emerging markets where, *The Asian Banker* complained, 'transparency is limited and it is very hard to discern the terms of the deal, and even if these are disclosed, they often contain hidden costs' ('Trade finance' 2001). Yet there too change is underway. In January 2002, the National Audit Office of China denied that executives at the Bank of China had embezzled money. In March, the Bank admitted that five officials had stolen almost $500 million between 1993 and 2000 – the tip of a very large iceberg. One motivation for the Bank's changed message was international ambition – its Hong Kong unit planned a global stock exchange listing later in the year and the global marketplace could accumulate and punish evidence of rampant corruption that would have been suppressed at home ('Bank of China admits' 2002a). 'Every bank in China has problems like this', an anonymous source told the *New York Times* ('Bank of China's mounting problems' 2002b: W01). 'There is', the Bank's incoming President had said, 'an urgent need to instil good corporate governance into Chinese enterprises', including 'a transparent and sound decision making process' (Kang 2000). Meanwhile, seven executives were placed on trial in Peking for 'stir-frying shares' – borrowing money from state banks to inflate prices on Chinese stock markets. The trial itself was also an interesting example of the government's understanding of transparency: it was set to last only three days despite the complex case, scheduled to coincide with new rules allowing foreign firms access to Chinese securities and fund markets, and hundreds of journalists were invited to attend. The impression was left of a traditional 'show trial' staged by a closed regime to send messages of globalisation and openness. In this connection, the trial may bear out the dictum that communication events are valueless unless accompanied by operational changes: 'The audience would be foreign investors', a Hong Kong investor cautioned, 'the ones less likely to be fobbed off by a public show and fanfare' ('Stock rigging' 2002).

Nor has the full meaning of transparency been grasped in developed markets. This is because of the emphasis on using familiar, controlled, tools – releases, webcasts, focus groups, print publications – to demonstrate operational and social transparency. The other obstacle is a natural fear of unmanaged messages, the risk of joining online debate or even encouraging the exchange of diverse views of your company within the anarchic web community. 'I'm still surprised at the large number of corporate websites who do not offer such an opportunity – or if they offer a feedback mechanism it is very limited and structured', Shell's Clare E. Harris told visitors to the oil company's 'uncensored space', TellShell, started in 1997. Without the internet, Harris reminded TellShell readers, 'you as a company cannot claim legitimately to be listening and engaging. You are far from a goal of having your finger on the pulse of society' (Harris 1999).

48

TellShell's lack of structure is striking. The tone ranges from reasoned to abusive and occasionally hysterical. The subjects range from human rights, pump prices, the environment, bad customer relations and shady appeals for business. Yet even uncensored and totally transparent communication must be provided and managed, and (as explored in Chapter 6) business must learn to exploit it. Yet the United Kingdom edition of *PR Week* warned that communications practitioners have not weighed the impact of such global changes on themselves, 'or the way in which their companies could be affected in the future' ('Quarterly reporting' 2002: 11).

Meanwhile, IT managers enjoy more detailed guidance which Business in general might also note.

> IT directors should work closer with business leaders to ensure they are complying with the law for corporate governance, and firms may even establish a database checklist in order to ensure they are fulfilling all their responsibilities . . . Risk assessment and effective business continuity plans will be essential to ensure that companies are run in a sensible way, and to protect the interests of investors.
>
> ('Management Week' 2002: 34)

Compliance must be married to communication. Cobra technology shapes financial information as it does other kinds of information, and lets decentralised stakeholders join in. The internet's role as a communications network, argued *The Asian Banker Journal*:

> Allows aggregation of parties involved in trade finance and provides greater visibility among them, which means better information and transparency. Better information can reduce apprehension and increase the level of trust, which in turn can lead to higher volumes of receivable trade and liquidity.
>
> ('Trade finance' 2001)

Financial transparency boosts social transparency. When transparency is absent, investors stay away, and instead, in the words of one journalist, 'reward reform' ('The era of' 2002: 50). Paul Reynolds, a net-based PR executive, assessed the knock-on effect: 'It's not just a question of [financial] reporting. People want more information and there is a quest for that information. There are huge opportunities for companies that get it right' ('Quarterly reporting' 2002: 11). In February 2002 the pension titan CalPERS (California Public Employers Retirement System), managing $148.5 billion for 1.3 million Californian public employees, retirees and families, launched new ethical review criteria for rating and weighting investment decisions in emerging markets, a list of countries that fitted the Fund's blueprint, and another list of countries from which CalPERS would 'eliminate its public equity investment position' ('CalPERS adopts' 2002). The top three measurements were:

- Political stability (including civil liberties, judicial independence, and political risk).
- Transparency (defined by CalPERS as press freedom, accounting standards, and listing requirements).
- Labour practices (Permissible equity 2002).

The review, a senior manager announced, 'is a living document subject to on-going change', and: 'Believed to be the first of its kind ever done by a public pension fund that looks beyond traditional economic factors and considers basic democratic principles' ('CalPERS adopts' 2002).

Financial, ethical and social transparencies are growing interdependent. Openness in one leads to similar expectations in the others, expectations which become necessities when stakeholders start taking key decisions based on what they can or cannot find out. The spread of transparency to finance, therefore, raises expectations about transparency in general. Some corporate communicators may struggle to meet these expectations. Nevertheless, delivering transparency must be a key plank in future crisis or issues strategy. Several proposals are offered in Chapter 6.

It will be seen in the next chapter that the joint impacts of a shifting power balance and increased transparency are rearranging the building blocks of public opinion, and creating new audiences and challenges for management. Public opinion is also becoming more aware that cobra technology makes companies vulnerable to new forms of 'shock'.

COBRA TECHNOLOGY'S THREATS

Some of the shocks are new; others refine existing threats. Cobra technology will either *react* to a separate issue or crisis event, or *be* the event itself, or both. The vulnerabilities created are either inherent in the technology, or from people not anticipating the implications of that technology.

These threats are universal, in that many different audiences in many different circumstances can apply them. Other threats are specific to particular audiences and circumstances, and are described in their relevant chapters.

Systems failures or attacks

'Advanced, post-industrial societies and economies are critically dependent on linked computer information and communication systems' ('Countering cyber' 2001/2: 16). A BT/IDC paper in May 2002 claimed that despite concerns about terrorism, 'human error and viruses are the most frequent causes of disaster within telecommunications companies', and estimated the cost of 'downtime' for companies at $9,000 a minute. Yet '60 percent of UK and 90 percent of European enterprises, with global revenues in excess of 66 million pounds, have no business continuity plans in place' ('Telecoms companies' 2002).

This book is not qualified to explain the technical mysteries of viruses and hackers, cyber wars between nation states, defaced websites or the defences against them like firewalls, patches, filters, encryption and authentication software. Those are referenced here, written about elsewhere (see References and Bibliography) and several examples appear in these pages. Indeed, if the increase in volume and sophistication of attacks continues at its current rate, today's methods will seem as distant by 2010 as modern fighter pilots are from their earliest predecessors in 1914 firing pistols from open cockpits. It is, however, worthwhile noting how the main trends affect crisis communication and issues management.

'We can't assume that everyone on the planet is going to be socially responsible', Sun Microsystems's Chief Scientist reminded a business audience ('From "long boom"' 2000). The likelihood of systems failures or attacks on all companies naturally grows with the growing online population, and their ability to disrupt the internet by accident, out of malice – like the hackers posing as Ford employees who in May 2002 stole the credit records, social security numbers and bank account numbers of 13,000 people from a reporting agency ('13,000 credit reports' 2002: C5) – or to make a social or political protest. Traditional terrorism has spawned political 'cyber terrorism', and Information itself is the victim. Examples include the 25 Israeli organisations targeted by the Palestinian worm 'Injustice' ('Israeli organizations' 2001: 4), sites in the United Arab Emirates defaced and pasted with a 'Zionist flag' ('Internet city' 2001), and numerous United States and Chinese confrontations ('Cyber terrorism' 2002: 16–18).

'Hate sites', some of which, like Dowethics.com have already been recorded in these pages, are a related phenomenon. Mi2g, the respected British 'digital risk specialists' conducted confidential interviews with 125 CEOs and CFOs in Europe, Asia and the Americas, finding that: 'The biggest digital risk problem keeping some senior executives awake at night is not hacking, viruses or network intrusion but corporate hate sites worldwide' ('The rise of' 2004). Their cogent report offered a useful definition as well as information:

> The corporate hate sites dissuade customers from buying a particular product or service and damage the revenue streams in a very measurable way. Corporate hate sites have also, in many well documented cases, caused a major public relations problem in terms of the resultant pressure from government watchdogs and access to capital markets. Other hate sites also include those that are anti-Semitic, anti-Catholic, anti-Islamic, anti-gay, anti-abortion, as well as sites that promote racism, hate music and culture, neo-Nazism and bomb-making.
>
> ('The rise of' 2004)

Mi2g declared that there were '10,500 hate sites against major global brands on the internet', compared with 1,900 by the end of 2000, 550 in 1997, and one in 1995 ('The rise of' 2004).

Since 9/11, close attention has been paid to 'cyber strikes', either against individual privacy or directed at government and other official sites, sometimes sparked by meetings of international bodies like the G-8 or IMF. The connected step – attacks on companies – has also been made. An FBI survey revealed that 186 US companies recorded a total of $377.8 million in financial losses from security breaches in 2001 ('The new look' 2002: 28–32). In 2003 a Government–academic survey estimated the cost in the USA had reached $666 million ('2004 e-crime' 2004).

'The entry costs for conducting cyber war are extremely modest', noted CERT, a US Government-funded internet security study group at Carnegie Mellon University in Pittsburgh, in an article about cyber-war between states ('Countering cyber' 2001/2: 16). The entrances may be existing 'interconnections between the enemy and its allies, using links for sharing resources or data, or through wide-area network connections' ('Countering cyber' 2001/2: 17). CERT has plotted a rise in reported attack incidents from 21,756 in 2000 to 137,529 in 2003 (CERT/CC statistics 2004). 'An incident', they advised, 'may involve one site or hundreds (or even thousands) of sites. Also, some incidents may involve ongoing activity for long periods of time' (CERT/CC Statistics 2004). United States research firm Computer Economics put the worldwide cost in 2000 at $17.1 billion, a 41 per cent increase on 1999 ('Protecting yourself' 2002: 24). Mi2g reported in 2004 that economic damage from 'all forms of digital risk manifestation – covert attacks, spam, phishing scams, DDoS, major malware, overt attacks – in 2004 has crossed $411 billion worldwide. The comparable figure for 2003 was $215 billion' ('Q3' 2004).

CERT's 'Overview of Attack Trends' in April 2002 had warned that attack tools were:

- Increasing in speed and level of automation.
- Becoming harder to discover.
- Finding more ways through existing 'firewalls'.
- Using other systems attached to the internet to attack a victim.
- Increasingly threatening the internet's infrastructure leading to denials of service, compromise of sensitive information, misinformation and diversion of time and resources to combat the attack (CERT 2002).

In 2004, CERT stopped publishing the number of incidents recorded: 'Given the widespread use of automated attack tools, attacks against Internet-connected systems have become so commonplace that counts of the number of incidents reported provide little information with regard to assessing the scope and impact of attacks' (CERT/CC statistics 2004).

From the perspective of crisis communication, the growing scope for systems failures and attacks is a striking sign of the power passing into the hands of nebulous groups, individuals, and countries. A joint CERT/US Secret Service/CSO Magazine survey in 2004 concluded: 'Nearly a third (30%) of respondents in organizations experiencing e-crimes or intrusions in 2003 do not know whether insiders or outsiders were the cause.' Of those who did know 'hackers were most frequently cited (40%) followed closely by current or former employees or contractors (31%)' ('2004 e-crime' 2004).

> When it comes to identifying specific types of e-crimes committed against organizations, the survey shows 36% of respondents' organizations experienced unauthorized access to information, systems or networks by an insider compared to 27% committed by outsiders. Both sabotage and extortion are committed equally by insiders and outsiders for organizations responding to the survey.
>
> ('2004 e-crime' 2004)

Michael Erbschloe, an American author and consultant, warned of the consequences of concerted action: a scenario he calls 'PH2', in which a group of terrorists from around the world 'launch a series of attacks in the month of December to disrupt commerce' ('The future of' 2001). In July 2001 'the head of the Australian Defence Forces told a conference that more than 30 countries had "advanced and aggressive programmes for waging war by computer"' ('The dangers of' 2001). But such attacks need not be the preserve of nations or established terrorist groups; everyday, online users scattered across the planet could mount them. These people may be goaded into action by many more individuals, the more extreme 'e-fluentials', or people 'who shape the opinions and attitudes of the Internet Community', tracked from 1999 by PR multinational Burson-Marsteller (BM) and researchers Roper Starch. It may be as hard to segment e-fluentials into shades of opinion as pinning down the actual attackers. Subsequent research estimated that 11.1 million adults fitted the broad category in the USA alone (Burson-Marsteller 2002). This group is examined more fully in the next chapter.

Much attention has been paid to the jobs of preventing accidents or attacks, minimising the damage and hunting down the attackers. Communicators also face several challenges as the number and intensity of disruptions grow:

- Increased monitoring of communication activity relating to a company and the issues connected with it.
- Maintaining the trust of stakeholders when systems are seriously compromised.
- Developing communication relationships with large numbers of 'e-fluentials', globally as well as nationally.

- Deciding how best to 'own' but not control the forum for such communication activity.
- Defining how to best establish a consistent, transparent and acceptable 'tone' that encourages frankness and meets demands for transparency, but discourages volatility.

See Chapters 5–7 for an examination of possible strategies and tactics, integrated with a general communication plan.

Instant boycotts

British Government and MORI Research findings in 2001 suggest 'that as many as one-fifth of consumers now boycott or select products on social grounds' (DTI 2002: 8). In that year one organisation alone, the British-based *Ethical Consumer Magazine* and website, promoted 45 UK boycotts from companies to countries and films to foodstuffs (www.ethicalconsumer.org).

Boycotts are a common and simple form of protest. They must have a target – usually a well-known company or institution; 'targeters' – usually a non-profit group; an action – usually a call to stop buying the target's products or services; a universal issue that can be understood – perceptions of animal cruelty, damage to the environment, or human rights abuses by subcontractors; and at least one audience – consumers, shareholders or students. Issues communication is both the brake and accelerator, used by protestors to keep the boycott momentum going or, by governments or companies, to slow, divert or stop the process.

Traditionally, boycott communication might involve colourful publicity like the plan by America's PETA (People for the Ethical Treatment of Animals) boycotters to dress up as cows and butchers and enact a 'cow-skinning with a papier-mâché ax' outside a Safeway shareholders meeting. Counter-cultural approaches include defacing posters or wrecking public space with graffiti. Sometimes companies apply counter-pressure. Their traditional responses include ignoring the issue; presenting their own side of the argument via websites, media and third party experts or, in the case of Safeway, entering into a dialogue with the protestors and agreeing to change business practices ('PETA withdraws' 2002).

At present the internet is used as a boycott publicity and information tool:

- To publicise special events.
- As a resource for downloadable 'leaked memos' or 'action packs' about 'guilty' organisations. Greenpeace's anti-Esso site includes both of the above.
- As a forum to exchange ideas, news, draw in support, subscriptions and maintain momentum.

The UK Greenpeace website uses all these techniques in its 'Stop Esso' boycott campaign ('Use your' 2002).

But the internet will move from promoting the boycott to *becoming* the boycott, exploiting new technology and e-commerce dependence. In May 2002 NGOs in the United Arab Emirates publicised, by the usual patchy publicity methods, a wider Arab boycott of American products ('Boycott of' 2002). 'It's not organized', said a Saudi businesswoman, 'I felt it from inside. It spreads by word of mouth' ('Arabs fuel' 2002: A11). In contrast BT's well-known scientist and futurologist Ian Pearson has raised the prospect of boycotting the same target much more dramatically, in a scenario where future environmentalists email everyone on the net, recommending economic sanctions against the USA because of its CO_2 emission policies.

> By pressing the 'I agree' button, the user's e-commerce preferences are automatically set to exclude products and services from the USA. The result could be a billion or more of the richest people on the planet excluding the USA from business, within a few minutes. No geographically based power structure can impose such a penalty so quickly.
>
> (Pearson 2000)

This is a 'reactive' boycott, *against* an organisation. A 'proactive' boycott may be just as possible, and more publicly acceptable, as NGOs and interest groups colla-borate and offer e-commerce settings *for* ethically 'approved' companies.

Addressing specialised issues in a 'holistic' environment

More information will lead to more discussion and information exchange, and more of that information will crystallise into issues. Some of these break down distinctions between discussion and response.

In *The Network Society*, written in 1991, Dutch academic Jan Van Dijk foresaw more connections between micro (private) and macro (public) levels of social life, connecting the spheres of personal life, work, study, recreation and travel (Van Dijk 1991; 2000 edn). This is certainly happening within the west's ever larger and more influential elderly population, part in work (in 1999, eight in ten US baby boomers expected to work at least part time after 'retirement'), and part at play, techno-literate and using IT to help them in every 'sphere of living' ('Technology needs' 1999: 53). The sick and the elderly, historically the most helpless and dependent in society, now number among the most influential. By 2005, over 100,000 Americans will be older than 100. Greater life expectancy brings greater risk of chronic illness – forecast to affect around 40 per cent of Americans by 2010. These enormous, revenue-eating socially ambiguous trends are an unambiguous business opportunity. On average, 'consumers use more than twice the amount of health services in each decade they live after 30' ('New technology' 2000: 33). Ian Pearson is among those anticipating a move to a 'caring economy'. 'We will value the human as a human, not as a cog in a machine. It will be the human skills – the interpersonal, caring skills – that we will pay for. For everything else, we will use a machine' ('Beyond digital' 2000: R20).

While estimates vary, the Asian edition of *Wall Street Journal* noted that around 100 million people had logged on to obtain health information in 2001. Many websites and patient groups are springing up to influence and guide the decisions of commercially significant audiences, and 'usher in a new era of patient activism' ('Technology Journal' 2001: T6).

The elderly are emerging as a leading exemplar of Van Dijk's analysis. Better-informed about health, they are relating personal well-being to macro issues of work, leisure, food and travel. Many companies already find themselves being judged by their attitude to issues in other fields. Those companies – whether in healthcare, biotech, hi-tech, fitness and leisure – will develop a 'holistic' communication strategy sensitive to wider, hard-to-measure, developments. 'I think I understand the need to hone our message so that it is more about the people we help now or in the future, and not about the money we do or don't spend', the CEO of Bristol-Myers Squibb pharmaceuticals told a Detroit business audience in 2002 ('The new leadership' 2002: 308).

Unexpected actions from once-silent groups

As technology spreads, it will offer isolated communities new powers. The Centre for Tomorrow's Company based in London has raised the prospect of confronting western consumers and investors with peasant farmers in Andhra Pradesh forced into penury and suicide by agri-business, using technology provided by develop-ment agencies or activists to relay their plight direct to the western world in 'real-time – as real-time as day-trading . . . Any self-respecting global company will offer stakeholders direct opportunity to talk to them about the impact they are having' (Goyder 2000: 4).

Global 'communication empowerment', forces rich sophisticated organisations to hear discomfiting messages from poor people with no further need to remain communication's 'subjects' or 'targets'. 'We can't accept the Government radio', Metlakunta, a village woman from India's Deccan region, complained in 1996: 'that radio will not allow poor women to dialogue on their own problems and issues.' Narsamma from the same district complained in a development agency film that the mainstream camera 'looks down' on rural people. She called this, the 'Patel Shot'. The agency's director agreed after arranging an encounter between local women and environmentalists and feminists from the city of Hyderabad. 'They made a royal mess of it. They could hardly communicate with the village people.' The outcome was a 'communication media centre consisting of a radio station and a video production facility', run by local women. 'For these women, communication is a means to extend their expression, articulate their ideas and concerns without any interference from an educated elite, whose language is alien to them' ('India: breaking' 2001).

This development will accelerate as more sophisticated technology becomes available. The women were struggling to get a licence for their radio station, but ultimately the internet will outpace foot-dragging local bureaucrats and project their message as far and as widely as they deserve.

Rumours

> A brand can be brought tumbling down in a matter of days through an offhand comment on a little visited web site.
>
> Nick Denton, Moreover.com. ('What can be done?' 2001: 12)

Posting internet rumours is a notorious and, for the internet, traditional activity. Other than ignoring them, companies sometimes respond by doing what Apple did in 1997, using legal pressure to shut down damaging sites ('Rumormongers' 1997: 54). Another method is to obtain disclaimers from respected third party sources, like the United States Food and Drug Authority's (FDA) public statement in 1999 that tampon manufacturers were not adding asbestos to their products ('Internet rumors' 1999: 7). Microsoft took the same approach in September 2001, after the World Trade Center tragedy, when the non-profit Anti Defamation League confirmed that the company's 'WingDing' font did not contain anti-Semitic messages ('ADL' 2001).

Absurd, malicious, or accurate servants of transparency, rumours can disrupt sales, shares, reputation and careful planning – or, as ICI found, all four at the same time. The United Kingdom chemical firm prematurely unveiled an £800 million rights issue two days after advance rumours started driving down its share price ('ICI confirms' 2002: 26). On 19 September 2001, an internet stock page suggested that a vulnerable Japanese supermarket chain, Kotobukiya, would be unable to cover a cheque the next day. The share price fell 35 yen to 17 yen immediately, and only rebounded slightly the following day after managers fielded a flood of telephone inquiries. Three months later, Kotobukiya filed for bankruptcy. 'We couldn't raise our share price after it had languished for so long. We'd been pushed down a path from which we couldn't return', remembered a former executive ('Fragile firms' 2002).

Nick Denton, an *Economist* and *FT* journalist who co-founded Moreover, a UK–US Internet monitoring firm, believes that 'the uncontrolled flow of opinion, comment and rumour across the web has reached an epidemic proportion and remains largely unchecked or unmonitored by the vast majority of firms' ('What can be done?' 2001: 12). Research in 2003 indicated that 81 per cent of 'e-fluentials' 'have used the Internet in the past year to discuss, post or forward hearsay information about a company, brand or CEO to their friends, family or

57

colleagues' (Burson-Marsteller 2003: 1). 'The study', claimed Burson-Marsteller, 'reinforces the need for companies to listen carefully to Web site visitors' questions and be prepared to provide accurate information about their operations and core values' (Burson-Marsteller 2003: 1).

Hearsay is not automatically accepted as gospel, with 86 per cent of online opinion leaders attempting to confirm rumour details through corporate and news websites, as well as other sources (Burson-Marsteller 2003:1). Cobra technology piles pressure on rumour management, by:

- *Speedier spread*. According to Denton, writing in 2001, 'the average time for information to flow from the bottom to the top of the gossip food chain can be as little as two to three days' ('What can be done?' 2001: 12). Given that faster-moving rumours already proliferate in hours not days, the reduction of any average seems likely as more people go online to spread gossip down faster and more individually tailored conduits. 'My wife', a Zimbabwean journalist complained in 2002, 'received a message on her cellphone that fuel prices would be increasing by 55% *that night*' ('If rumours were energy' 2002; emphasis added).
- *Increasing the sources*. As Denton explains, some online journals currently 'operate to lower journalistic standards than established publications and in this way uncorroborated rumour is treated as fact' ('What can be done?' 2001: 12). More online users in more countries will spawn more news outlets with less time or inclination to check their sources. They may knowingly post a rumour to scoop competitors, serve social or political agendas or attract a bigger audience.
- *Squeezing time*. Growing ability to dump or purchase shares, and buy or sell products online squeezes the time available to check truth for fear that others may act first. Unscrupulous companies may contribute to this cycle by timely deployment of rumours to lift share prices, raise expectations about new products, or prepare markets for a bad quarter.

Up to now, rumour-mongers have used sources external to the targeted company; but this could change. In its April 2002 'Attack Trends' report CERT warned: 'Intruders might be able to modify news sites, produce bogus press releases, and conduct other activities, all of which could have economic impact.' Misinformation injected *into* a company may also, if it happens frequently enough, weaken the whole concept of transparency, and perhaps trust in the internet itself.

Treating technology 'technically'

The final threat is really the sum of all the others. Technology cannot be treated as a servant of existing public relations methods or as a tool to win various operational advantages. It will force corporations to re-evaluate what communication means to them.

This is because technology opens new spaces where companies must talk, listen and occasionally fight. It may be a distorting, contradictory, frustrating, inaccurate space or it may provide clarity, wisdom and more mature levels of public knowledge. It will certainly be fast and volatile and shaped by social trends and sentiment as much as by financial statements or marketing campaigns. It is the new arena for deciding power relations between a corporation and its publics. The manager of Shell's uncensored internet forum 'TellShell' told the company's online public: 'We have to remind some people [in Shell] . . . that it is OK just to write without having your response checked and double-checked by all the right people. It is OK to think aloud, or on-line' (Harris 1999).

The information revolution can be an uncomfortable place for Business, but it cannot simply pick out the good bits and ignore the rest. When new technology is switched on for the first time, its impact goes far deeper than simply doing the job faster, better and more cheaply. The internet lies in many hands and is hard to destroy. Corporate information and attitudes are inscribed on it, perhaps forever. Good digital forensics will extract it; good communicators will use it. That challenge is more than technical.

Denial, misunderstanding and failure to integrate all the changes made by the information revolution expose Business to the force of an accompanying revolution in public opinion (Moore 2004: 36). This is the subject of Chapter 3.

The future for public opinion – 'an imitation of closeness'

But there is no such thing as man in the world. In the course of my life I have seen Frenchmen, Italians, Russians etc.; I know, too, thanks to Montesquieu, that one can be a Persian. But as for man, I declare that I have never met him in my life; if he exists, he is unknown to me.

Josef de Maistre. *Considerations on France* (1797: 53)

INTRODUCTION

'Public opinion is formed and expressed by machinery', Churchill wrote between the two world wars in his essay 'Mass effects in modern life', adding: 'there is neither the need nor the leisure for personal reflection' (Churchill 1932: 194). Since then, the movement towards the mechanisation of opinion has clearly intensified and, at the same time, amoeba-like, continuously divides into new technologies which multiply points of opinion. So, while information remains the raw material for the global economy, and public opinion one of its major products, technology is changing the constructions, tastes and expressions, and the sheer quantity, of public opinion. The way firms find and influence that opinion must therefore also change, and executives who have never engaged in opinion management and have no professional knowledge of communication. They cannot escape its tides, under-tows and eddies, or their growing role in its formation.

Public opinion has always been tapped to build sales and value, awareness and assent. Transparency and interactivity means that: 'In the future, rather than being focused on effectively communicating to the public, PR professionals will become increasingly involved in communicating with the public' (Cooley 1999: 41). Not just PR professionals. 'Journalists and other relevant publics can access information without going through us' a United States PR veteran foresaw in 1999 (Freitag 1999: 36). Although online publics can go anywhere for material to form opinions, some of their corporate ports of call still do not know how to interest and accommodate them.

It is intended here to explore three questions:

- What is happening to the public?
- What is happening to opinion?
- What should Business do about it?

WHAT WILL HAPPEN TO THE PUBLIC?

A business's 'publics' are the various individuals and audiences (or stakeholders or constituencies) that collectively comprise a company's 'general public'. They matter because the company wants to do business with them, because they want their active support or passive goodwill, or because certain 'publics' are forming influential opinions. An organisation's usual publics might include – quite possibly but not always in this rough order of priority – customers, employees, investors, regulators, suppliers, distributors, subcontractors, trade and general media, local communities, sponsored celebrities or theoretically independent-minded experts like academics or consultants, activist or industry groups. Within these categories are 'opinion leaders', who help shape the perceptions of the others.

Within these broader publics other distinct groups are important to inform or commune with; perhaps children, pension fund managers, parents, business travellers, diabetics, analysts, activists, tourists, doctors, banks, neighbours, cultural groups, ethnic minorities, influential journalists, company directors, senior citizens. Communications with these audiences varies with fortune or fashion. If a company gets into enough trouble, peripheral audiences may step in and exert a powerful impact on 'public opinion', which here means stakeholder perceptions of a company's overall reputation. Those perceptions are powerfully affected by the company's actions and communication during a disaster or a long drawn-out issue.

Business audiences and technology together decide the warmth and depth of the relationship, with technology forcing the pace of change. If it has done nothing else, IT does this because it has given meaning to the prefix 'micro'. Large numbers of people and the media that serve them can now be micro-segmented and micro-targeted with progressively more personal messages. This is the latest stage of a process accelerated by the Enlightenment, widened throughout society by the industrial revolution, professional specialisation, and urbanisation, and deepened by the growth of media outlets demanding more detail to win a competitive advantage for their particular readers. It ushered in today's sophisticated communication management disciplines: mass marketing, financial PR, media and community relations, political campaign management or crisis management.

Now the scene is changing again. We noted in the last chapter that many 'publics' are reconstituting themselves because of:

- Access to information technology.
- 'Globalisation' of markets, issues and events.

61

These trends expose the publics to two immense and opposed forces:

- The force of coalescence – to group on a massive, perhaps worldwide scale around a product, belief, brand or point of view.
- The force for fragmentation – the power to act online as an individual, seeking out tiny clusters of like-minded individuals whose interests are limited or highly specialised.

These forces feed off an ability to find out more, and the power to act on what is found out.

At the same time, audiences will continue to be identified by traditional characteristics.

- Shared geographies and social features.
- Common cultural factors such as ethnicity, age, diet, gender, class, religion, and leisure activity.
- Shared vocational or other professional features.
- Mutual economic or political interests.
- A shared approach to a particular issue or organisation.

But these conventional clusters are tugged in new directions by technology, global-isation, fragmentation, and coalescence. The character of some audiences is changed by new online arrivals from other countries and cultures; other audiences, as we have already seen, are transformed by technology's power to lobby and act. Totally new clusters with a hi-tech focus are also on the scene. Some audiences are pulled out of the 'real' world into a purely 'virtual' world of communities to pursue causes that might simultaneously be fluid, confusing, clarifying, personalised, empowering, alienating, addictive, overwhelming and highly stimulating. Richard Edelman, CEO of Edelman, argues that such 'splintering of audiences' is creating 'individual webs of trust and triangulation among multiple sources of information' ('PR must embrace' 2001). This transformation is most apparent among con-sumers. UK retail analysts Verdict Research warned in April 2002:

> If there is to be one defining attribute of retailing in this new millennium, it is that mass markets are dissolving into highly fragmented micro-markets. . . . The rolling out of a formulaic approach is now obsolete. Today, the 'devil is in the detail': skilfully tailored propositions will reach more of the target customers more often. The scattergun of old must be replaced by a collection of rifles aimed at more segmented customer groups.
>
> ('Micro retailing' 2002)

In an information age crisis this need is urgent since customers are only one of many 'micro-segmented' audiences, and events and feelings move too fast to allow firms the luxury of a planned and scheduled campaign. Yet even in that segmented environment, collective communication exists. Public spaces are still needed to find and share opinions and information. Forms of 'collective' rather than totally 'individual' perception therefore exist, and can be reached.

The desire for public fora pre-dates recorded civilisation. In more modern times, the German philosopher Jürgen Habermas believes public opinion was given momentum in late-seventeenth-century England, several 'public spheres' appeared for informed persons to communicate. These were pamphlets and the press, salons, Masonic lodges, coffee houses or reading societies (Chisick 2002: 48). Now the 'public sphere' is entering the limitless spaces opened by the internet. Knowing *where* stakeholders and others go to communicate will be as important as knowing what is said when they get there. Corporations will need to keep track of the multiplying spaces where public opinion about them is formed, and learn new communication rules.

At the same time, because of micro-segmenting and message personalisation, many individuals accessing collective spaces will nonetheless tend to imagine themselves as autonomous and independent-minded. Whether this is true or not, it means they will certainly be independently empowered. Marketers are already catering to an enhanced and perhaps unreasonable or unrealistic sense of empower-ment. Text messages, screens in grocery stores, trains, waiting rooms, stations, airports, or toilets are touted as advertising tools for the era of consumer 'micro-retailing', but future issues and crises must be driven by much more intense, focused interactivity. Chapter 2 noted how the balance of power is being changed by interactivity. 'In an interactive communication world', notes a PR academic and practitioner, the former receiver of messages 'usurps power'.

> The receiver determines when to accept a message, when to process it, how much of it to process, and what related messages to seek and retrieve. Further, the receiver, in a truly interactive environment, may choose to provide immediate feedback. Immediate feedback, in turn, has its own consequence: It shortens the decision process.
>
> (Freitag 1999: 36)

But the 'receiver' need not only provide feedback to a 'sending' organisation. He or she can also change and pass on impressions to other receivers.

Does fragmentation, transparency and empowerment always mean information age publics are reaching independent opinions? Probably not. To make fast sense of the diversity and detail of information, and to feel secure about sources, online audiences turn to 'independent' specialists from within their own ranks, people who claim to make sense of the detail needed to construct opinions. Technology is already creating a new audience of opinion formers who influence stakeholder perceptions. A picture can be painted of the emerging opinion formers, according to research in the most 'mature' internet region, the USA. They must, to begin with, be active contributors to the online environment. A Pew Internet and American Life investigation of these 'content creators' in Spring 2003 concluded that 53 million Americans (roughly 23 per cent of the United States adult population and 44 per cent of adult users), 'have used the Internet to publish their thoughts, respond to others, post pictures, share files and otherwise contribute to the explosion of content available online' (Pew Internet 2004: 2). Most (67 per cent) did not regularly update their thoughts and materials, either every few weeks or even less; 28 per cent did so 1–2 times a week or more (Pew Internet 2004: 5). The Pew survey classified this constituency as younger, open 'power creators'; 'older creators' (average age 58) who are most likely to build their own websites, and 'content omnivores' who 'log on frequently and spend a considerable amount of time online doing a variety of activities (Pew Internet 2004: 3). The United States study briefly noted in Chapter 2, conducted in 1999 and 2001 by the large PR multinational Burson-Marsteller (BM) and research firm Roper Starch, sought the communication keystones of the new community, describing these '*e*-fluentials' as: 'a group of men and women who are much more active than other internet users in terms of their online influence, using e-mail, newsgroups, bulletin boards and other online vehicles to convey their messages' ('The e-fluentials' 2000: 3). The project was intended in part for BM to blend issues and branding needs, and build business by customised e-fluential surveys for particular firms or industries, opinion polling, web development counsel and campaign management. This new public, it was argued, was important to the process of 'building a trusted brand' ('The e-fluentials' 2000: 4).

BM and Roper Starch studied these 'change agents', at least in America. Many are also 'influentials' offline – categorised as people who conducted at least three political/social activities in the past year such as speech making, local committee service or holding political office. Online, 'they are significantly more likely to provide feedback to Web sites, post to bulletin boards or actively participate in newsgroups' ('The e-fluentials' 2000: 7). Compared with typical users, 'more than twice as many e-fluentials are asked for their opinions on new technologies, business and jobs or careers'. 'One in two (51%) e-fluentials provides insight on current events, compared to just 25% of general users' ('The e-fluentials' 2000: 4). 'Eight in ten (79%) find the Internet the most effective mode of information exchange, in contrast to five in ten (49%) in the general online population' ('The e-fluentials' 2000: 8). This curiosity and flexibility complements Pew's finding that internet 'Content creators are likely to have higher levels of education – 46% have a college degree or more compared with 26% of all Americans' ('Pew Internet' 2004: 6). In *The power of online influencers: your company's newest stakeholder group* (2002), BM produced more detail. Between 1999 and 2001, the number of e-fluentials had risen from 8 to 10 per cent – 11.1 million of America's online adults, with 'a say in the purchasing decisions – online and offline – of approximately 155 million consumers' ('The power of online influencers' 2002: 2). Noting that e-fluentials spread news about a negative experience to an average of 17 people, and pass on positive experiences to 11 people, BM claimed:

> The far-reaching effect of this powerful group of men and women can make or break a brand, marshal or dissolve support for business and consumer issues, and provide insight into events as they unfold. For companies and marketers, there is an urgent need to earn e-fluentials' trust, approval and support.
>
> ('The power of online influencers' 2002: 2)

The rise of e-fluentials is unlikely to confine itself to the United States or to market-ing communications. As a result of fragmentation of stakeholders and therefore opinion-forming, and the added complication of many more e-fluentials emerging in other countries as the world online population grows, important new relation-ships must be built by Business that only technology can mediate.

In this way, the more interactive, spontaneous, empowered and online audi-ences rely on the opinions and agendas of relatively small, often unaccountable, groups of people. Micro-knowledge of e-fluentials clustering around particular brands, issues, beliefs, regional loyalties, causes and industry sectors, and their communication preferences, will become critical to resolving crisis and issues at internet speed. 'I think it is a little frightening that one is able to set the political agenda with five people who are able to do some good research, write convincingly and who have good contacts with the media. It is not really very good for democracy', a Danish human rights activist admitted to a researcher in 2001. 'The problem is, though, that that's the way to do it' (Backer 2001: 235).

Twenty-first-century businesses must identify these new stakeholders, and closely engage their free-ranging, time-starved, empowered and overloaded publics.

WHAT WILL HAPPEN TO OPINION?

Fifty years ago the potato had an easier life. Certainly Idaho growers would not have pondered such esoteric matters as potato perception management. Their product, the Russet Burbank, was 'the most sought after variety in the frozen processing industry', and is still 'used mainly to make French fries' ('Potato Growers'). Matters, including the Russet Burbank itself, had grown more complicated by 2002, when the Idaho potato farmers' conference heard a biotech executive dismiss food firms' belief that consumers would shun genetically modified (GM) French fries, but admit that managed perception had nevertheless made a big impact on the product. 'Basically, public relations sealed the fate of potatoes' ('Public perceptions' 2002).

Perception, image and potatoes are now definitely sharing the menu. 'What is the biggest dietary fallacy about potatoes being disseminated by the food communication/media business at this time?' *Potato Grower* magazine asked farmers in an online poll (70 per cent answered: 'Potatoes are loaded with carbohydrates and contribute to obesity') ('Potato poll' 2002). Today growers, food manufacturers, agro-chemical and biotech companies, fast food chains, bureaucrats, scientists, dieticians, crusading journalists, environmentalists and consumer groups include the potato in campaigns crossing national borders and time zones. They must influence consumer perceptions by distilling scientific research to simple messages, but transparency sometimes makes information harder to render into agreed opinion.

For opinion-forming about food in general is also less simple than it used to be – or used to appear, and transparency takes much of the blame, partly in the form of 'improved' labelling. In the United Kingdom of 2005, even the decidedly low-tech food label carries data on nutrition, storage, allergenic ingredients and recommended daily amounts. Some manufacturers go further than the law and add extra information. Elsewhere, authorities keep up with a perceived public requirement for highly disparate information. In April 2002 the Japanese Government announced plans to jail and fine deliberate mislabellers ('Government to send' 2002). The Australia New Zealand Food Authority in March 2002 proposed forcing food makers to tell consumers about naturally occurring salt and sugar in food labelled 'salt free' or 'low in sugar' ('Cleansing salts' 2002: 29). The EU now expects food manufacturers to list whether their products include any of the top twelve allergens ('EU ruling' 2004: 8). German retailers opposed, in late 2004, Government plans to label fresh cheese and sausages, which they claimed 'could lead to the loss of as many as 100,000 jobs' ('Food labelling' 2004: 27). In the United Kingdom, there is support for labelling to promote sustainable fisheries by differentiating between seafood products (Jaffry *et al.* 2004: 215–28). Swedish academics have investigated the value of 'negative outcome' labelling, where the label shapes decisions by being a social warning: 'Do not choose this product, it is worse for the environment than the average product' (Grankvist *et al.* 2004: 213).

Most consumers, though, cannot cope with existing transparency levels, as a Safeway UK customer survey found in 2002: 'Our research suggests that one in four people don't read the label. Second, those that do have a limited understanding of what a lot of it means' ('Information overload' 2002: 42). In fact, '93% said working out the nutritional content of food was more difficult than changing a plug, reading a map or setting a video', and 78 per cent did not know that RDA stood for Recommended Daily Allowance ('Many consumers' 2002: 12). But what is the solution? Surrendering yet more of our precious time to accommodate yet more helpful transparency, according to the Consumer Association, which says food labels need 'an education programme so consumers can understand the information'. According to Safeway UK: 'there are 30 million regular shoppers out there and what they want to know will vary from one extreme to the other. Catering for all is damn near impossible' ('Information overload' 2002: 42).

The effort now needed to reach a truly informed opinion about what consumers consume itself consumes unreasonable amounts of time. Rarely is society able to spare it. Do shoppers shun GM potatoes out of hand if a newspaper reports that they caused 'intestinal lesions' in lab rats in a covered-up experiment, or do they investigate the methodology of the experiments ('CropGen reports' 2001)? Do they simply accept the headline that 'half the nation would eat GM food', as suggested by an NOP survey in the UK; or order a copy of that survey to investigate its less publicised findings ('Public opinion swings' 2001)? Or do audiences rely on experts or activists whose opinions chime with a pre-existing bias, fear or prejudice?

Whether the subject is food safety, health and well-being, the environment, human rights, social responsibility or financial probity, more 'bits' of information – the ingredients of opinion – are now in rapid and ceaseless circulation, colliding or splitting like electrons in a particle accelerator, and placing immense demands on organisations and on us to respond. Peter Denning, a prominent computer scientist, believes the Internet is 'stealing' our time: 'As our communication circle enlarges, the collective rate of events from it rises. Even if the diffusion of Internet technology into society is slow, it is inexorable, and it enables an ever-increasing flow of messages.' 'Time', he continues, 'has become our most precious resource. Every email message, phone call, or Web page link is a request for our time' (Denning 2002: 15). Information's demands on our time and perception, already intense at the office, will reach further into the home by 2010 as 'one-way' media like television – which 71 per cent of Europeans describe as the medium that best brings their family together – folds its still unique power to provoke feeling and shape perceptions into interactive digital technology ('TV the most' 2002).

The time-pressure information and interactivity creates, tests everyone, not least those keeping the information highways open. Research in 2000 indicated 77 per cent of UK companies published out-of-date information on their websites.

> In the vast majority of cases, the sheer volume of information on a site that has to be updated leads to problems and delays, as the webmasters simply cannot cope with the amount of content needing to be published, causing bottlenecks.
>
> ('Don't trust' 2000: 7)

Unsurprisingly, a 2001 survey by Gartner Consulting's People3 group discovered US IT departments 'should expect workloads to increase 50% in the next four years' (Fox 2002: 9). 'This cannot happen', a consultant to the IT world protested, 'all my customers are "maxed out," regularly working genuine 70–80 hour weeks, tired all the time, ignoring their lives at home' ('Already maxed out' 2002: 12).

Companies do not use technology to effectively engage with public opinion. But

67

to place pressure on IT professionals and treat the information challenge as a technical blockage to be cleared is to miss the point of public opinion in the information age. Peter Drucker argues, with the aid of capitals: 'So far, for 50 years, the information revolution has centred on data – their collection, storage, transmission, analysis, and presentation. It has centred on the "T" in IT. The next information revolution asks what is the MEANING of information, and what is its PURPOSE?' (Drucker 1998).

Drucker looked at the impact on regular business activity. The trend, he noted, 'is leading rapidly to redefining the tasks to be done with the help of information, and with it, to redefining the institutions that do these tasks' (Drucker 1998). The prospects for *irregular* business activity – epitomised by a crisis or a drawn-out issue, may be very similar. As Drucker remarked, the amount of information about the outside world now able to come into a company, and the amount of inside information about the company now going out:

> Have aggravated what all along has been management's degenerative tendency, especially in the big corporations: to focus inward on costs and efforts, rather than outward on opportunities, changes, and threats. This tendency is becoming increasingly dangerous considering the globalization of economies and industries, the rapid changes in markets and in consumer behavior, the crisscrossing of technologies across traditional industry lines, and the increasing instability of currencies.
>
> (Drucker 1998)

In an issues-driven or crisis environment, stakeholders deploy information to present opinions that suggest a desired course of action. Lack of time, multiplicity of sources and reconstituted micro-publics all have an impact on the future meaning and purpose of information, particularly as IT gets better at rousing emotion.

> Broadband Internet communication will soon allow inexpensive simultaneous real-time interactive visual, oral, numerical and textual messages, creating a much more powerful imitation of closeness than has heretofore been possible.
>
> (Leamer and Storper 2001: 641)

The academic authors of that remark feel these trends will not stop people clustering in traditional localised ways, since the internet cannot deliver the complexity of a face-to-face encounter. This is little comfort to crisis and issues managers, where interactivity will exploit the globalisation of issues, risks, crisis and increasing numbers of empowered internet stakeholders. Together, these factors suggest localised clusters may indeed occur, but on a massive, hard to track and international scale.

'Imitation of closeness' may affect opinion in two contradictory ways. First, it may act as an agent of transparency, assisting opinion by making masses of complicated information more vivid and memorable. Second, it will over-simplify information into something that feels deeply believable, and 'guilty' organisations will struggle to repair the damage without immense effort. Even before IT's rise, opinions did not necessarily become more accurate whenever they aroused emotion and felt more personal – now as then, opinions entrench in times of tension, and fuel volatility with escalating emotion.

What then is in store for opinion, as far as crisis and issues management is concerned?

- Opinion will be widely distributed and tailored to suit multiple and empowered audiences.
- It will depend on and exploit IT for this wider influence.
- It will become more interactive.
- It will be condensed from detailed and voluminous quantities of information.
- It will compete with many other opinions to attract stakeholder interest.
- It will be fed by volatile, instant, unanticipated and time-pressured swings of rumour-stoked emotion.
- It will put more pressure on audiences to act fast.
- By taking concrete shape it can inflict instant damage on targeted companies.

WHAT SHOULD BUSINESS DO ABOUT PUBLIC OPINION?

How can crisis and issues management accommodate the new demands made on it by public opinion?

Intense stakeholder emotions have always filled the opening stages of a crisis or issue: concern, fear, expectation, anger, hate, trust, anxiety, panic. These feelings are unlikely to be quelled by the effect of IT on public opinion, let alone the knowledge that IT allows critical actions to be taken in the opening stages of disaster. Consequently, many stakeholders, especially those unfamiliar with the threatened company or industry, may grapple with strong emotions in the face of an IT-sparked information deluge, and will use the technology at their disposal to effectively fan the flames.

The public then, will seek help online about how to feel and act. In the new public spheres, overflowing with information – general and specialised, permanent or the fleeting product of a particular incident or issue – new systems of trust will form, and new trustees of opinion and feeling will come forward. Ben Schneiderman, a scholar of Human–Computer interaction concludes: 'Now, new social traditions are needed to enhance cooperative behaviors in electronic environments supporting e-commerce, e-services, and online communities' (Schneiderman 2000: 57).

Trust, Schneiderman argues, must be designed into online experiences. Certainly, a firm threatened by risk or crisis must participate credibly in the new online models of Trust and Transparency. Away from the crisis discipline, this activity is touted as an obvious business opportunity. Gartner Research observes: 'Online groups and chat sessions between customers or between customers and enterprise employees can be very valuable. Communities can leverage customers' collective knowledge and allow the enterprise to better understand its customers' (Kolsky 2001). When it comes to retaining customer loyalty in economic downturns: 'Shared systems of trust, validation and manifested praise support organic structures that allow community users to interact transparently and productively' (Andrews 2001). 'Enterprises', the report advises, 'must prepare to deal with these new trust systems' (Andrews 2001).

These criteria can be applied to crisis management in the information age. Intervening in existing trust networks and constructing new ones raises the prospect of continuous interaction with diverse stakeholders, many marginal to a firm's day-to-day fortunes, but with the potential to intervene in a crisis with devastating effect. The right model for business, according to Harvard's Shoshana Zuboff, might in future lie with ' "distributed capitalism," in which ownership will be more widely spread and organizations will be as responsive to their employees and communities as they have been to their shareholders in the past decade' ('After Enron' 2002: 68).

Whatever the final extent of the swing towards a broader community of stakeholders, cobra technology forces firms to grasp the nettles of both 'public' and 'opinion'. They must pay closer heed to information provision. This must, we propose here and more fully in Chapter 7, go further than the blanket provision of transparent data, and involve shaping the meaning, and paying heed to the emotional capital of language, content and style less hedged around by legal caveats or marketing-speak. 'We need', declared Richard Edelman, 'to provide the client's perspective in a way that is fact-based and that acknowledges other points of view. We call it "modified advocacy"' ('PR must embrace' 2001: 3). This approach must overcome a bruised company's natural fear of 'unmanaged' messages and of participating in and even encouraging, diverse views in the uncontrolled setting of the web. 'To share our dilemmas and problems before we have worked out a solution requires a great deal of self-confidence', a Shell public affairs manager recently admitted ('Do the right' 2001: 33). TellShell's Clare Harris went further when replying to a highly abusive post:

> As you have already recognised Shell has a culture that is not used to going out and asking people what they think or in some areas empowering all of their staff to be part of this engagement process. There are a lot of people in Shell who are worried that if we enter into a[n] open public debate the world will fall around our ears if we say what we think and don't only deploy 'trained

spokespeople'. I think this nervousness is only natural in the company that communicated so badly with Brent Spar [see Chapter 1, p. 33]. But I do think we're learning and I believe that we want to do it better.

(TellShell, 1999)

It might also be dangerous. Can a communication plan that truly engages stake-holders find a way between vapid statements about corporate social responsibility, promoting trust on key issues and surrendering control to e-fluentials and other activists? Part Two investigates potential steps for engagement with public opinion in the decade ahead.

Public opinion is changing its relationship to communication. Instead of expand-ing intellectual independence, the time-pressures, segmentation of sources and detail of information expands the authority of key influencers and the potency of information suffused with memorable emotion and argument, but not necessarily clarity.

Change to communication is therefore essential. But it must be asked if Business as a whole can change its approach to public opinion, and fit the change into their crisis plans, when so many companies are broken up and outsourced across countries and continents. How will the rise of decentralised, loosely organised enterprise affect the future of issues, crisis and crisis management? This is where we turn next.

Chapter 4

The fragile corporation

It is the transfer of ownership that defines outsourcing and often makes it such a challenging, painful process. In outsourcing, the buyer does not instruct the supplier how to perform its task but, instead, focuses on communicating what results it wants to buy; it leaves the process of accomplishing those results to the supplier.

From the website of Dimensioni, an Indian outsourcing provider (2004)

THE OUTSOURCED IDENTITY

The prospect of a knowledge-driven, devolved, global corporation dominates the thoughts of leading commentators. Peter Drucker famously foresaw that success in the information revolution would depend on 'the manipulation of symbols' (Drucker 1986: 768); D. T. Quah has stressed the need 'to organize understanding into forms that others will understand' (Quah 1997: 4). Remarks like those antici- pated, as a prominent Japanese management professor later observed of Drucker:

The uncoupling of the primary-products economy and the industrial econ- omy, the uncoupling of production and employment in the manufacturing industry, and the near uncoupling of the real economy and the symbol economy.

('The man who' 2001)

It is helpful to examine several aspects of this uncoupling process, and their impact on corporate crisis. We must first remind ourselves that we have already discussed powerful new influences changing the task of 'organizing understanding' in a crisis. Step changes in technology, target audiences and public opinion are reshaping and relocating the places where companies network and interact with their publics. Stakeholders are more if not better informed, and – perhaps less apparently – more exposed to emotional demands from other stakeholders. They also feel entitled to greater quantities of corporate information but must fend off emotional and informational overload in a restless and charged communication environment.

Consequently, companies in crisis are more porous, and need to give access to information that was once protected and denied – before critics find the same information and craft less favourable messages of their own.

To meet the new conditions for corporate messaging, information access and stakeholder perceptions, companies in crisis will need to devote more effort and resources to monitoring and responding to what might be called 'symbol manipulation': an attempt to reshape the elements of identity by external opinion, speculation and information. This requirement comes at a time when relations between employees and employer are more tenuous, despite the former's growing responsibility for corporate messages and reputation. One of the main reasons for this decline is outsourcing – the uncoupling of corporations from their functions and their employees.

While the much-vaunted virtual organisation may consist of individual or corporate partners joining over cyberspace, outsourcing is the more obtrusive section of the new model. Admittedly it is not a new concept. There has been a mushrooming of consultants (in management, marketing, accounting, public affairs, public relations and other fields). That, and the need to spread a company's insurance or borrowing over several financial institutions demonstrate a longstanding requirement to tap external niche resources. Firms have always sought knowledge or resources that cannot be economically retained in-house but must be harnessed from time to time to connect to people, technology, money and ideas.

IT has drastically accelerated this phenomenon through the redistribution of the company over an array of subcontractors. Forrester Research predicts that 3.3 million IT jobs will be lost to outsourcing from the USA alone by 2015, and doubles that figure when other G7 countries are included. IT outsourcing was touched on in Chapter 1, but this development facilitates outsourcing activities in, *inter alia*, production, accounting, customer relations and human resources, a trend termed Business Process Outsourcing, or BPO. 'Just because we developed something first doesn't mean that someone else can't do it better, faster or cheaper', warned one British correspondent to *Computer Weekly*. 'Just ask a coal miner, steelworker or shipwright. The IT and related industries are simply following suit' ('Outsourcing is inevitable' 2003: 32). Technology now permits third-party management of many tasks once reserved for in-house professionals. United States hospitals outsource PET and CT scanning; Ernst & Young outsource work to Indian chartered accountants at half the salary of their American counterparts; routine data entry is outsourced to Ghana by a Dallas firm that processes claims forms ('Philippine Leader' 2003). Top London hotels outsource their catering to restaurants run by celebrity chefs. The Pentagon outsources laundry, food, recruiting, and less mundanely mine clearance and some maintenance of planes and helicopters. An outsourcing contractor helped Pentagon staff write their manual dealing with outsourcing contractors (Schwartz 2003: 100). Brookings Institution Fellow Peter W. Singer, author of *Corporate Warriors: The Rise of the Privatised Military Industry*, estimates that ten times as many contract employees were used by the Pentagon in the second Gulf War than in the first, twelve years previously. In that time the number of American PMCs (private military companies) has gone from ten to over thirty ('Outsourcing the dirty work' 2003: 17). 'You could fight without us, but it would be difficult; because we're so involved, it's difficult to extricate us from the process', said the CEO of DynCorp, a major contractor of services to the United States military (Schwartz 2003: 100). Sensibly, the PMCs – like any sector with sensitive issues to manage – operate their own trade group, the International Peace Operations Association (IPOA), whose members 'are involved in all sectors of peace and stability operations including mine clearance, logistics, security, training, and emergency humanitarian services' (IPOA 2004a). To this list may be added prisoner guarding and interrogation. Naturally enough, the IPOA strongly favours outsourcing: 'The prospect for long-term, sustainable peace in many of the world's troubled spots today increasingly depends on skilled private companies and organizations specializing in peace operations' (IPOA 2004b).

Outsourcing either goes abroad – offshore – or remains near-shore with a contractor in the company's home country or a familiar near neighbour. Collaborative technology and interconnectivity are consolidating corporate systems, which enlarges the scope for cheaply managing BPO offshore. This at any rate is the hope of overseas subcontractors. 'We see the future of all communications infrastructure in being converged networks', prophesied Indian outsourcing giant Tata Telecom's Vice Chairman ('Focus on converged' 2003). India, Philippines, and Russia are at present well-known offshore destinations. The second, non-technological motivator is cost savings. 'Indian salaries are about one-seventh of their equivalent London posts', *Computer Weekly* alerted readers in 2003 (Fowler 2003: 33). Such convergence and cost savings help Tata Telecom win business from banking and finance, healthcare, education, the hospitality industry, manufacturing, retail and transportation. China is cheaper still.

In the rise of G7 BPO offshore as well as among near-shore western European and North American subcontractors, potential crises go unnoticed. Risk management is certainly discussed, but can have a different meaning in this context. Outsourcing is often seen as a way to reduce or defer some risks, especially the type that nag at chief financial officers, insurers and lawyers. 'We can beat any legitimate European or American bid and reduce your exposure. Lower cost is lower risk', urges one CEO at an Indian web development firm ('6 ways' undated). A perhaps self-serving survey by the Outsourcing Institute, an American body 'dedicated solely to outsourcing', found risk reduction one of the 'top ten' reasons companies outsourced: 'Outsourcing providers make investments on behalf of many clients, not just one. Shared investment spreads risk, and significantly reduces the risk borne by a single company' (The Outsourcing Institute 1998). This view continues to be voiced. 'Companies today are averse to embarking on big-ticket projects that risk insufficient returns or even outright failure. They just don't feel that they can afford a big IT mistake', declares an article backing 'tactical' IT outsourcing of customer relations services ('Tactical outsourcing' 2001: 50–1). The risk of not catching the wave in time was highlighted in a survey for a British outsourcing consultancy: 'it would appear that a significant number of FDs [Financial Directors] are suffering from the NIMBY syndrome and are missing an opportunity to reduce costs, improve quality and become more core business focused as a function' ('Are Finance' 2002). The risk of supervisory over-stretch is also cut: 'Outsourcing non-core competencies also saves management from spreading itself too thin' ('5 keys' 2003: 10).

Such promises and prospects spur outsourcing's cheerleaders. 'Any function that is non-core to a business's profit generation is eligible', says the head of a South African outsourcing firm ('Letting go' 2003: 42). '[V]endors have a tremendous opportunity to expand their client base in these tough economic times by providing efficient, cost-effective outsourcing services', urged a manager at internet research firm IDC ('Top 100' 2003). 'Any job that is English-based in markets such as the USA, the United Kingdom and Australia can be done in India. The only limit is your imagination', proclaimed the CEO of GE India ('GE champions' 2003: 11). Even risk management itself – or rather the version concerned with managing uncertainties in price, credits and volumes – can be outsourced. Energy firms 'can save 20% to 40% by outsourcing offshore' risk management functions, declares the co-founder of a software development company (Riabokon 2002). No stone is left unturned. 'Possibly', *eWeek* speculated, '[HR is] the next big wave of business process outsourcing' ('Study: Outsourced' 2002). A 2002 study of big firms in the USA and Europe found two-thirds outsourcing HR activities. 'HR restructuring', said one of the research team, 'has been partially enabled by technology, which frees up resources to do more strategic things' ('Study: Outsourced' 2002).

The 'strategic things' outsourcing enables include more outsourcing, but how this model will work in a future full-blown information age crisis remains uncertain. While outsourcing needs may be met by near-shore and offshore locations, and on occasion coordinated through a Project Management Office (PMO), the fact is that elements of corporate identity are being devolved to subcontractors, regions and cultures. North American and European companies have sent much of their manufacturing to Asia, via subcontractors in Indonesia, Vietnam and of course China, where labour costs look good even in comparison with low-wage neighbours. Novelist and travel writer Paul Theroux visited a southern Chinese development zone and found that 'Barbie lived in Dongguan, and so did Ken – they were produced in vast quantities in the Mattel plant there' (Theroux 2000: 225).

Subcontractors in China, India and elsewhere control perceptual and operational factors important in crisis and risk communication. Dongguan Barbie is Chinese, but the retail Barbie is perceived as an American. She will nevertheless be unable to deny her Chinese heritage. If something goes wrong in China it is as an American that Barbie must defend her reputation, along with Ken, Batman, plus products made by (or for) most well-known firms including Dell Computers, Kodak and Raytheon (Theroux 2000: 232) which all operate out of Xiamen, on the south-eastern coast of China. Operationally, Infosys and other Indian software firms are discovering the attractions of a 12–15 per cent wage differential between India and geopolitical rivals China, and are starting to outsource their outsourcing. 'Philippines and China could pose the strongest competition to India and challenge India's supremacy in the medium to long term', reported Nasscom, India's software and service business association. 'Only China and the Philippines, other than India, have a sizeable, low cost talent pool, which could meet global ITES [IT-enabled services] manpower needs' (Nasscom 2003).

'Outsourcing takes place when an organization transfers the ownership of a business process to a supplier. The key to this definition is the aspect of transfer of control', advises the Indian outsourcing firm Dimensioni (Dimensioni 2004). But, however far and however many functions disperse, blame will continue to concentrate, especially around sensitive industries or well-known brands. A pharmaceutical industry journalist remarked:

> You can transfer risk, but the ultimate responsibility is with the party that owns the product. At the end of the day, it's not the vendor's name that is on the NDA [new drug application] or product marketing application – it's the sponsor's name.
>
> (Miller 2001: 82)

Some instances of 'blame convergence' fuelled by outsourcing are familiar, like the criticism of sports apparel firm Nike over its own labyrinthine subcontracted labour arrangements – the company 'maintains contract relationships with over 900 factories, representing 700,000 workers in 55 countries around the world' ('Nike Statement' 2002) or the 'Sweatshop of the Year Awards' dished out to the Hudson's Bay Company and Wal-Mart Canada at the end of 2002 by a Canadian labour rights group ('Bay, Wal-Mart' 2002: C09). As Nike found, issues combust when the match of corporate outsourcing touches the gunpowder of global politics, stakeholder fear or international activism. The general trajectory is well established: the issue, the corporate response, high-visibility activist protests, which if successful escalate media attention and expert comment which in turn affect other company activities – these are common characteristics and challenges of global issues and crisis management.

More outsourcing continues to shape the nature of this exposure, and some observers are awakening to the implications. One *Harvard Business Review* contributor controversially asserted in both the journal and later a book that IT's competitive advantage is vanishing, and companies must switch their focus to managing vulnerabilities raised by IT outsourcing (Carr 2003, 2004). In Chapter 1 several of the vulnerabilities connected to outsourcing were bulleted. How might they and others thrust companies into public disaster when considering BPO as a whole?

Anticipating malicious behaviour and criminal activity may play a greater role in crisis preparedness, particularly as smaller companies join the outsourcing movement. Proponents of outsourcing claim that fraud is easier to detect in an isolated unit. GE for instance, outsources internal fraud checks to Indian accountants. However, offshore outsourcing has made CVs harder to vet, especially for small or medium sized firms. 'Many employers do not have the internal resources to do a thorough background check, which makes it easy for less honest applicants to disguise problems in their career history', warned a pre-employment screening firm's spokesperson ('Data laws' 2003: 6). Some regions seeking to attract outsourcing business may also prove more prone to fraudulent activity than others. In South Africa for example one CEO lamented: 'fraud levels are unbelievable' ('Letting go' 2003: 42). South Africa's Standard Bank's 2002 decision to end an outsourcing contract for credit card processing may not have been related to similar concerns, but it was apparent that the bank felt it had surrendered one 'non-core' operation too many. 'We need to own that customer interface', said a director of the firm's Card Division ('EDS "Not Prejudiced"' 2002). The more formal announcement noted: 'customer contact and its associated processes are core business competencies and important contributors to its competitive advantage, and should therefore be directly managed by the bank' ('Standard Bank' 2002). Several months later, a virus attacked the same bank's processing contractor, an event unlikely to dissuade Standard Chartered from its decision to reclaim the affected systems and networks.

Supply chain protection will also occupy a larger place in crisis management and communication. The chain that brings companies raw materials and carries their finished goods to market, becomes more exposed as it disintegrates among far-flung subcontractors, with the end result that the chain itself is now outsourced. Third Party Logistics – 3PL – places a company's supply chain distribution, warehousing and transport in the hands of contractors. A new model – Fourth Party Logistics or 4PL – is also emerging, whereby the chain's entire management, including orders and manufacturer coordination, is outsourced to consultants with analytical and IT capabilities. 'According to the 4PLs, their 3PL cousins cannot deliver ongoing supply chain savings and efficiencies because they lack the optimal combination of technology, warehousing capabilities, and transportation service. The 4PL, on the other hand, is free to find the best of breed in each category' (Foster 1999: 35–6). Or, as the *Financial Times* put it: 'The logistics industry these days is as much about technology as trucks' ('A vital part' 2002: 5).

The vulnerability of outsourced supply chains was highlighted by the SARS virus, which fell most heavily upon China. In the wake of the disruption caused by the crisis, one expert warned that firms outsourcing in China 'have been left highly dependent on distribution operations going in and out of the region' (Swaminathan

2003: 38). 'The fact is, vessels are not full', warned the managing director of Unaffiliated Shippers of America, a group that negotiates rates for about 200 importers. 'There is no doubt in my mind that the impact of SARS on eastbound volumes will be much greater than anyone wants to admit' (Peak season 2003: 8). In the information age, of course, *perceptions* of such problems may also have a measurable impact to parallel the reality. Europe's largest bank, UBS, reacted to the possibility of slowdown in global container trades by cutting its demand growth forecast 'due to a slowdown in outsourcing brought about by SARS concerns' ('Peak season' 2003: 8). The United States Semiconductor Industry Association also cut its 2003 forecast, noting the impact of SARS on electronics manufacturing and consumption in China, and admitting that this all too non-virtual virus 'certainly dampened demand for the end product, hence the supply chain has been impacted' ('Global chip' 2003).

Blame does not *have* to converge exclusively on the outsourcer, as it did with Nike. The reverse will also happen: the subcontractor inherits the outsourcer's legacy, assumes responsibility for key capabilities and becomes vulnerable to the outsourcer's issues. Evidence of this appeared at the end of 2002, when a Saudi investor in Ptech Inc., a small US company, was placed on a US government 'blocked list' as a suspected terrorist financier. Ptech, located in Quincy, Massachusetts, a town with a significant Middle East population, maintained software for managing the personal and structural assets of several Federal entities including the FBI and the Pentagon. After a high-profile federal search of the firm's offices four employees had their bank accounts cancelled, others received a slew of hate messages and as business fell away the company shed 17 out of 27 personnel. One Chicago-based employee had his home described as an al-Qaeda HQ in the local media (Verton 2003). Ptech Inc. fought for survival in a climate of ruptured trust and damaged perception. 'I feel like I'm not allowed to dream', chief executive and co-founder Oussama Ziade said ('Software company' 2002). 'I could not sleep in my house for three days', he told *Computerworld*. 'It was ambushed by the media. And I couldn't send my kids to school for a week' (Verton 2003).

Coordinated relationships will pose problems. During a crisis companies will need to manage a web of communication with multiple subcontractors. Regular information sharing about vital corporate capabilities between in-house and contractors will require a taut, intricate and highly sensitive communication network able to cope with countries, cultures and time zones. The main guardians of the company's reputation and credibility – key companies in resolving the crisis – may be independent entities. In a field like pharmaceuticals, where drug development tasks are outsourced, the need for such effective coordination will be particularly important.

The same conditions apply to the workforce. Part-time or subcontracted employees make message consistency more challenging, raising problems of loyalty and commitment from personnel some of whom may have, at best, divided allegiances or, at worst, resentment, particularly if accompanied by lower pay and worse conditions, or when the outsourcing firm sends its own workers to the client company at the expense of existing employees. The Financial Services Authority (FSA), which regulates UK financial service providers, was among those warning against such 'mindless use of outsourcing', though without naming any particular companies. FSA's Managing Director cautioned that firms were retaining too few staff with vital skills; and too few were supervising outsourcing, which would make them unable to recover from disaster (Campos 2000: 6). Americans disgruntled at the arrival of cheaper foreign workers sent by subcontractors are more direct in their criticism of the 'enemy within'. 'How do you know for sure whether your outsourcing provider is using domestic, H1-B [a US temporary work visa] or offshore IT workers? Sometimes, it's not easy to tell', warned *eWeek* in 2002 ('Where's your contractor's work force' 2002).

At the same time, managing the new vulnerabilities depends on the new sub-contracted and existing workers, for the more the core of an organisation disperses, the greater and wider the volumes of circulating information. Real people, not functions, software or job descriptions, see and control this information. What could they do with it?

THE OUTSOURCED WORKER

The answer partly depends on what the workforce thinks of outsourcing. A 2003 survey of British supervisors and junior managers in several fields found uncertainty, with over two-thirds worried that outsourcing damaged job security, but over half believing that being outsourced would be 'a valuable, CV enhancing experience' (Cap Gemini 2003). Elsewhere there is hostility or fear. 'Corporate America is quickly learning that a cubicle can be replicated overseas as easily as a shop floor can', noted *Fortune* magazine. 'Increasingly, supereducated and highly paid workers are finding themselves traveling the same road their blue-collar peers took in the late '80s ('Down and out' 2003). 'The days of the 300-strong marketing department could soon be over', *Marketing* advised in March 2003, 'as many functions and the people who perform them are hived off to third-party suppliers' ('Opinion: Outsourcing' 2003). Those third party suppliers may have better quali-fied personnel than the people they replace. 'India produces 230,000 engineers every year, out of a total of 1.5 million college graduates. I can't see a situation where we will ever be short of skilled young labour', reported the head of a major Indian IT firm ('British corporations' 2003).

The mix of labour and skills outsourcing arrangements is important. People are outsourced from personal choice, persuasion or force. The relative balance between choice and compulsion will affect future crises by influencing how outsourced workers use the tools and knowledge at their disposal.

79

Whatever their expertise or qualifications, workers who choose to outsource themselves as telecommuters may number themselves among the perpetually learning, flexible, mobile middle classes of tomorrow. In the US, the sluggish economy and the 9/11 tragedy gave impetus to telecommuting, some arguing – typically for any economy in times of peril – that a dispersed workforce was better for continuity and security, tilting the balance away from concern about lack of supervision, obstacles to teamwork, and isolation. A 2004 report from market researchers In-Stat concluded that 12 million United States employees were 'full-time teleworkers, a segment it expects will increase moderately to reach 14 million by 2008' (Kistner 2004: 28). In Australia, the number more than tripled from 308,000 in 1992 to 980,300 in 2000 (Braue 2002). The Institute for Employment Studies found 6 per cent of employed Britons were teleworkers, around 1.78 million people in the spring of 2002 ('Teleworking' 2003: 433).

Voluntary teleworking has zealous proselytisers (Canada once designated a national Teleworking Day) who push, like the United States-based group Telework Connection, benefits that include reduced traffic congestion, cleaner air, 'more jobs (and hence income) in rural areas', and even 'improved safety from stronger neighborhood watches' ('Telework connection'). More directly, it is also said to empower disadvantaged groups like the disabled, caregivers, or parents with small children. BT is one of Europe's largest employers of teleworkers, with over 5,000 of 108,000 employees. Ninety per cent of BT's teleworkers reported that they were 'satisfied or very satisfied with teleworking' ('BT employees' 2003: 17).

Other workers may number themselves among the vulnerable, benefits-less, relentlessly monitored, insecure part-time helots of tomorrow, and are unlikely to be comforted by pro-outsource rhetoric. 'In the current marketplace, workers have to realise that they will have to make themselves relevant to the workplace', warned the CEO of a Malaysian bank's outsource subsidiary ('Controversy over' 2003: 1). 'Every week Computer Weekly publishes letters from people with job titles such as "director" or "consultant" trying to convince us of the need to send IT offshore because UK workers are greedy and expensive', complained an unhappy correspondent ('Offshore outsourcing' 2003: 32). 'Many big investment banks, accountants and consulting firms are farming work out to Indian-based sub-contractors, even if they are shy about admitting it', commented the *Economist* ('Backroom deals' 2002). UNIFI, the European finance sector trade union, cata-logued the transfer of workers refusing redundancy packages to out of the way 'warehouse-type' buildings without work or facilities; others were allegedly moved 'to different parts of the Bank outside their home state and linguistic area' ('Support Indian bank workers' 2003).

Inevitably, unions or other activists will target unhappy employees, along with high-profile companies and industry sectors. They will be spurred by economic downturns, periods of articulate white-collar labour unrest, by concerned politicians, and also by the impact of unexpected events such as the software programmer who killed himself because, his father reported, not only was his contract terminated but he was required to train his Indian replacement. They will make use of technology to fight the issue that technology has created. The Washington Alliance of Technology invited web visitors to play the Tech Worker Challenge, in which digitised tech workers are helped across a busy street with speeding trucks marked 'Intel', 'Microsoft', 'HP' or 'Sun'. 'Try to avoid getting laid off with no notice, having your job shipped overseas, being illegally blacklisted, having your pension robbed, and more . . .' (Washtech 2002). Aside from the impact of outsourcing on domestic employees, even offshore contractors will be forced to manage the issue, and crises arising from it. Indian bank workers struck in 2002 against Britain's Standard Chartered Bank over plans to cut the permanent workforce and increase short-term contract and agency labour.

Outsourcing is thus firmly connected to wider white-collar concerns. The rise of a business model which promotes employee shrinkage as a means of economic expansion has, for many, and despite rising rewards overall, created a difficult new environment. A report for the Economic and Social Research Council found that feelings of job security dropped from 70 to 48 per cent in the United Kingdom between 1985 and 1995 (Taylor 2002: 13). The 2000 European Survey of Working Conditions (ESWC) reported that '42% of the workers consider their jobs as non-sustainable, stating they do not think they will be able to or want to do the same job when they are 60 years old' (OECD 2003: 45). Sixty per cent of European workers, the OECD recorded in its *Employment Outlook 2003* said they worked to 'tight deadlines' in 2001, up from 50 per cent in 1991; the percentages who reported working at 'very high speed' rose from 48 to 56 (OECD 2003: 46).

The influence of corporate cultures dominated by either voluntarism or compulsion, with – in both cases – a rise in personal insecurity – must be accepted by the company that is outsourcing, and taken into account when planning for crises. But other factors will also contribute to workforce behaviour:

- Diversity. A workforce that reflects the diversity in society is socially just and – as e-commerce spreads around the world – commercially essential. Companies are able to cast a wider net to find the skills they need, and to find the expertise to reach segmenting audiences. It must however also be remembered that the more diverse the workforce, the more diverse will be their decisions and thus their actions and reactions in uncertain times.
- Recognising and responding to diverse emotional and communication needs. The united urgency of a traditional crisis team in one locale will be hard to replicate among scattered outsourced workers. The upside of this may be a more rational approach to critical decision-making. The downside may be a problem identifying with stakeholder feelings. An urgent concern or deadline in one locality may not be fully recognised in another. The problems of uncomprehending and subcontracted company representatives far from

either the scene of the crisis or the corporate headquarters dealing over the computer or telephone with angry, scared victims or media will need to be incorporated into future crisis plans. Wherever and whoever they are – outsourced workers representing the company and its message must be attuned to the levels of feeling, and able to anticipate reactions of external audiences at ground zero: whether they be victims, expert commentators, the media or concerned regulators. This will require global knowledge of e-fluentials, local cultures and the incorporation of outsourced workers into crisis preparedness plans.

- Independent communication activity. The coming crisis, thick with the exchange of messages and viewpoints, mediated by new technologies, will create more clutter and noise than ever before, increasing the capacity of external stakeholders to dominate the flow of events. Internal stakeholders will also be able to participate more fully, and less controllably, from offshore locations and home offices. They will have access to internal documents, the means of distributing them *en masse*, and the possibility that some can whistleblow from home with greater freedom than from the corporate office.
- Cross-networking. Alienated from the company as a whole, or hostile to particular corporate key messages, outsourced workers may feel freer to network with external audiences, with consequences for their client company's communication strategy. The pressure on communication discipline, already strained by global scale crises, will be exacerbated by scope for independent intelligence gathering and damaging action by scattered workers.

The challenge of successfully managing internal crisis communication – working with employees and subcontracted workers – in the outsourced world is to provide cohesion and coherence. As their trust management with external audiences is being revolutionised, so also must corporations re-examine the relations of trust with their own workforce. They must reconcile the tension between managing information and messages, encouraging virtually empowered workers to feel they are receiving untainted and unvarnished truths. The dilemma attracts little attention at business schools; a mistake, since aggrieved individuals and campaigning nonprofits – major players in a crises and issues – take this task very seriously indeed.

These new conditions join those set out in earlier chapters. They force damaged companies to take a fresh look at communicating issues and risk, and consider approaches that go beyond customary corporate advocacy. Many of the affected companies will be small, attracted to e-commerce but without the resources to manage their reputations through an information age crisis. Nevertheless, they must make more room for a communication function that is no longer a suspiciously 'soft', tough-to-measure activity 'scattered' across media relations, marketing, investor relations or human resources, but something more central to their fortune.

Two other consequences must be recorded. The appearance of virtual and dispersed co-workers calls, say some, 'for re-examination of traditional controls over employee ethics' (Ariss *et al.* 2002: 22). A less rigid, devolved approach to ethics may indeed prove crucial to helping employees trust their crisis-hit company. Finally, outsourcing's effect on reputation management must be considered. Reputation's sometimes nebulous components now depend on the activities and attitudes of subcontractors and their workers. However redistributed, a company must continue to create, manage and therefore – in times of vulnerability – guard a reputation that attracts stakeholders and sells products.

These and the other developments described in Part One change crisis strategy and tactics. What are those changes? This is the subject of Part Two.

Part Two

Organising for crisis

LABADDIA II

Thirty minutes late. Jennifer Stone, fighting an escalating global health scare at her new employer, had read somewhere that commuters regularly experienced higher stress levels than fighter pilots going into battle. Fortunately, she was armed with her new London ticket, her computer link and her mobile phone. The first class Quiet Coach was thankfully silent except for an occasional tut or exasperated hiss as the train slowed yet again. Stone tried to ignore her complete lack of control over the progress of her own journey and concentrate on the situation online. There too she felt powerless. At the moment, for example, she was asking herself: *what is the Centre for Food Initiatives?*

'Tea, Coffee, light refreshments?'

'Tea, please. What's in that baguette?'

'Pork and Herb Wychwood & Stevenson Gold Medal Pâté – exclusive to our First Class customer service, Madam. Four pounds.'

Stone recalled that Labaddia had the contract with the train caterers. 'Go on then.'

She took a bite out of the baguette and mused whether they might be still for sale or off the trolley for good before their train reached London – if they ever got to London.

Then she thought of the train caterer – who was it? And then she thought of all Labaddia's big buyers. Who's talking to them?

She chewed slowly and stared morosely at the homepage of CFI, the Center for Food Initiatives. On it was a link to the webcast she had just heard, a 'declaration for global food transparency', a discussion forum, some rather unsavoury pictures of unclean meat factories in Asia and Europe including pictures of decomposing flesh, and a list of boycotted companies including her own. It was, it seemed, a joint effort by campaigners around the world.

Labaddia's site had been hijacked and diverted to this CFI group – whoever they were. The company's Indian outsourcer was struggling to reclaim the site but in the meantime the company had no way of offering an instant response to the world. The people – and who knows how many thousands of them - now trying to get to Labaddia would instead find themselves on the site of their opponent. Pretty clever. Stone shuddered as she thought about all the media, investors and customers now seeing the same site she was looking at.

'But who are they?' Stone muttered. It was hard to find any names on the site – anyone she could contact. How come activists got away with concealment when they expected everyone else to be transparent?

Three names she had noted. The three lead figures on the webcast: Adam A. Berenson, formerly of the US Food Security Agency; Karen Eaton, formerly of the British Food Quality Unit; Ms Etsuko Takino, formerly of the Japanese Health Inspectorate now, apparently, a campaigning activist.

Three whistleblowers, all blowing the same whistle: Labaddia's Chinese facility was a major health threat — threat was the exact word they used — and with pictures to prove it.

Stone stopped staring at CFI's website and went to the BBC. There it was. 'British food giant "ignores basic hygiene" and mistreats employees claims sacked official.' Of course, the fact it was about the Far East was left for the opening paragraph, but the animal rights and food activist protest planned outside Labaddia Durham was startling. Stone wondered for a moment if she should return to deal with any media who may show up. Was it a big demo? Was it still raining up there and would that keep the numbers down?

Why was this happening?

The earlier webcast had attracted a limited number of international media — it sounded like Japanese, Chinese and one or two Europeans including the *International Herald Tribune* and a couple of tabloids. No Americans. It was very well done, with translators and a transcript instantly available along with an online release, copies of the original emails, production details and authentic looking temperature charts showing continual undercooking of meat products and, worse of all, soundlinks extracted from a couple of telephone conversations between the subcontractors ITYO, a Chinese official and Ms Takino which — if the translation did not lie — appeared to include the offer of a bribe if Takino kept quiet.

*

'Sarah? Jen. What do we know about ITYO?'

Her immediate superior interrupted: 'I've heard from Tatsuo Fujimori again. Most of our big account buyers in Japan have pulled the products and temporarily stopped all orders. Apparently there was a big protest in the food halls at Isetan's and Mitsukoshi's flagship store just after the webcast — '

Stone assumed they were important department stores. 'Sarah — '

'And have you seen our website anywhere?'

'Sarah — '

'I've had Harrods on the line in the last five minutes. *Harrods.* We can't mess them about. It's our flagship.'

Stone took a deep breath, and closed her eyes. She was stuck on a slow train, her company was under what appeared to be a globally coordinated attack, she had no crisis plan, she had only been in the company two weeks and did not know who she needed to talk to, her boss was about to be surprised by the event at a meeting of European analysts, the corporate website had been hijacked and she couldn't access her email.

For a moment, her head and body felt frozen in a numbing limbo. The other passengers sipped their tea, ate their Wychwood & Stevenson Gold Medal Pâté baguettes, and read newspapers as Jennifer Stone contemplated the disaster that had unfolded about her in a few moments. It was worse than the crisis she'd suffered in her last job five years before – now there was no time to meet because crucial decisions were already being taken by stakeholders in seconds.

She found ITYO's address on the web. It meant nothing to her. 'Listen, Sarah. Who's looking after us in China?'

'Lloyd Davis – he's an Aussie. I'll get his number and text him to call you.'

*

On the BBC website, meanwhile, an ambitious and far left MP was calling for an inquiry to investigate the BSE allegations and a criminal investigation into the bribery allegations. CNN Business reported that the World Health Organisation announced plans to host a conference about the international food industry and its 'regulatory environment'.

She could not bring herself to see what was happening to the share price, but when they finally reached York Jennifer noticed a press statement from a competitor clarifying the magnificence of its own outsourcing arrangements and quality controls.

Megan had left a voicemail saying rumours were going around that Labaddia's site had been hacked but their Indian IT service provider said it was okay and they'd wrested the corporate homepage back from whoever stole it. Jennifer replied by telling Megan to get the news out in blog space – don't wait to run it by anyone first. She'd deal with the internal criticism if there was any.

*

Finally: 'Hi – Lloyd Davis. Nice to talk with you.'

'Did Sarah get you up to speed?'

'Yeah – just seen some of it. Unbelievable.'

'Listen: I'm new here. Who are ITYO?'

'They're about five years old. Do a lot of food preparation work for our labels – all over Asia but mostly Japan. It's pretty significant. Twelve hundred workers make boiled, smoked, semi-smoked, and semi-prepared meats, pâtés and sausages. Quite a fashion for European type gourmet foods at the moment. I think Labaddia signed the deal with them three years ago. Before my time.'

'When did you join Labaddia then?'

'I didn't. I mean I haven't. I'm a consultant employed by you lot to manage quality issues until you get a full-time person on the spot. Not that that's easy to do – everyone's going flat out in this economy. You didn't have an Asian presence until little old me – I've been in the Asia Pacific food business, oh, seven, eight years. Don't ask me to speak to reporters, by the way', he added. 'A couple have already sniffed me out: Brits. I've referred them to Sarah.'

'Okay.' Stone felt impatient. 'Let's not mess around then: in your opinion, is ITYO safe?'

Davis paused noticeably. 'Well', he eventually said, 'they are when I'm there, but I can't be there 24 hours a day can I? Thing about outsourcing out here is, you can't take your eyes off suppliers and subcontractors for a moment or they'll take you for every last cent. Not that I'm about to put that in writing.'

'Not that I want you to put that in writing. I do need the truth as you see it – we've got to know what happened.'

'Good. It's like this: as long as you're watching them they're doing it right. When you're not – well, that can be a different story. It's all about money here. They didn't have much of it before, and they like the taste of it. Can't say I blame them altogether.'

My God, she thought. 'So . . . so those allegations might be true? What about that low temperature stuff from the Japanese official?'

'Absolutely not on my watch', Davis said firmly. 'I've only seen good production standards with back-up records but it's true to say the quality argument hasn't fully sunk in yet. Two of those whistleblowers on the webcast said they'd resigned in protest and one says she was sacked because of Labaddia pressure on the local authorities. I thought you could tell me the answer to that one.'

'What's going on at the facility now?'

Davis sounded surprised. 'The usual. They're doing what they're there to do – making overpriced European pâtés and sausages for Japanese department stores. There's no reason to stop. We've got Korean customers who couldn't care less about panic in Japan.'

'Don't you think they should stop for health and safety checks at the very least?'

'You'll have to get Production to tell me that. I can't just flick the off switch without hearing from the right person.'

'We're fixing a conference call about that – you'll be hearing shortly.'

'Okeydokey. But like I said, get someone here if you want to talk to the media – if we get cameras outside the gates I'm not going down in flames for you lot.' Food outsourcing in Asia Pacific was taking off: work elsewhere was easy to get and good people were in short supply - sometimes good people weren't even necessary.

All Jennifer said was: 'Just wait for our call.'

'Right. And by the way. I heard the Durham plant got firebombed – did you hear about that?'

The refreshment trolley was passing again. Stone noticed that the baguettes were finished - or were they removed?

*

In a hotel in Frankfurt, David Corio, who had finished a good-news analyst briefing on new meat processing plants in southern Argentina, Belgium and China, stepped from the lift and walked into the lobby alongside his Director of Investor Relations. A friendly looking woman went up to them with a placard in English and German.

'Meat monoculture?' Corio hissed to the IR Director. 'What's all that about?'

*

'Because of staff shortages this train will now be calling at Newark North Gate. We apologise for any inconvenience this may cause you.'

*

According to a food industry website, a takeover bid was being considered by several EU competitors, and a large American food manufacturer. Labaddia's shares were off 10 per cent so it was scarcely surprising.

Some progress was being made. The switchboard had been told to route all media enquiries to Megan and Stone's mobile. By the time the train had left Newark Stone had won Sarah Collins's reluctant permission to respond to rumours as and when necessary, and not wait for corporate or legal clearance. Megan was pushing their application maintenance provider in Mumbai to finish content on food safety and breaking news for Labaddia's website. Others were adding extra connectivity – or whatever it was called – as the site was periodically crashing due to an epic surge in traffic.

It was almost a relief to have a normal crisis call from a normal journalist.

'John Mallinson – Channel 6 online. Calling about your mad cow crisis in China – '

'I think that's a little premature, John – not that we're taking it lightly.'

'What about those Japanese schoolkids diagnosed with CJD?'

'Pardon me?'

'Some man at your Tokyo office – Yamada – know him? Says these kids have been eating undercooked pâté for years at some posh European style school somewhere. It's no secret there: online buzz already pretty developed – that's why I called him.'

'CJD? You do mean CJD?'

'Human variant Mad Cow. Yes. You're telling me you don't know about this?'

'John – we certainly take any allegation about people's health very seriously. That's the only priority for us right now, but I'll be honest and say I've never heard that one before. You appreciate there's a lot of things flying about at the moment and it's hard for us to deal with it all at once. I'm going to look into this, and I will certainly get back to you as soon as I can.'

'My report is going online in an hour. Sorry but you know how things work nowadays. No deadlines anymore etcetera. Can't lose good stories to the competition.'

*

The activists were checking in once again via Instant Messenger.

What's next?

We've put a protest together in Frankfurt. Threw rotting meat at their CEO.

The thing's got its own momentum now. They were so overleveraged with all that expansion – it won't take much to send the whole thing crashing down.

Yes – some of the old media are taking it up now. It was on CNN and the BBC – websites and newscasts. Saw a couple of things in India as well – their Information Systems provider in Mumbai is under a lot of pressure.

Your website hijacking quality move!

110,000 hits in four hours. They came from everywhere. Mainly Japan.

Helped build phenomenal chatroom traffic on our website also.

Awesome how the rest of the world wants to join in. Etsuko and Adam knew to go to us. It's like the whole planet is suddenly feeling the same thing and knows what to do.

Yes. I wonder why that is?

And what else do we know?

Watch – leave it to the miracle of free enterprise.

*

By the time the train had finally reached Grantham, the first lawsuits were being predicted. David Corio had warned her about that in the course of a long call from Frankfurt, half of which Stone spent listening to him, the other half viewing her email in horror: media; Labaddia customers trying to talk to someone, anyone; managers from half a dozen sites around the world; and yes, a couple of company lawyers.

In a way, the sheer volume was comforting. There was absolutely no way Jennifer could deal with them all, so she didn't; instead, until David's call, she'd been talking to India, trying to add some messages to the corporate website now it was functioning: information, a holding statement, updates about the situation in China – mainly that a team was going out there to work with authorities and investigate: at least *that* didn't sound defensive. They even added a rumour section where instant clarification could be posted – she'd just thrown a body from her office at that problem; and a soundbite section with comments about the crisis from senior executives extracted from them by her over the telephone, with Corio's backing. Stone even got support from the shellshocked legal department.

'We can't communicate enough on this.' Stone was relieved to hear him say that after she described her activities, rather nervously since there had been no time to get anyone's go-ahead.

She wasn't surprised though, Corio understood communication. 'You're doing the right thing. This is why we hired you. What else could we be doing?'

'Definitely a webcast – a reasoned credible response to the one aimed at us. I think I can guarantee an audience.'

'What if someone tries to disrupt it?'

'We can control the participants – but we can't dodge the tough questions. We've got to say that the rumours about our other plants are totally malicious and the allegations about Durham's negligence in particular are utterly untrue – the place won an award for goodness sake. But I do stress – we can't avoid the difficult ones about our Asia Pacific suppliers: were we really doing enough down there, even if it turns out that there isn't a problem?'

'I'll get the board together', Corio decided. 'I'll use conference calling from here.'

'That's fine, but, er, from my perspective it's not going to help unless one of my people is there to offer communication input. I need a team of people willing and able to talk fast, online and offline, to stop this from going ballistic. We're starting to talk back: the more we talk and the less reluctant we look, the softer the landing.'

'Okay – so we talk about what we're doing – '

'And planning to do – and dealing with online audiences: several influencers are reacting with knee jerks, not reason, and it's damaging us. It doesn't help when politicians stir up the flames in real time. We need to show we get the message and can put out this fire. We've got to take risks about what we say to show that we're believable.'

Corio did not give a straight answer for once: 'Three hours ago, I was talking to satisfied analysts about our growth, success and future. Now three hours later I've got to convince them about our survival. Our market in Asia is collapsing in front of us.' Corio stopped for breath. Stone waited for the rest of it, but all he did in the end was present the simple question that nobody else from Argentina to Japan was asking, because they were too busy reacting:

'What the hell happened?'

Everything, thought Stone.

Chapter 5

Descent into the maelstrom: the unexpected crisis

> Emotional occasions, especially violent ones, are extremely potent in precipitating mental rearrangements.
>
> William James. *The Varieties of Religious Experience* (1901–2: 220)

INTRODUCTION

'The art of appealing to crowds is no doubt of an inferior order, but it demands quite special aptitudes', declared the social psychologist Gustave Le Bon in 1895, in his influential work, *The Crowd* (Le Bon 1895: 23). Now such aptitudes are not only special, but essential. Appealing to crowds – large or small, scattered or concentrated, virtual or real – no longer depends on mob oratory, but on a winning synthesis of technology, research, information, luck and emotion. It is ideally, if not realistically, a full-time task, but one that corporations do not always have the time, resources or inclination to undertake. What then should be the reaction of an unprepared company that has not tried to manage an issue or risk in advance, and is suddenly ambushed by an information age crisis? Here ideas are offered for the new conditions of disaster – not that they can be definitive, since the most convincing and uncompromising teacher is alas experience. A major crisis, global and online, is assumed to display the full range of elements needed in lesser degrees for less severe events.

It has been argued earlier that the accelerating crisis drags participants into unfamiliar communication surroundings, and increases the chance that, somewhere in the world, unprompted or not, damaging behaviours and actions will be observed and copied. We have also argued that for stricken firms to understand that setting, let alone master it, pivotal decisions must be agreed and executed in an instant. Do these pressures mean taking chances about what to say and how to say it? Can a company, a non-profit organisation or even a Government – irrespective of size – act fast enough to successfully protect falling stock prices, failing products or tarnished reputation or maybe the existence of the organisation itself?

94

PRESSURES, NEEDS

Although the pace of events quickens, not all crises will move at the same speed since, as of old, they attract different levels of attention and therefore action from stakeholders. Some may rumble and smoke before erupting, while at the other extreme, high-profile crises might unexpectedly explode. Whatever the situation, though, the general acceleration of events and the reasons for them given in Part One allow us to anticipate the varying pressures, waxing or waning according to the scale and story of the disaster. Understanding those pressures helps to anticipate the operational needs, and knowing those needs helps to structure the responses which could include:

- Critical requirement instantaneously to identify, track and perhaps respond to diverse crisis participants.
- Pressure imposed by heavier financial and product damage at the earliest stage.
- Demands to release unmanaged or at least minimally vetted detail in the opening moments of a crisis in an attempt to end or contain instantaneous damage.
- Urgent requirement to assemble a team to coordinate and agree a crisis communication and recovery strategy, again instantly.
- Need to obtain decisions and information from inside a corporation when their human sources are paralysed by fear, large volumes of stakeholder activity and public hostility.
- The related difficulty, in a large crisis, of knowing how to intervene *credibly* in the eruption of opinion, speculation and activity inside and outside the company, which in combination will be hurtling into the minds and hands of alien and powerful audiences.

This unstable environment offers few options for Business: it must learn more about crisis communication, about the new rules, and about placing them in an overall communication strategy ahead of disaster. It is likely though that even if more companies do prepare, many others will be unprepared and surprised, and face hard and possibly decisive tests of nerve, discipline and culture.

RESPONSE: PRINCIPLES

The critical questions involve the task of responding to unexpected events. Response shapes operational and reputation survival, since responses to events and claims by all participants, especially in a big crisis, influence the speed and direction of the crisis and the size of the initial 'punishment' stakeholders may inflict upon the embattled corporation. It is the wind, filling the sail of the original event – and deciding its ultimate destination.

But the response means accepting the crisis revolution. Their effects, as we shall see in the remaining chapters, go far beyond the perimeters of crisis communication, and recoil to change it profoundly.

Learning to respond

Because they must habitually exercise caution, the modern crisis team is peculiarly exposed to the future's pace and volume, when responses will be instantaneously expected. No crisis team trying to prise information out of their complex and perhaps scared and confused and dispersed company can sift, sort, synthesise and summarise in the time that will be available, unless external publics reverse the current of human affairs and use new technology to slow down rather than speed up communication, grow more not less patient, and less not more insecure and volatile. Falling into their hands are tools to rapidly extract answers – of some sort – and shape perceptions. Where are those answers and how will they be supplied?

To some extent, the response depends on ensuring that Business uses technology as deftly and loosely as other crisis participants. This is a risk of course, exposing the business more than its critics. The pressures described earlier, however, point to a solution in this direction by illuminating new needs:

- A crisis management structure that at least gives a business the option of accelerated communication, while trying to minimise the associated risks so far as is feasible.
- An accompanying precondition is the need to agree message content faster – as near instantly as possible.
- And preceding that is the job of generating ideas for those messages, in a forum crowded with noisy, hostile, alternate and shifting opinions.
- These needs are joined by the traditional essential – much enlarged by cobra technology – closely tracking multiple speculation, rumours and discussion among participating e-fluentials, to react credibly before unhelpful viewpoints become the accepted perception.

Business must use communication to keep pace with its critics: to drive technology at the same speed, and to some degree mimic stakeholder communication practices, as Shell is learning to do. The basic coordinating and decision-taking group, the team drawn from within the company, ideally no more than ten-strong, must adapt to these circumstances.

Organising to respond

However fast vital decisions are made and executed by the most alert crisis teams, its members, despite being small in number, meeting together and sharing a common corporate identity cannot act with the instantaneous unity and over-whelming authority of large, disunited, diverse, scattered, spontaneously generated, emotionally engaged information age 'crowds' relentlessly tracking events and sharing opinions.

As it is now organised, the crisis team and its support cannot – should not – achieve split-second reaction. Their *raison d'être* is to graft prudence onto the temptations of rapid response. For this reason its members are not mere neurons, blindly flashing unfiltered data back down hi tech nervous systems. They must be alert to the counsel of other company officers; must rightly help check high emotions that may produce inappropriate, inaccurate or legally exposed communi-cation; must work at adapting technical information and raw data to the sentiments of stakeholders.

That working together in a team remains relevant is partly explained by another technological by-product: increased specialist knowledge. No person, no group sharing one identity can hold every technical, communication or operational thread of the information age crisis. Specialist support grows more vital: to ensure the crisis is properly coordinated inside and outside the company.

The new teams will therefore need familiar skills – albeit magnified and accelerated – and new kinds of communication expertise which we identify as:

- Understanding of global communication tools with the ability to deploy them quickly.
- An understanding of the motivations, emotions and potential behaviours of tech-armed stakeholders.
- An ability to provide information in the volume and unedited detail demanded by stakeholders anxious for 'truth'.
- The ability to embed complex messages into the greater volumes of raw information.
- Instant access – particularly if the disaster is big and/or global – to third-party counsel on the culture, beliefs and communication preferences of unfamiliar crisis participants.
- Authority to place, if circumstances require it, confidential information quickly into the public domain.
- Authority to make core decisions based on diverse, shifting currents in stakeholder perception.

The contradictory demands placed on future crisis managers are apparent: more niche experts needed for a team, which ideally needs fewer people in it to speed up decision-making in an intensified communication setting. Answers are wanted for:

- The membership of the information-age crisis team.
- The way it handles information and reaches decisions.

97

- The team's future structure.
- The team's future responsibilities.
- The team's relationship with senior company officers.

Audience diffusion

Theories of one-way communication from company to stakeholder – often via the traditional media – and of two-way communication exchanges between company and stakeholder are known to many organisations even if not always practised.

But a third principle is upon us: all-way communication – the ability of millions of individuals to reach in all directions for data, views and courses of action. The insightful report prepared in 2000 for the Council of Public Relations Firms, and cited in an earlier chapter reminded readers: 'the impact of the Internet on global communication has been logarithmically large: in the space of a decade the number of people communicating online went from thousands to hundreds of millions' (IMT 2000:1). 'Quality and authenticity will be self-regulated', warned the report. 'People will vote by mouse click as to the sources of information they trust most, which in many cases will not be traditional media outlets' (IMT 2000: 3). In other words, the company that best contains the crisis damage, or that contains a flammable risk or issue, will be the one most adjusted to all-way communication with multiple outlets and stakeholders, and incorporating it at the highest operational levels because as we have suggested, communication technology must influence corporate decisions at the operational level – containing and resolving the physical causes of the crisis must remedy the perception of the crisis. Preferably, the company has made this highly disruptive adjustment either before a crisis, or failing that afterwards, as Shell has recognised; but not, if possible, *during* the crisis.

What does such an adjustment mean? It means – as much as possible – blending corporate and stakeholder approaches to the point where in certain aspects they *feel* indistinguishable, yet in others are sufficiently *differentiated* for the business to reap a reputation benefit. How can this be done? Probably by:

- Accommodating chaos and volatility instead of seeking to expunge or control it.
- Unbuttoning strategy and perhaps confidentialities to permit that accommodation.
- Finding elements in the chaos that help the acceptable 'corporate face' to emerge naturally, wherever possible unencumbered by corporate livery and language – often unsubtle, unhuman, clumsy, invasive eyesores of the unauthentic.

Crises will involve Business in replicating the activities of multiple crisis participants, and showing the confidence to put messages in the public arena semi-finished or unfinished, within range of groups and e-fluentials well able to harness 'love, jealousy, guilt, fear, remorse, or anger' (James, 1901–2: 220) to deliver their own perspective. Many other stakeholders, acting singly or together, vy to achieve the momentum that delivers 'mental rearrangements', a phrase aptly used in William James's account of the conversion experience, whereby 'emotions that come in this explosive way seldom leave things as they found them' (James 1901–2: 220).

ORGANISING FOR TOTAL CONNECTIVITY

> The power of words is bound up with the images they evoke, and is quite independent of their real significance. Words whose sense is the most ill-defined are sometimes those that possess the most influence.
>
> Gustave Le Bon. *The Crowd* (1895: 61)

Learning to respond, organising to respond and achieving greater diffusion with stakeholders obliges Business to accept the non-business scope of technological connectivity. Technological grip by itself is no guarantee of emotional connectivity – presenting images and arguments that make the targeted business more likeable during a crisis. However, emotional connectivity in a crisis cannot be achieved without technological connectivity which depends on the unprepared company's existing attitudes: whether IT is treated, for instance, as a servant for other activities – a useful tool for transmitting data or gathering marketing intelligence; or whether IT is used as a strategic not tactical instrument, as a major participant in message shaping, and as a self-standing 'total environment' in which the fate of the crisis – communications and operations – is decided and which must because of that influence the highest levels of decision-taking. There must be recognition that the soft power of technology-mediated words and images affect investment and purchasing decisions, employee loyalty and stakeholder behaviours.

Technological connectivity expresses that moment when unprepared companies hit by unexpected disaster accept – immediately – IT's power to decide their fate, and use that understanding to arrange themselves around the needs created by information technology.

Whether total connectivity – striking the optimal blend of stakeholder engage-ment and technological exploitation – is accepted as a guiding principle or not, business must still reorganise. Once-intangible, irrational elements in the crisis lifecycle should in the twenty-first century be treated seriously, as seriously as a stalled production line or damaged product. Because of the information revolution, business in crisis must accept as a hard, measurable, practical fact, William James's comment on religious experience:

> All our attitudes, moral, practical or emotional, as well as religious, are due to the objects of our consciousness, the things which we believe to exist,

whether really or ideally, along with ourselves. Such objects may be present to our senses, or they may be present only to our thought. In either case they elicit from us a reaction; and the reaction due to things of thought is notoriously in many cases as strong as that due to sensible presences. It may even be stronger. The memory of an insult may make us angrier than the insult did when we received it.

(James, 1901–2: 61)

Response: action

With these precepts a crisis-struck company may breathe meaning into its response. Communication, because it can now cause both perceptual and physical problems, must play a bigger part in reaching resolution. How should the crisis response be organised?

The 'crisis group'

A big information age crisis will demand the decision-making advantages of a small unit and a larger group to negotiate the audiences and their technology.

In an international crisis, the crisis team will also continue to need people in all affected countries.

In a crisis dominated by technology, either international or domestic, but with marked cultural or regional content among its defining characteristics, the company will need specialists in communicating meaning via technology, to online partici-pants from cultures or regions engaged with the crisis.

Since stakeholder conclusions may be reached and action taken at hyper-speed, the business must be able to exchange, discuss and decide critical actions and responses at equal or greater speed.

Crisis team members should therefore receive in-depth training in corporate communication strategy to help them assess the communication and operational implications of hostile activity, take the initiative and react instantaneously without referral or deferral to others. If this training has not happened, they should work with as limited a number of senior decision-makers as possible.

These demands suggest that the traditional crisis team of senior executives digesting information and issuing directions for responses will be simply over-whelmed by volumes of fluctuating information and the reactions demanded of them in open, transparent, unmediated and 'believable' online settings chosen by stakeholders, not the corporation. It would, in fact, be unfair and disastrous to put a small crisis team head-to-head with stakeholder groups who are 24-hour communi-cators with passion or experience on their side: masters of using IT in pursuit of their objectives.

Cobra technology demonstrates how disunity in opposition can be more powerful

100

than unity, by enlarging the activities of diverse groups, sometimes acting together, sometimes separately and sometimes even in disagreement with each other, but all bringing their technology to bear on a single harassed and exhausted target.

To deal with this, the present corporate crisis-fighting model that accommodates monitoring and message delivery, message planning and overall strategy will need some refinement. Because technology and its impact on behaviour changes the size of the communication tasks, it also changes the size, structure and scope of the company's crisis communication team:

- Today, a crisis team tries to divide management of the disaster from regular corporate operations. In an information age crisis, the explosion, the volume and the potency of incessant activity may demand that the team's communication tasks are split into three, to protect strategy formulation from the near-constant task of response.

- Although the precise name probably does not much matter, it helps (with a wry nod to Dante) to view this threefold approach as concentric circles, into which external audiences and internal audiences from within the company can penetrate a determined distance. The first and innermost circle must have space and time for broad operational decisions and basic communication needs including message creation and coordination. Yet this circle, shielded from most of the distracting noise and action, needs information. This is supplied by a second circle of managers, again with time to receive in return the basic messages and strategy, and adjust them to the volatile demands of the crisis, as defined by the participating technology, cultures and key audiences. They too, though, cannot engage in this task as well as that of providing constant communication, or presenting themselves to diverse stakeholders as the company's public 'face'. If, then, the crisis is big enough to draw in online and offline groups beyond familiar corporate contacts in the trade media, investors, lawyers, and regulators, a third and outermost circle must be constantly engaged at the unfamiliar frontiers of perception shaping: monitoring shifts in opinion and unfamiliar key players, identifying e-fluentials, refining and actually delivering the messages and building credible, open, informal, continuous, trust-driven relationships.

- The diverse participants exploiting IT raises an additional prospect of providing multiple corporate 'faces' as general spokespeople in an international crisis, complementing the expectations of particular audiences grouped by faith, nation, online and offline culture.

We must examine these 'circles' in more detail; communicating rapidly with one another but performing different tasks:

- Circle One: a small number of senior decision-makers, agreeing global plans and consistent key messages for containment, recovery and reputation protection in the light of major shifts in the crisis lifecycle. This unit also includes a fully-empowered representative from each of the following:

- Circle Two: takes minute-by-minute responsibility for refining messages to familiar audiences, cultures or technology; coordinating with familiar crisis stakeholders already noted, and outsourced subcontractors; and keeping the first Circle informed of major shifts in stakeholder activity and attitudes. Circle Two may need to establish:
- Circle Three: a tactical unit whose size is defined by the number of new audiences, regions, cultures that need to be engaged, and the cobra technologies that dominate online activity. Team members may be embedded with subcontractors and authorised to deploy emotion tactically, listen and monitor communication activity, consult with Circle Two about message content and reshape messages to reflect evolving attitudes of stakeholders.
- Company spokespeople sited in cultures and regions, coordinating major public announcements with second and third circles.

These groups will operate more loosely than the former, tightly coordinated system pumping out plans and messages. Corporate credibility will require a greater effort to avoid being seen as the 'Other', or the 'Them', by 'tribal' micro-audiences, which means cohabitation in their technological milieu.

Online and offline spokespeople

The lead spokespeople and their appointed deputies – each with their own personalities – must as far as possible mirror the culture of less familiar participating stakeholders.

This 'mirroring' must cover online cultures – language, tone, attitudes – as well as any traditional participating cultures defined by geographical region, social and political customs or belief system.

There is a role for other spokespeople embodying the corporation's message for these additional audiences. This might be undertaken by those within the tactical sphere of Circle Three – but the job of handling incessant flows of opinion may sometimes have to be divided from the task of being a visible lead figure on large corporate announcements. Personal preparation time might not be available to someone locked into perpetual messaging with online audiences. Larger announcements raise the need for a separate senior representative, able to absorb occasional damage to their public persona without hurting the credibility of those in Circle Three involved in a continued communication process.

The spokespeople must also, as the company's face and voice with a selected audience, project a virtual personality that complements their preferred public personality on television, radio and newsprint.

They must work with Circle Three to decide the best platforms for message delivery to their target audience, and to adjust the message to their own online/offline personalities.

The spokespeople and their deputies must be capable of building credibility and trust as individuals, rather than corporate representatives.

They must have a continuous presence, since the time between many stakeholders receiving information and some of them being moved to take damaging online action will to all intents and purposes be non-existent. As a minimum, misperceptions will need to be corrected, or rebutted by sending out holding responses, with equal celerity.

Circle Three

Circle Three members must be able, and enabled, to see past the business, the product and the emergency to the social currents that shape their company's fate.

The team members will assume regional responsibilities as well as responsibilities for online stakeholders, and general communication with traditional audiences essential to the company: investors, customers, employees.

- They must be responsible for instantly adjusting general corporate messages to the online setting for which they are responsible.
- They must act as monitors and participants, passing on signs of a swelling current of hostile speculation or action, with response recommendations.
- They must identify and if possible, build relations with or isolate key influencers.
- They must study and understand the motivations of the groups they are dealing with.
- They must provide messages frequently with the aim of establishing a constantly credible corporate position, partly by constantly demonstrating – by weblogs, mobile phones or IM for example – their own autonomy and the company's high comfort level.

This group will be in regular contact with Circle Two, reporting shifts in stakeholder perceptions and proposing refinements to corporate messages.

Circle Two

Circle Two mediates between Circle Three's regular interactions with diverse online stakeholders and Circle One's development of overall corporate strategy.

The managers here, few in number (between one and ten) to speed decisions, provide a corporate perspective to ensure Circle Three does not identify too closely with external audiences; and a stakeholder perspective for Circle One; ensuring that senior company officers understand stakeholder attitudes and its likely consequences. For these reasons, this unit also includes representatives from Circles One and Three.

With these responsibilities they are corporate 'interpreters': amending the general messages and strategic recommendations crafted by Circle One to the needs of the company's micro-segmented publics, without compromising the main themes.

Circle Two also coordinates these messages to employees generally, especially those at the interface with external publics – the salesforce, reception staff and customer relations managers.

They take additional responsibility for relations with more customary crisis participants, such as important media and investors, since Circle Three is engaged with less familiar and volatile audiences, and because important media or big investors expect a higher level of corporate contact. For this reason, Circle Two must possess strong communication expertise, a chief spokesperson with one or two deputies, and should be able to call on senior company officers if major communication events are needed.

Circle One

Here is the heart of the information age crisis group, steeply inclined to the company rather than its external publics. Consisting, like the traditional core team, of not more than ten senior executives from the most important and afflicted operational sectors, law, finance, marketing and corporate communication, along with representatives speaking for the other circles.

This unit must guard and develop the company perspective to the crisis, and ensure that the messages are not lost in the pressure to adapt to the demands and actions of hostile stakeholders.

Circle One members take strategic and operational decisions, decide key messages, plan for containment and recovery based on information presented to them. Any stakeholders they deal with directly must be few and highly important, given the information volumes and the speed at which decisions may be demanded. Their points of contact beyond the crisis group mainly consist of the most senior corporate officers, biggest investors and if need be senior regulators and politicians.

The traditional task of splitting the crisis from the regular business of the company must remain in the hands of Circle One. To them flows a constant stream of information:

- The cause of the crisis.
- The operational actions taken to fix the physical cause of the crisis.
- The reputation status of the business/product in light of periodic reviews of stakeholder activity.

- Major emerging threats online and offline.

To them falls the aforementioned task of liaison with the CEO and senior officers. From them flow:

- Requests for information from Circle Two.
- Redirected inquiries from less senior external stakeholders to Circle Two for allocation to online or offline spokespeople and Circle Three.
- Key messages and response line for adaptation by other circles.
- Recommendations for managerial/operational action or reform in light of evolving stakeholder activity.
- Final report on crisis and lessons for the badly surprised business – including, perhaps, a new understanding of communication strategy?

They also continue, as formerly, to liaise with other support teams responsible for logistical tasks like recall, quality assurance or damage repair.

The outsourced crisis?

The proliferation of diverse, scattered, active stakeholders also suggests companies surprised by a large-scale information age crisis cannot always deploy the human resources to engage with them. The hopefully rare prospect of a crisis would naturally stop an individual business investing resources in a permanent staff of niche expertise, though large, wealthy and vulnerable sectors may do just that for some audiences. The rest must trust to a steep learning curve and to finding the right people at the right time.

Where are such people found? If they are not already employed by the company, the free market and the trend towards outsourced expertise must provide a solution in the shape of experts in particular stakeholders, technologically sophisticated, strong communicators and available as consultants. Perhaps they will emerge from the stakeholders themselves; perhaps they are already influential among the group – a valuable asset for a distrusted and inexperienced company.

These people are, ideally, experienced in online activism, message adaptation and in weathering issues and crises. They know their stakeholders' opinion leaders. Since they will be retained in Circle Three by the company, their loyalty must lie there – and ensuring that it does in all cases must be a task of crisis managers inside the business. Loyalty is naturally assumed from the current generation of crisis consultants, but may require revision for a new generation of online experts whose experience might not lie in building crisis communication strategy but in empathising with angry stakeholders, and who may not want to be perceived as a hired corporate gun. Yet the model for their role already exists in the shape of the lawyer who must build relations with a jury. The jury know full well that the lawyer is hired, has a paying client and a case to represent, but nonetheless is open to his or her arguments (Bernays 1928: 64).

Tale of a crisis message, construction of a perception

> The patience with which mankind suffers the authority of logic is simply inexhaustible.
>
> Hermann Broch. *The Sleepwalkers* (1930: 482)

Isaiah Berlin once commented, 'Orwell's 1984 merely echoes the crucial thesis that control of language is essential to the control of lives' (Berlin 1959: 143). With a crisis group at last in place, if only at the eleventh hour, let us then track two basic manifestations of language seeking to control the tone and outcome of a crisis – initial messages and formed perceptions. Let us try to discover what may be done with them over the next ten years, when disaster has unexpectedly struck and IT is participating in the event. The company's opening posture is reactive but made with a view to regaining the initiative, and to shaping perceptions at greater-than-internet speed in the opening moments.

For our purposes, it does not matter what the crisis is about. The purpose is to see what the communication must be about. Here, as always at such times, the crisis will illuminate and supercharge and rearrange the communication process.

The crisis cause then, is generic, as is the company. Whatever the cause, it must be sufficiently important and compelling to attract and involve several audiences. Let us assume that these audiences, each in its own way, are violently seized by a perception of the crisis event and are rapidly – perhaps in seconds – making 'logical' extrapolations about its impact on themselves and the things that matter to them. Obedient to the authority of this logic, they obey its injunction to counter an apparent threat, or to vent the violent emotion that has gripped them.

From these conditions the first message emerges to push the crisis forward. This message – perhaps an account of the event, or the verbal distillation of a perception – eventually appears, exclusively in one guise or in various combinations, written, aural, oral, pictorial, visually static, moving, novel, unchanging, or rapidly metamorphosing as many participate in 'growing' it. This message – with its inevitable identification of the degree of outrage, a target for blame, a channel for emotion leading towards an acceptable public sanction – is certainly tailored to the instincts of the audience, and participation in its creation by members of that audience will add to the sense that it is absolutely true and justifiably impatient to get its way.

Whatever technologies provide the medium for germinating and nourishing the messages, they satisfy the activist adage about being both global and local. They possess global reach but with the option of local adaptation. Even as the crisis-causing event unfolds, perhaps from the opening seconds, those with an opinion are, pre-meditatively or unconsciously, pooling thought that will distil itself into a view, then a message, then – hopefully – a truth, and last of all, rapid technological punishment of the kinds forecast in Chapter 2. If it is premeditated, the information exchange and message-creation might be an internal collaborative effort by workers at an activist group bent on using the event to draw attention to a wider issue. A less concerted form of message creation may be simultaneously underway, between groups and individuals with nothing in common beyond the event itself, perhaps using third-party IT platforms owned by providers that may respectively be unaware, neutral, supportive or hostile to the company in crisis.

Whatever the circumstances, the third circle of the company's crisis group should already be at work, perhaps retained by the firm or quickly identified and recruited from the more respected or sympathetic of the early crisis participants. They would be open about their affiliation, yet accepted as participants in the debate about what to think because they are:

- Providing valuable corporate information.
- Presenting the company response or view without excuses or obfuscation, critically where necessary.
- Employing the vocabulary and culture of their stakeholders to the extent needed for credibility.
- Engaging transparently with the leading online opinion formers, to ensure where possible the propagation of a 'fair' perception.
- Providing objective references and general support for the crisis information exchange, even where it may be neutral or contain reasoned criticism.

Meanwhile, they are also fulfilling their company responsibilities:

- Notifying circles Two and One when an out-of-control message is escalating rapidly towards a 'sanction', like an instant boycott, malicious rumour, hoax website or cyber-attack.
- Advising the crisis group when major changes to a corporate message or communication tactic might be needed to maintain effective relationships with certain stakeholders.
- Cementing close relationships with individual active e-fluentials during the crisis.
- Providing – as is already customary – updates about information content and volume, and any other organisations including competitors or subcontractors.

SUMMARY: TOTAL COMMUNICATION

These activities are needed because as we have seen, in the crisis of the future there may be little or no time between agreeing a message and the sanction it seems to demand. Companies may not be able to wait for the first messages to 'appear'. They must, as soon as possible, begin the process of public advocacy with their segmented, scattered, all-too-powerful audiences armed to punish the stricken firm easily, instantly and significantly.

External stakeholders cannot be left to themselves. It will be harder for companies to reverse a global e-commerce attack than to stop it before it gets started. Audience segmentation, globalisation and technology's proliferation forces companies to attend to personalised message-formation among important audiences.

The task for Business is to help construct perceptions, by shaping the fate of the crisis in participation with key publics, and not in reaction to them; to create the possibility of a moderating logic that triggers fairer public reactions that the company can – or should – accept.

The scale of the coming struggle for language, and the rising stakes involved, will make heavy demands on the crisis-hit business. In order to handle the catalytic circumstances of a crisis, managers at all levels will need better understanding of the direction and momentum of a stream of communication:

- They must understand the basics of strategic communication. This requires a sea-change in corporate attitudes towards transparency and reputation management.
- They must understand in detail the motivations and ambitions of important stakeholder groups.
- They must learn to forecast how their stakeholders are likely to behave in a communication-filled crisis and be able to forecast likely reactions and consequent actions.
- They must know how to get the most out of the IT tools at their disposal.
- They must know how to use words and images under pressure: in writing, verbally, powerfully, democratically.
- They must be able, and enabled by their employer, to see past the merely business and product dimensions or the physical aspect of the emergency to take into account broader social currents that shape their fate.

The future crisis is even less well-behaved than its wayward predecessors: less pliable, reluctant to be nudged into 'proper channels'; more likely to spill into the lives and technologies of everyone in the company; more likely to tempt them to enter the fray themselves, anonymously or publicly, from guilt, loyalty or indignation.

Preparation is the best antidote to such untrammelled and unregulated activity within, alongside a management that grasps the new conditions. Fresh approaches to the crisis preparedness are set out in the next chapter.

Chapter 6

Learning conversational transparency

What will happen when young people, or the more intelligent and energetic among them, begin to see through this modish and profitable fraud? What will they think of the mass communicators, verbalisers, manipulators and purveyors of fashionable rubbish they now allow to speak in their name?

Peter Simple. *More of Peter Simple* (1969: 190)

INTRODUCTION

In *Our Final Hour*, Sir Martin Rees's catalogue of scientific and natural catastrophes menacing the World, he proposes alternative counter-measures – 'concealment' or 'openness' (Rees 2004: 82). Concealment would attempt to guard certain research by secrecy, regulations and oversight, 'selectively denying new knowledge to those who seem likely to misapply it' (Rees 2004: 82). The other option: 'maximum openness in communications, and a high rate of international migration [of science students moving between institutions], would render even small-scale clandestine projects harder to conceal' (Rees 2004: 83). Under the openness umbrella, scientific codes of ethics to stop biological weapons proliferation and encourage 'whistleblowers' have been proposed by some scientists as part of a more general control initiative. Although an anonymous panel of senior US industry experts working with the non-partisan Henry L. Stimson Center doubted openness would 'be much of a barrier, especially in the absence of any specified, enforced consequences for rule breakers' (Henry L. Stimson 2002: 42).

In business and in communication, the same debate faces exposed corporate managers: suppression and control of information to shield it from whistleblowing employees, the competition and other hostile groups or individuals; or engagement by installing systems and codes encouraging a more open approach.

As managers and scientists ponder, communication technology and globalisation force a solution by making a world that expects organised pursuit of openness. There is widespread yearning for 'authentic', equal encounters with organisations

109

and a belief that technology can see through 'the mass communicators, verbalisers, manipulators and purveyors of fashionable rubbish'. The desire, whether realistic or sentimental, is being converted into business opportunity. Public relations giant Hill and Knowlton tell website visitors that 'brand loyalty is under siege, and there is growth of both brand cynicism, driven in part by the lack of corporate transparency, and advertising avoidance' (Hill and Knowlton: 2004). One response to the yearning and cynicism has indeed been the rise of the 'transparency' concept, recounted briefly in chapters 2 and 3. Transparency, the word generally used to advocate the fullest and open provision of information, attracts interest and influencers. Canadian author, consultant and business commentator Donald Tapscott evokes it as an essential corporate objective for the new millennium: 'in a world of instant communications and transparent corporations, the emerging color to aim for is blue, a color that evokes the clarity of a cloudless summer sky' (Tapscott 2002: 18). Firms that do not heed transparency will be exposed to attack and destruction; firms that understand constituent and community values will develop sustainable business models (Tapscott and Ticoll 2003). Certainly, activist groups use transparency as a general values-based campaign lever, prying responses from governments and businesses, as when a coalition of activist groups including Friends of the Earth, Greenpeace and the World Wildlife Fund For Nature publicly called for 'a fully transparent chemicals policy' in the EU ('Transparency demands' 2002: 1). This incidentally did much to raise awareness of the transparency value of proposed 'REACH' (Registration, Evaluation and Authorisation of Chemicals) regulations in the European Union, under which 'businesses that manufacture or import more than one metric ton of a chemical substance annually would be required to register it in a central database' (EU 2004).

But transparency is not readily transparent. It is indicative of this point that the coalition's chemical transparency campaign was a demand for industry information they required, coupled with a demand for inclusion in EU Commission policy-making ('Transparency demands' 2002: 1). Two years later, the incoming President of the European Chemical Industry Council (Cefic) countered with 'Trust', a transparency initiative aimed at advocacy and dialogue with nonprofits, governments, industry and the public: 'The trust theme is not new. It is as old as mankind, but we feel it has never been more relevant than today . . . A solid license to operate is built from two elements – business performance and reputation. It's our job to realize improvements on both counts' ('Cefic aims' 2004: 9).

Adversarial notions of transparency and the subjective preferences that surround it means transparency's inherent virtue cannot be taken for granted. Baroness Professor Onora O'Neill noted in her 2002 BBC Reith Lectures: 'This high enthusiasm for ever more complete openness and transparency has done little to build or restore public trust. On the contrary, trust seemingly has receded as transparency has advanced' (O'Neill 2002).

This chapter is about managing transparency as a crisis prevention mechanism.

110

MANAGEMENT OBSTACLES AND COMPROMISED TRANSPARENCY

How can transparent crisis models be developed? Unfortunately for communicators, transparency, like the infinite universe, has no fixed centre or boundary. A scholar of international regimes notes: 'transparency depends upon both the demand for information and the supply of information' (Mitchell 1998: 109). A crisis moreover is sensitive to the impact of fast, transient and diverse overt and covert stakeholder manoeuvres. There is usually no single set of convincing, truthful words and phrases for all stakeholders to unite around. To adapt Tapscott's phrase, there are several shades of blue but little discussion about how much or what kinds of information equals transparency, which methods of delivery are transparent or even whether transparency is much more than a veil for use in public relations messages. Ronald Mitchell commented in 1998: 'Almost no work to date has investigated the determinants of transparency' (Mitchell 1998: 110). Now in a more vulnerable world that effort must be made. In 2004, many businesses are exposed to the complex influences of transparency, communication technology, and 'non-business' spheres like international relations. Tapscott and Ticoll examine many aspects of this in their pro-transparency invocation *The Naked Corporation* (2003), but the content of transparency when planning against crises or threats is unresolved. The challenge for suddenly stricken or slowly vulnerable organisations and their critics is not just one of discovering where transparency is hiding. Other questions must also be asked, and will now be explored.

- Transparency is something that either is or is not perceived by crisis participants – which audience's perception will dominate, and why?
- Can transparency ever be satisfactorily harnessed and communicated by an inherently distrusted and vulnerable corporation?
- If transparency is to truly occur, the subject that is to be communicated must in principle be minutely understood. Is that objectively possible during a disaster? If it is not, must crisis transparency be subjective? Can subjectivity be transparency?
- Can transparency simultaneously satisfy changeless constituent and community values, and sudden, emotionally volatile and highly transient constituent and community events?

Transparency does depend on supply and demand, in this case for information, and so it has commoditised. It is also a commodity because a value is now attached to it. It is a perceptual commodity because it must meet divergent and politicised notions of openness held by the company and among its various audiences; notions covering information and also operations. We have seen that the EU chemical policy activists unsurprisingly wanted transparency to serve their agenda, so providing transparent information was not enough: their idea of transparency included the right to join in decision-making.

Transparency is also a divisible commodity: the EU activists did not demand transparency *per se* – there is no such thing – but selective information that met their strategic needs. Transparency therefore is a frangible, highly sensitive commodity that can add to or detract from a company's value. Because of its ambiguous and influential nature, transparency needs attention to an extent yet to be grasped by most business leaders.

Despite widespread confusion or ignorance about what transparency actually is, there is intense competition to 'own' it – or rather the perception of it. Von Furstenberg studied transparency's 'hopes and delusions' in international relations and finance:

> The main message that emerges is that greater transparency, far from having the characteristics of a simple public good which yield non-rival benefits to all consumers of this quality, is bound to be a contentious issue between the parties jockeying for control. While greater transparency of political agents can be helpful to principals even when not necessary or sufficient for improved governance, greater transparency of the principals themselves often harms them.
>
> (Von Furstenberg 2001: 105)

Transparency's integrity is also compromised by other factors, among them a time-sensitive information 'supply chain'. Technology encourages and/or forces audiences or individual opinion-leaders moved by fear, suspicion, curiosity or anger, to demand more information on key subjects, which once it arrives simply raises expectations for information extraction from deeper inside the company's decision-chain, presumably until – in theory if not in practice – satisfaction is reached. The targeted business is correspondingly pressured to supply 'believable' and 'authentic' transparencies at earlier phases before data checks are complete. Sooner or later it reaches a point where, for the company, transparency release is dangerously unpredictable because its impact is harder to anticipate, or meaningless as the data becomes more speculative. 'The more I've explained, the deeper the uncertainty has become', complains the German physicist Werner Heisenberg about perceptions of his wartime activities in Frayn's drama *Copenhagen* (Frayn 1998: Act 1 Scene 4).

Technology simultaneously enlarges the possibilities of 'transparency', and puts it in the position where stakeholder uncertainty can only be relieved – if at all – by increasing uncertainty within the company, and creating dangerous hesitancy as the permissible time between decision-making and action-taking shrinks.

Transparency must overcome deep contradictions in our economic and social roles: for instance as consumers, employees, parents, activists, investors, cultural or religious adherents – as one, some, or all of the preceding audiences. Individuals often want more transparency about someone or something. That need for uncertainty-reducing information and opinion escalates in a crisis. Few stakeholders in personal or collective trouble choose to know less about the subjects that affect them when they are armed to discover more.

The more information, the more there is to interpret, so corporate transparency, and even the rawest data, finds itself burdened by an accompanying need to offer opinion and persuasion. Natural curiosity and habits of interpretation infect the objectivity of the best-intentioned data whether or not the company's transparency plan is prepared for it to do so. In a crisis or long-running issue, communication is more than usually 'transformative' rather than simply 'informative', because participants are in opinion-conflict. One group of communicators 'attempts to link ideas and symbols in ways that contribute to the creation or maintenance of an existing pattern of social relations' (Phillips and Brown 1993: 1548), while another either tries to disrupt an existing pattern of social relations, or is accused of doing so. A plethora of participants, views and potentially transformative data draws stakeholders into competitive attempts – for imagined, real personal or societal advantage – to establish their information as the 'truth' and which adds weight to the quantity, variety and confusion of crisis news. In this arena, transparency shifts to become a swirling fog of rumour and speculation. Heated claims and sidebar issues flower; transparency's promise of clarity is compromised, and drags down with it established audience relationships that act as a calming brake on events. Attaching a persuasive, interpretative component to transparency is for corporate leaders a fair and very necessary precaution.

In a corporation, therefore, fear of transparency's impact might grow when 'shocks' worry the system; but elsewhere transparency's scope widens amid multiple tremors caused by determined, maybe small and sporadic groups of twenty-first-century stakeholders using openness to harm reputation and operations more comprehensively than even their late-twentieth-century counterparts.

CURRENT APPROACHES TO TRANSPARENCY AND 'THREAT' MANAGEMENT

But as more of us demand and get transparency, contradictory circumstances exist where we want to retard and supervise its supply as employees, interviewees, homeowners, parents, immigrants, taxpayers, company directors, or public officials. We may even at times resent and suppress it. As proselytisers for a particular cause we may stress one fact as opposed to another that might be more ambiguous or even flatly contradict our position. As employees we could feel degraded by technology-enabled demands for more information on our daily activities, seeing it as invasiveness of a sort that former Iron Curtain regimes could only have imagined. 'It would be a big mistake for companies to conclude that corporate transparency should be applied to individuals – that customers should get used to being naked', warn Tapscott and Ticoll (2003: 181–2). Nevertheless, that is what is happening, not only to us as customers, but to us as the other audiences already mentioned, including employees. 'Alison, the head of a "community" of teams (about two hundred CSRs [Call Centre Representatives]) at Orange, can see with a glance at her computer screen what everyone is doing . . . Everything is monitored: the length of calls, the time spent on "off-call work" and the number of calls put on hold' (Bunting 2004: 65–6). In a comprehensive investigation of management surveillance, Graham Sewell remarks:

> Such intense scrutiny not only extracts information about the activities of individuals, it also goes a long way to shaping their subjectivity as they come to see themselves in the ways they are defined through surveillance (e.g. sick versus well patients, reliable versus delinquent borrowers, productive versus unproductive workers).
>
> (Sewell 1998: 403)

Such tribulations ensure that where we have control over data about ourselves, we occasionally pause before releasing it into the public domain, unwilling to submit to more 'measurement, enumeration, and rationalization' (Sewell 1998: 403) without offering explanation or interpretation of the material. We engage in transparency management and direct our audience towards particular arguments, wrapped in particular sets of words, sounds or images. We pursue 'subjective' transparency: data infused with overt or covert messages.

If reflecting on content is unavoidable and choosing a way to wrap and distribute information is unavoidable, it is also unavoidable, and not necessarily deceitful, to give premeditated consideration to tools and content. Supervised and controlled transparency does not of itself compromise its authenticity. Unfettered transparency is not the only measure of truthfulness. While one company under pressure may offer more information, it is misguided in a crisis to confuse quantity with belief that an organisation is being more 'spontaneous', 'natural' and therefore 'open'. It could also be a worrying sign of ignorance, loss of control, or an attempt to bury the truth deep inside a mountain of information. Material eventually released might be called transparent by those who agree with it, but even with a large amount of data it is more accurate to say that inescapable subjective, selective influences of setting, time, existing perceptions and tools have produced an 'impression' of transparency, dependent on the pre-existing legacy of trust between the corporation and its audiences, whether the information offered does what the company says it does, and the history of the vulnerability. It is in any case expecting much of managers facing personal or corporate disaster to release large quantities of transformative information without consciously trying to shape its reception and subsequent perceptions.

114

Future managers must make rapid judgements about releasing very large masses of crisis material, which could effectively generate unhelpful heat rather than shed light on complex issues and situations. They have an obligation publicly to interpret the material they release, especially when under global inspection. Businesses reacting to threats are learning how – and how not – to manage their transparency so that it addresses their own and society's vulnerabilities, and to become credible participants in debates that threaten to engulf them.

Full transparency

At the most 'reactive' end of communicating around transparency is the corporate website of tobacco giant Philip Morris USA, which does not even mention its products. It has instead become an information board about smoking and disease, addiction, smoking and pregnancy, quitting smoking, under-age smoking and secondhand smoke (surrendering its attempt in former times to popularise the more measured label of 'Environmental Tobacco Smoke'). The site design is notably unadorned, consisting of simple colours and text, unblemished by product marketing but with attention to applying a frank, responsible 'look' to issues communication – to convey openness, seriousness and earnestness. The menu bar concentrates, not on self-promotion, but on facts about tar and nicotine numbers, health issues and responsible marketing. Links are provided to impartial sources such as the United States Food and Drug Administration and the Surgeon General's 1998 Report on Nicotine Addiction. Even where a corporate identity is offered by Philip Morris, it is subject to the conditions set by transparency. The mission statement does not open with the customary pledge to provide stakeholder or customer satisfaction. It barely mentions cigarettes.

> Our goal is to be the most responsible, effective and respected developer, manufacturer and marketer of consumer products, especially products intended for adults. Our core business is manufacturing and marketing the best quality tobacco products to adults who use them.
>
> We will support our mission by proactively engaging with our stakeholders to enhance our ability to act in a way that is consistent with society's expectations of a responsible company.
>
> (Philip Morris USA 2004)

Philip Morris USA's website, and its separate international website – offering a little more 'soft' design but still stressing that 'what it doesn't include is marketing materials for any of our products' (Philip Morris International 2004) – have become transparency pioneers reactively, after thirty years of political and regulatory pressures, threats of litigation, legal restrictions, medical science, hostile media coverage and cause group attacks. This transparency is a logical communication

115

outcome of the prevailing and now largely uncontested activist communication environment. Information and resources on quitting smoking are offered as an act of strategy; managing and defending reputations matters more than overtly selling the product. In this way, transparency is deployed and managed to help Philip Morris to continue selling its products, to fend off being legislated out of North America and other countries and ultimately to avoid the fate of the asbestos industry – similarly marginalised and finally destroyed by escalating public ill-will. Here, the commodity of transparency, for all its presumed objectivity, attempts to act as a life belt for the storm-tossed company.

Proactive transparency

Transparency can also be proactive, wrapping facts and messages to help organisations take early ownership of issues or risks. The Body Shop, multinational personal care manufacturer and campaigner on various global challenges to society, wraps its identity into a public exposition of its campaign activities, which has become a marketing platform or springboard for sales activities. The impression is that The Body Shop is not all about money, but the material is less transparent, and couched in a less transparent format, than Philip Morris. There is less raw data on product ingredients beyond marketing information, because the lack of demand currently makes total transparency superfluous. The Body Shop, by taking the initiative, has more choice about where it wishes to be transparent and seizes hold of social issues, presenting them to stakeholders as issues that should matter to them also, and providing reports on the company's campaigning activities. The issues include the use of animals in research and testing, community trade, human rights, self esteem and the environment. The Body Shop deals with the rather closer and less comfortable issue of animal testing in cosmetics by universalising the problem, pointing out that 'almost all cosmetics ingredients have been animal tested by somebody at some time for someone' and broadening the issue by opposing the legislation that put the industry in this position, boycotting cosmetic companies that continue to use animals and petitioning the European Union.

The Body Shop uses transparency on its own terms. It has not yet been forced into openness. Philip Morris was forced to accept and integrate transparency. Other companies operate in the space between.

Reluctant transparency

In 2003 in the wake of the Iraq War, Halliburton learnt about the perils of a deficit in public perception, and took the first steps towards transparency and, potentially, large-scale culture change to accommodate it. The United States provider of oil and gas services was pulled irreversibly into the domain of public comment and speculation in 2001 when media reports, notably the *Washington Post*, highlighted its links to the incoming US administration led by oilmen George W. Bush and Vice President Richard Cheney, both pushing a new oil-inclined energy policy for America. Halliburton subsidiaries were also alleged with Cheney's knowledge to have signed contracts to sell over $73 million in oil production equipment to the regime of Saddam Hussein, despite a policy against trading with Iraq (UPI 2001; 'Firm's Iraq deals' 2001: A01). Halliburton shied off public communication until the United States-led invasions of Afghanistan and Iraq provoked speculation, fanned by a six-month study from the United States Center for Public Integrity, about its donations to the Bush election campaign, and its place among a group of 70 companies securing 'no-bid' contracts for reconstruction work in the oil fields, 60 per cent of which employed 'former senior government or military officials or had close ties to government agencies and to Congress' ('The struggle for Iraq' 2003: 8). 'The root of these problems', asserted Henry Waxman, a critical US Democratic Congressional Representative 'is the administration's insistence on virtually absolute secrecy about how it is spending the taxpayer's money' (Center for Public Integrity 2003).

Halliburton, its preference for silence compromised, started a consistent and objective-leaning public response of sorts. Online it was led by the company's website, which simply carried on the homepage third-party links to supportive media articles. As in any escalating issue, however, audiences soon began drilling into promising new topics. Misgivings were voiced about Halliburton's preferential prospects in the Government's new energy policy; no-bid contracts in war zones; overcharging for those contracts; latterly, bribery and corruption in Nigeria, and an emotive vein of human interest stories, flavoured by the difficulties and issues surrounding outsourcing explored in Chapter 4. Comment mushroomed over the fate of kidnapped employees of KBR, Halliburton's fuel distribution subsidiary in Iraq; and the possibly illegal treatment of 30,000 non-US workers whose hiring was outsourced by KBR to subcontractors in India (where, according to KBR itself, up to five levels of subcontractors and employment agents managed recruitment), Pakistan, the Philippines and 35 other countries. Allegations ran in the *Washington Post* and elsewhere that KBR's subcontracted workers were misled about conditions and locations, worked in proscribed occupations on one-tenth of US wages, and were kept short of food, water, healthcare and security protection – although some received a certificate of appreciation for their trouble. KBR's response, made in July 2004, was that it 'had been unaware of the workers' concerns until recently' ('Underclass' 2004: A01).

Halliburton could no longer ignore these multiple and even subcontracted threats to its corporate position. The company advanced – or was dragged – further down the path towards a fuller and managed communication strategy. Non-commercial corporate releases appeared in quantity as 2003 progressed. Occasionally they struck a defensive note: 'to allege that KBR is overcharging for this needed service, insults the KBR employees who are performing this dangerous mission to help bring fuel to the people of Iraq' (Halliburton 2003). By 2004 Halliburton's releases had metamorphosed: they now included responses to critical news coverage, further explanations of KBR's activities; empathetic accounts of its work to improve the lives of soldiers and Iraqis; tributes to slain employees (41 by June 2004); continual updates on the 'current Iraq situation' (Halliburton 2004a). A Frequently Asked Questions page now included Halliburton's moderately expressed views on whistleblowers: 'KBR questions the factual nature of many of these assertions'; testimony to the Congressional Committee on Government Reform (ranking Democrat Member: Henry Waxman): 'KBR was invited and is pleased to have the opportunity to appear'; and responses to accusations of secrecy with key documents: 'the company is exceptionally forthcoming' (Halliburton 2004b). 'Click here', visitors to the company's homepage are asked, 'to send a note of encouragement to KBR employees in Iraq'; 'Click here to check on the status of a KBR employee currently working in the Middle East' (Halliburton 2004c).

At the time of writing, 'Halliburton has become a byword for the cosy links between the White House and Texan big business' declared the *Guardian* ('Inside story' 2004: 16). The communication value of this perception has not escaped Osama bin Laden, who in his October 2004 videotape referred to 'the size of the contracts acquired by the shady Bush administration-linked mega-corporations, like Halliburton and its kind' ('Bin Laden' 2004). The *Guardian*'s perhaps inevitable scepticism contains at least one central communication truth – fair or not, a promising target has been found by diverse audiences from America to the Middle East, and it is Halliburton.

Corporate transparency, as suggested by Philip Morris, the Body Shop and Halliburton operates anywhere between the aforementioned poles of compulsion or voluntary initiation. These poles support the argument that voluntary transparency is perceptually more laudable but not necessarily less opaque. Philip Morris started with communication denial and ended a generation later with a near total surrender to the forces of transparency. It offers visitors large quantities of raw unrefined information about the dangers of its product, stripped of the distracting seductions of design and presented as understated advocacy. On the other hand, it must be asked whether a business should dally until its reputation lies in shreds and hostile audiences force it to expose itself on highly unflattering terms.

The voluntary alternative, represented by the Body Shop, helps companies convey transparency on their own terms, and constrict transparency more effectively. Prepared corporate messages can be folded into a full informational programme on valid issues of public concern that offer no direct harm to the corporation, and do not appear to test its internal culture or corporate activities because the bulk of key influencers and other stakeholders are satisfied by this social commitment alone, while others believe this commitment actually helps the bottom line.

Between these two poles companies shuttle reluctantly or often hopefully back and forth, adapting their approaches to transparency by impulse, design, events and the brightness of the public spotlight. Halliburton is still trying to align transparency with its commercial ambitions. Simply opening up and communicating in public was a large concession; another was the company's decision to present third-party media information, provide information on congressional scrutiny and recount the dangers to their employees in the Middle East. The interplay of corporate-speak with positive language – how many people or organisations are honestly 'pleased' to be summoned for public interrogation by a congressional committee? – and the paucity of online links to critical or impartial sources of information nevertheless suggests that Halliburton regards openness as a tool for getting its own message across, rather than for enhancing its general believability by accommodating criticism and 'objective' information release. It will be instructive to plot Halliburton's evolving attitude towards transparency to see if management will reach a more complete understanding and initiate a cultural change within the company to facilitate an impression of less partial messaging and optimal disclosure.

Compromised or partial transparency

Transparency's ever-changing nature makes understanding hard to achieve in a defensive position. The Energy sector generally is familiar with the intense stress on communication created by price volatility, political scrutiny, globally distributed activity and activist attention. In this high-profile field lie clues to the future for issues, risk and crisis containment and perhaps globalisation itself.

Shell's own advance to open engagement, described in Chapters 1–3, have included a notable online movement – by no means over – to convey the transparency necessary to give substance to their message. With platforms like TellShell, and online material on human rights and the environment, Shell took transparency further than Halliburton, even pushing the experiment of open and unfiltered communication to the point of testing corporate comfort levels, and providing information on social issues that – in contrast to the Body Shop – directly affect the company's operations. Shell UK addresses its presumed vulnerabilities on its website, where a detailed 'Issues' page recounts Shell's activities in the area of Corporate Social Responsibility (CSR), without attempting to dismiss public sensitivities. Shell tackles animal testing by covering the issue, regulations, its own record and standard practice. The company also describes its ill-starred attempt to decommission the Brent Spar oil rig, stalled since 1995 by intense activist, media and political pressure (see p. 33). Other subjects deal with the general problem of disposing of industrial legacies, climate change, sustainable development and fuel prices. The tone reflects to some degree Shell's place in the transparency spectrum – neither combative because, unlike Halliburton, the company is not reacting instinctively to a flood of unfamiliar criticism; nor assertive and campaigning, as with the Body Shop, which desires to be seen as more or less possessing the same values as Shell's potential critics. Shell poses the questions, presents the issues and sets its tone as 'non-confrontational', 'informational', 'responsible' (Shell UK 2004b).

This approach to social transparency complements traditional corporate efforts, including the launch of a new CSR 'Academy' with the UK Minister for CSR and Shell UK Chairman. The framework of the Academy project recognises that successful transparency and communication are inseparable. The project's six 'core characteristics' for CSR include, at number four: 'Stakeholder relations – identifying stakeholders, building relations externally and internally, engaging in consultation and balancing demands' (Shell UK 2004a).

But Shell's own journey to transparency has been signally interrupted by a failure to rise to unexpected demands. On 9 January 2004 (a Friday and a time less experienced companies use for dribbling out bad news), the company issued a public statement: 'Proved reserve recategorisation following internal review: No material effect on financial statements' (Shell 2004a). An innocuous headline to the average motorist but a massive shock to informed stakeholders – the opinion-leaders in any big crisis. Shell was making a 20 per cent reduction of its oil and natural gas reserves, one of the vital signs of an oil firm's potential. Somehow or other, the company had overestimated its reserves by one-fifth.

Despite emphasising that an internal review and not external whistleblowing had prompted the announcement, the impact inside Shell was exaggerated by a series of missed communication opportunities, leaving the impression that Shell had left too many unanswered questions. The Chairman, Sir Philip Watts and Finance Director Judy Boynton did not attend the teleconference of the announcement, hosted by the heads of Investor Relations and External Affairs, and a Technical Director of Exploration and Production. A separate message to staff – 'dear colleagues' – from Sir Philip did not appear until the following Friday, ensuring that the 'colleagues' heard the news through the media, the same way as the public. Sir Philip tried to explain his absence from the teleconference: 'Given subsequent reactions, to some this might not seem to have been the correct decision but we did achieve the objective of giving the facts unclouded by personality issues in the first instance. I will of course', he continued, 'be at the forefront when we next meet with investors and the media on 5 February' (Shell 2004b).

Between the teleconference and Sir Philip's letter, waves of controversy rippled decisively outward into the energy sector. 'Any resemblance between Shell and a clam is entirely coincidental', commented a *Financial Times* reporter as Sir Philip attempted to explain himself ('Shell needs' 2004: 20). 'Can we still be sure of Shell?', asked the BBC in February as criticism continued even after healthy financial results ('Can we still be sure of Shell?' 2004). Shell's shares dropped 7.5 per cent on worries that the company would not produce its previously stated reserves. ChevronTexaco took the opportunity to remind investors and would-be investors of its own 'rigorous review process' for determining reserves ('ChevronTexaco response' 2004).

In the months following their announcement Shell made more downgrades arriving at a final reserve reduction figure of 23 per cent. Investors, the *Sunday Times* reported on 11 January, were 'incensed' at the absence of Watts and Boynton. Sir Philip 'has four weeks to save his career', as the traditional crisis-fuelling and anonymous 'source close to the company' said it was 'make or break time for Watts', who 'has until February 5 when the group publishes its year-end figures to pull a rabbit out of the hat and show he is in charge, otherwise investors will be clamouring for change' ('Ultimatum for Shell chief' 2004: 1). Speculation spread to the company's executive bonus system, and the possibility that it stimulated the overbooking of reserves.

Sir Philip Watts was failing to locate a rabbit. On 3 March Shell announced he had 'stepped down' as Chairman, by 'mutual consent', along with the head of exploration and production and, a month later, the finance director (Shell 2004c). The non-executive Chairman of Shell's UK holding company 'pleaded for investors' forgiveness', *Forbes* reported, offering in his words, 'a sincere apology for the failures that led to the significant restatement of the group's proved reserves earlier this year' ('Oxburgh: Shell Chairman apologizes to investors' 2004). This did not end it. By July 2004 at least 30 employees had been questioned by the United States Securities and Exchange Commission. Stories ran in the *Wall Street Journal* and elsewhere that 'company insiders had alerted [Shell's external auditors] to the possible need for downgrades two years ago' ('Shell auditors' 2004: 39). Auditors KPMG and PWC responded by referring all inquiries to Shell and standing by their work. Shell, meanwhile, as it had done once before after the Europe-wide firestorm over their failed 1995 efforts to dump the old Brent Spar oil rig in the North Sea, yet again initiated a major review of its internal structure; another step perhaps, on its long journey towards acceptable levels of transparency.

The incident bore the marks of a large-scale reputation-damaging crisis: a well known brand, a big company, a large amount of money, and Information Technology to drive the speculation far, fast and wide. But there is more to it than that. For all Shell's commitment to the open engagement demanded by the information age, with platforms like TellShell, with generous expositions of the company position on sensitive social issues; for all that, Shell's 'mud level' remained thick enough to block transparency where it really mattered: in the heart of the company, at top levels of financial decision-taking, in explaining fiscal and operational blunders as they happened. Such reluctance is a large obstacle to Tapscott's true 'blue' corporate world.

IDENTIFYING, PLANNING, MANAGING TRANSPARENCY

Transparency is shaping the worlds of crisis, risks and issues communication. It cannot be treated as a supplementary PR tactic, in which messages dominate selective data; because of the new age of crises and vulnerability management, it must become the foundation of the organisation's internal culture and external reputation. Transparency is malleable and dangerous to leave to chance – which really means that control over it has been ceded to others. Yet messages must be present. Data may be provided, but so should the viewpoint of the business. Both must appear as frank, open and as unmediated as possible for it to be credible; both require premeditation and craft, both require businesses to adjust their approach to communication. Believable bridges between the subjective and objective must be built by crisis planners and senior company officers, who must all be imbued with realistic views of the observers and critics focusing on their businesses.

Along with assisting the crisis response mechanisms described in the last chapter, these conflicting demands upon transparency must also operate effectively in a 'pre-crisis' space briefly introduced in Chapter 3. Traditional crisis planning tries to carry companies through disaster once it has broken. Issues and risk management offer communication for long-running but not yet explosive or highly public threats. Between these two, a 'pre-crisis' area is becoming crucial. As technology heats the arena for public communication, it is able to suddenly seize upon an issue or risk and escalate it to crisis levels. The laws of this space assume that a dangerous issue may or actually is finally metastasizing beyond circles of experts and other advocates and on the brink of entering a more public area dominated by mass online media and speculation. It is the last relatively temperate zone where caution, reflection or the correct emotional formula may stop a volatile risk or issue from achieving crisis. Transparency is needed to succeed in that debatable ground, to raise levels of audience belief in the shaken company and give it the precious gift of time. It must involve senior management and where necessary immediate reform of the corporate communication structure.

Transparency strategy therefore has new needs, as experienced global companies like Shell are discovering. They affect all entities coming into contact with information age, whether public or private, whether companies, activists or national governments.

- The need for companies to see transparency as something that not only embraces work project effectiveness, but anticipates the firm's external vulnerabilities.
- The need to identify the correct elements for successful transparency.
- The need to ensure that larger numbers of outsourced employees can understand, work in and communicate the new transparency.

Meeting these needs will deliver the perception of transparency. One entrant in this field is Burson-Marsteller, the US Public Relations/Public Affairs multinational, which offers clients a '62-item audit named PRePARE' that 'provides an overview of homepage functionality, online leadership strategies, contact accessibility, information distribution and transparency tactics' (Burson-Marsteller 2004).

Subjective transparency: likeability via 'conversation'

Burson-Marsteller's transparency service includes guidance on 'disseminating select internal memos, legal glossaries and other relevant sources online' (Burson-Marsteller 2003), but companies are not necessarily ready to take this route without knowing how to mediate between the information they are expected to divulge, and the audiences who use it. In their considered account of transparency, Tapscott and Ticoll admit: 'Even when the spirit is willing and the money is there, few firms have a culture of transparency and most need to invest time and money to build the required processes and infrastructures' (2003: 39). Processes and infra-structures can be erected from the wreckage of a crisis, or less painfully by accepting that transparency can help not hinder the communication of a corporate message. 'How can a company, government or NGO get their message across in a world of non-stop media and incessant commercial bombardment?', asks an internal paper for a large public relations consultancy: 'Sophisticated networks of consultants exist to help answer this seemingly central question. But it's increasingly the wrong question. People don't want messages anymore, they want conversations' (Knobel 2004: 1). Regardless of transparency, organisations still need platforms both to provide a simple one-way flow of information to some audiences, and more complex information and transformational conversations with others. To succeed in future, all must be gathered together. Transparency must accommodate humanity's subjective instincts.

Subjective transparency must forge a subtle relationship with messaging. Its work is to focus on tone and transmitting media, and convey likeability within a looser conversational framework. There is of course nothing unusual about treating likeability as a tangible asset. Academics, business professionals and the popular media do it frequently. Many professionals – with politicians perhaps the most prominent – know likeability is a strategy. Headlines from the 2004 US Presidential Election: 'GOP to play Bush's likability card' (2004: 1); 'Kerry and the "likability" index' (2004: 1); 'The "likability" issue takes center stage' (2004: H12) demon-strate the commoditisation of likeability by professional communicators. Advertisers, for better or worse, conduct likeability surveys for commercials while academics have for many years assessed likeability's relation to advertising success (for example Leather et al. 1994), or the effect of celebrity likeability on product endorsement (Kahle and Homer 1985; Tripp et al. 1994). Consultants stress the value of likeability in job interviews ('What's the key?' 2004: 1) or its value to customer relations: 'Recruit people who customers like – not just ones who fit the description' (Freemantle 1999: E8). Even academics are not safe from likeability investigations conducted formally by psychologists (Brady 1994) and, somewhat less scientifically, by US and Canadian students on www.ratemyprofessor.com or www.myprofessorsucks.com.

Likeability matters in marketing, in viewing personal and corporate performance, and in meeting the sophisticated needs of political communicators. Futurist and business consultant, James Bellini, has argued that businesses must be 'liked' to succeed in a crowded and noisy market (Bellini 1999). 'Conversation' and 'likeability' fill holes that *Naked Corporation*'s Tapscott and Ticoll fell into when they discovered that fear of the subjective and uncontrolled meant that business needed more persuasion about transparency. The authors recorded the problem in a 'transparent' analysis of their book's unexpectedly low sales: 'The book's hypothesis is counterintuitive: Everyone looks around and sees all this horrible behavior by companies, and they think that big corporations are in a sorry state and getting worse. This makes our core recommendation more problematic – why would any company want to expose itself to more slings and arrows?' One solution: 'Emphasize to the corporate community that transparency is not a development to be feared but, rather, a force that can be harnessed for growth' (Tapscott and Ticoll 2004: 9).

Deploying likeability for crisis survival and managing vulnerabilities is harder still, yet it must be done. 'Deputy Secretary of State Richard Armitage worried to us', reported the 9/11 Commission, 'that Americans have been "exporting our fears and our anger," not our vision of opportunity and hope' (9/11 Commission 2004: 377). How can likeability be knowingly communicated, building conversational relationships without compromising the impression that the organisation is offering unfiltered, unmediated, transparency?

Research into the nature of brand credibility offers insight.

> Brand credibility is broadly defined as the believability of an entity's intentions at a particular time and is posited to have two main components: trustworthiness and expertise. Thus, Brand credibility is defined as the believability of the product information contained in a brand, which requires that consumers perceive that the brand has the ability (i.e., expertise) and willingness (i.e., trustworthiness) to continuously deliver what has been promised.
>
> (Erdem and Swait 2004: 191–9)

'In fact', the authors continue in parenthesis, 'brands can function as signals since – if and when they do not deliver what is promised – their brand equity will erode' (191–9).

Believability, trust, credibility – the words are intimately related and trying to arrange them in an exact hierarchy may be unnecessary, giving too much credit to mere words and too little to related yet inexpressible currents of human feeling. For us they are sufficient in any order. Marketing aside, there is a parallel need to reconcile these feelings with technology and human needs in crisis or attritional threat situations. When there is a trust deficit, targeted companies and countries cannot conduct conversation or project likeability without first winning acceptance through believability.

Believability and acceptance in crisis management means – ideally – that key publics trust and believe what the company has to say, accept it can fix the problem and feel confident that it will take responsibility for its mistakes. If believability means an acceptance that the corporation should be allowed to resolve operationally its crisis helped by transparent public communication platforms, then those technology platforms must offer democratic access. The democracy of a crisis is full-blooded and predominantly self-regulating. Chief among those characteristics is seeing the business as an equal whose view is as believable as any others. In the late 1920s Ortega y Gasset offered a pessimistic view about this development. It was a time when others, some of whom were discussed in Chapter 4, wrote about the industrialisation of public opinion:

> Today . . . the average man has the most mathematical 'ideas' on all that happens or ought to happen in the universe. Hence he has lost the use of his hearing. Why should he listen if he has within him all that is necessary? There is no reason now for listening, but rather for judging, pronouncing, deciding. There is no question concerning public life, in which he does not intervene, blind and deaf as he is, imposing his 'opinions'.
>
> (Ortega y Gassett 1930: 71)

In the keynote speech for his CEO summit in May 2004, Microsoft Chairman Bill Gates preferred an optimistic, 'post-industrial' version of this in his forecast of 'bottom-up empowerment', when companies formed conversational relationships with customers because of:

> software advances that allow you to have the best of both worlds – that is, let people build the individual Web sites, communicate on an ad hoc basis, and yet have the kind of control you want [for] that information if you decide only a certain group of employees should see it, that it's retained within that group, even if they're e-mailing around, or building Web sites.
>
> (Gates 2004)

A crisis or threat fuses both sentiments in a principle that will not confine itself to helping firms improve customer relations and product quality. An afflicted organisation must recognise the conjunction of Gates's bottom-up empowerment with Ortega y Gasset's intervening citizen, and deliver transparency with conversational technology to establish the perception that it:

- Is capable of frankly admitting errors.
- Can take criticism.
- Either shares the same feelings or empathises with those who feel most damaged.

125

- Attracts broad and disinterested support from 'average' people and experts.
- Puts all relevant material in the public domain, both background material and explanation of crisis-fighting activities.
- Reacts instantly to discuss online rumours, statements and accusations.
- Creates, encourages and engages with spontaneous expressions of opinion.
- Is prepared to applaud good or popular ideas emerging from external audiences and adapt its plans accordingly – or at least explain why those ideas would not work.
- Is open enough to freely entrust communication to employees acting online, on their own initiative.
- Uses natural everyday language, stripped of jargon, legalese, marketing hype and PR spin.
- Is comfortable – but at the same time respectful of and not over-familiar with – the online and offline cultures with whom it engages.
- Is represented by communicators who meet the diverse expectations of external crisis participants.
- Attracts partnership or support, as in traditional issues management, from online third parties: other companies, regulatory authorities, non-profit groups, or individual experts or e-fluentials.
- Delivers credibility through communication or technology routes that are familiar and preferred by each target audience.

Planning conversation

The consequence is a top-to-bottom reform of communication strategy as it currently exists. For vulnerable companies, a new system would be installed that is sensitised to:

- Destabilised public opinion.
- Sudden shifts in perceptions of issues.
- Potential sanctions inflicted by stakeholders and other audiences.

Integrating transparency into a technology-focused crisis audit

An audit is traditionally used to identify combustible risks or issues, potential crisis participants, and a business's related communication readiness. Ideally, it does this by exploring every area of corporate activity, by talking to employees at all levels, by desk research of attitudes towards the company, its products, and the industry to which it belongs. Now, however, there is a case for widening auditing so that it embraces technology separately, not simply using it as an additional communication tool in an overall strategy, or as source for problems, but to analyse its worth as a crisis enabler and deterrent. New auditing needs include:

- Reviews of existing company readiness for effective online crisis communication.
- Employee and subcontractor understanding of strategic and tactical communication needs.
- Identification of online stakeholder communication platforms for opinion-forming, speculation and information exchange.
- Knowledge of e-fluentials with assessment of their attitudes, activity and impact on company or issues affecting company.
- Assessment of the language and style of online platforms and e-fluentials.
- Recommendations for preparedness or immediate participation in main communication platforms.
- Creation of online crisis teams identified in the preceding chapter.

Other questions that the organisation's audit must resolve stem from its comfort with the prospect of greater and continuous openness, and the pressing need to distil transparency into the communication programme:

- Where might transparency be expected of us? Involving which areas of corporate activity? For which issues or risks connected to our operations?
- Where might transparency be initiated in advance of audience knowledge or expectations?
- Is our organisation culturally and operationally equipped to recognise transparency and deliver it at the levels required?

The answers must be translated into a communication policy, centred on delivering a perception that culminates in the achievement of 'likeability'. The audit's recommendations for strategy will reflect a blend of:

- Continuous engagement. Open dialogue with participating audiences in weblogs.
- Information provision. Offering corporate data, in conjunction with other comparative data from fully referenced official and even critical sources.
- Opinion provision. Consisting of fair and frank corporate interpretation of external and internal data; corporate interpretation of issues; alternative fair interpretations of data and issues.

The outlets for this transparency must, more so than in former times, reflect the audiences and the experts and the most credible common voice of the company. The diversity of platforms, and of audiences, obliges business to consider the place of potential communicators in the twenty-first-century transparency plan. A crisis will continue to demand human voices, faces and accountability. Managing longer-term issues must though deploy technology, to audiences impatient of mediators standing between themselves and the 'facts'. As far as possible, an audit should recommend which material should be detached from human spokespeople, and how a virtual setting could reflect that material more appropriately.

Human factors in transparency delivery

Continuous engagement – conversation – on a far-reaching scale will be needed. The transparency audit must recommend a permanent mechanism on the scale demanded by a major issue or full crisis. Similar steps are being taken in other areas of corporate activity. They depart from the principle that messages must be coordinated and controlled as far as possible.

This control principle existed because it was essential to maintaining believability. Now, though, the conditions that underpin believability are changing; the balance is tipping away from a highly visible suspiciously seamless message. The test is the business's willingness to release material from the heart of the decision-chain, and place it in the hands of people who feel able to analyse the data themselves and act on their conclusions. Selecting and interpreting that data inside the company must be conducted by managers free to act at speed, to talk informatively about the data instead of relaying statements crafted by committees for public consumption. 'PR people not getting blogging', a PR blogger worried (Ochman 2004). This followed a pithy blog on the same topic by a well-known executive and blogger in the same business: 'The best CEO bloggers are Conversational Executive Officers. They're the ones who are conversing with other bloggers by linking/commenting on their posts' (Rubel 2004). The task of the audit is to find such people throughout the company at all levels, and where necessary to prepare a training programme for them that combines communication with use of information technology; a programme designed to bring out the characters of the participants, rather than reducing them to standardised corporate mouthpieces for spin and hollow sentiments. That search must not restrict itself to particular names and positions – which would imply, unfavourably, a status as corporate mouthpieces. Preferably, spokespeople should be spontaneously generated, by providing the communication facilities for employees and external endorsers to use as they like.

The presence of online conversation from 'non-official' participants on corporate rather than external platforms would offer greater 'conversational' advantage, particularly if it includes e-fluentials from the audiences involved. The object is to secure a spread of reasoned, participating, e-fluentials who demonstrate the company's issue or vulnerability is:

- Open to change brought by external stakeholders.
- Sensitive to significant movements in opinion.

- Grounded on substantive independent third-party evidence.
- Focused on an appreciation and understanding of the attitudes and feelings of stakeholders.

The steps needed to build conversation are relevant equally to Governments with public diplomacy problems, companies and cause groups. Many such groups, including political parties worldwide, are seasoned communicators, and could be studied by corporate leaders who have not had to think much about transparency.

The options should include corporate encouragement of employee weblogs; uncensored discussion fora on all issues, as practised by TellShell; assigning technology to open personal conversation with particular targeted online 'e-fluentials'.

Weblogs – posting comments and information on a shared webpage – are currently attracting much attention, both for product development and promoting social issues. 'Creating an impression of openness isn't the same as actually being open', commented an American journalist and grassroots activist for his profession. 'Establishing a corporate weblog can change that' (Gillmor 2004: 14). Correct or not, this is a common perception of weblogs and it is certainly true that senior executives and other opinion leaders take advantage of that by choosing it as a means to communicate. Ever alert to the need to be liked and accessible, politicians and campaigners are enthusiastic early adopters. The United Kingdom Labour Party 'overhauled its plans for online coverage of the 2004 annual conference in the past few weeks, lining up a virtual conference complete with blogs from party members, web chats with government ministers and a daily conference newspaper' (Kiss 2004). In countries where opinions are constrained and communications restricted, blogs act as a crowbar; Iranians are using them to prise open protest and also evade media censorship, including Hossein Derakhshan, based in Canada, who runs blogs in English and Persian (Derakhshan 2004).

The blog phenomenon is patchy at present. The 2003 Pew Internet and American Life survey cited earlier (p. 64), which reported 53 million Americans (roughly 23 per cent of the United States adult population and 44 per cent of adult users), used the Internet for posting their thoughts and opinions, also found the actual percentage of internet 'bloggers' was small: between 2 and 7 per cent. Eleven per cent reported visiting other people's blogs – just under half went to blogs written by others.

First adopters include Microsoft, which in the spirit of Gates's previously mentioned pronouncement actively encourages technical or personal weblogs among its employees. In April 2004 five company software developers started Channel 9 to provide conversational personal platforms with other software developers and customers interested in Microsoft who, said one of the channel's founders were 'sick and tired of all the PR talk . . . how do we become part of the conversation?' (Channel 9, 'Video introduction' 2004). They use small handheld cameras and other tools to promote conversation and participation: blogs, wikis (websites that can be written by users) and discussion forums. 'They're going to tell us what they want to see' (Channel 9, 'Video introduction' 2004). The layout is carefully informal, even amateur and dominantly mid level, peers talking among themselves: 'it's not about the rock stars all the time' (Channel 9, 'Video introduction' 2004) and the intent is similarly plain:

> We are five guys at Microsoft who want a new level of communication between Microsoft and developers. We believe that we will all benefit from a little dialogue these days. This is our first attempt to move beyond the newsgroup, the blog, and the press release to talk with each other, human to human.
>
> (Channel 9, 'The 9 guys – who we are' 2004)

Channel 9's 'doctrine' begins:

1. Channel 9 is all about the conversation. Channel 9 should inspire Microsoft and our customers to talk in an honest and human voice. Channel 9 is not a marketing tool, not a PR tool, not a lead generation tool.
2. Be a human being. Channel 9 is a place for us to be ourselves, to share who we are, and for us to learn who our customers are (Channel 9, 'Channel 9 Doctrine' 2004).

'You know', said one of the founding 'guys' in their introductory video – an informal 15 minute chat amongst themselves, 'very few companies bigger than 10,000 people have blogs and we have more than 300 employees blogging' (Channel 9, 'Video introduction' 2004). The team noted that most big companies forbid or heavily control blogs: 'the PR methodology of the old school is to control the messaging, control everything that's presented about the company, and here we're in an experiment where we have no control' (Channel 9, 'Video introduction' 2004). 'Why do most big companies keep secrets?' (Channel 9, 'Video introduction' 2004). 'Stop thinking of "distribution" channels and start thinking of "conversation" channels', advised an alert marketing communication director at a local US bank:

> Bloggers use a mechanism called 'syndication,' which is a fancy name for linking to other blogs and news sources. This incestuous information sharing is sometimes derided as creating an echo chamber effect. From a PR point of view, it also amplifies a message, spreading it in real time. People don't just read blogs; they contribute to the post, tell others about them and link to them.
>
> (Fernando 2004: 11)

The connection between blogs and crisis or threat containment is readily apparent. Open platforms for 'authentic' interchange not only help software developers or product marketers; they assist scared customers, worried employees, community groups or crusading media bypassing 'PR' messages in search of opinion, information and action.

Blogs may be a fad: but fads have a place in communication. Blogs will eventually lose their novelty and authenticity, becoming more 'tainted' as organisations tighten censorship or use them for marketing and propaganda but other attractive, conversational and transparent platforms will appear. As far as crisis management is concerned, those platforms must be deployed and meet the principles advanced by the blog phenomenon and Channel 9's founders.

THE GOAL: MUTUAL TRANSPARENCY BETWEEN ALL COMMUNICATION PARTICIPANTS

In a world of ample information and modified advocacy, there seems no reason why *all* crisis and issues participants should not be beholden to the same ethical expectations and furnish transparency, not only by broadcasting their principles, but by practising what they preach. The decisions behind activist campaign choices and fundraising activities are valid subjects for transparency, which should cover areas that nonprofits are uncomfortable about divulging. In their case, 'maximum openness of communications', to borrow Rees's phrase (2004: 82) would probe their internal workings – to enable wider publics to understand the rationale for their campaigning decisions. Activists must be ready to explain the logic behind selecting one target over others – why target, to take two semi-hypothetical instances, Nike over Reebok? Or Shell over Total? Why whales and not tuna? Why this product or corporate action over another? What research was involved, who conducted it, where are the sources, where are the links to alternative arguments and data, can anyone access this research and the discussions leading to their campaigning decisions? Corporations must surrender more detail about their works, and activist groups will find themselves in the same position with their basic product – communication. How do they use it to raise the emotional capital that funds and fuels their activities?

Organisations using transparency to converse, be liked, to defend themselves, make a profit, or to proselytise and criticise, will take reputation management to a higher level. This is explored in the next chapter.

Chapter 7

Devolution and fission: the future for reputation management

Reputation, reputation, reputation! O, I have lost my reputation! I have lost the immortal part of myself, and what remains is bestial. – My reputation, Iago, my reputation!

Cassio (Shakespeare. *Othello*. Act 2 Scene 3 lines 256–9: 832)

INTRODUCTION

The changes to technology, public opinion, transparency management and crisis planning change the ways organisations are perceived, and this affects their reputation and its management. It remains to explore why and how.

The expectations attached to Reputation go far beyond the usual parameters. The *Guardian* reported in August 2004 that recruiters Glenn Irvine International sought applications from Iraqis who could help Shell bring ' "suitable opportunities to fruition on behalf of the company" and draw up a "reputation management plan". They will ideally have "strong family connections and an insight into the network of families of significance within Iraq"' ('Business: Shell advert' 2004: 16).

This example is symbolic as well as real: like every other aspect of disaster and communication, reputation generally must henceforth work in a less stable world. It must learn to accommodate technology's unpredictable, free ranging and occasionally anarchic impact, and the benign and malign activities of e-commerce and global business. This ultimately means:

- Ending the unproductive subordination of reputation to brand issues in crisis or threat environments.
- Understanding the uses and limitations of Corporate Social Responsibility (CSR) and applying them to reputation rather than brand needs.
- Accepting the risk of delegating more reputation responsibilities to volatile external audiences.
- Ensuring that corporate oversight adapts to these changes, and is marked by

extensive strategic, tactical, political and social understanding of communications and not merely through narrow knowledge of technologies or professional functions.

REPUTATION MANAGEMENT, CSR AND BRAND MANAGEMENT

In a deceptively clear and prescient paper two consultants credited the rise of the reputation idea to pressure on brands to distinguish themselves in the era of globalisation, transparency and rising corporate citizenship expectations:

> For these reasons, more and more organisations are recognising the link between corporate reputation and competitive advantage. A strong corporate reputation can attract and retain the best stakeholders – whether they be consumers, investors or employees. It can attract customers, ensure a licence to trade and, in times of crisis, win 'the benefit of the doubt.' A sound corporate reputation allows an organisation to achieve its business objectives better.
>
> (Rankin Frost and Cooke 1999: 22)

'But', they continue, 'what exactly is "corporate reputation," and how do you manage such an intangible asset?' (22). The lack of substance presents problems. Academics have often struggled to isolate and dissect reputation by detailed research, only to cede the field to the diverse claims of consultants. Nevertheless, in spite of frustrating intangibility, reputation management grows inside business as a phrase, a hope, a concept and a practice.

One reason for reputation's intangibility is that it is the sum of many independent parts and has no life independent of them. For this reason, a 2003 survey of over 100 large European companies by the Chicago-based multinational insurance brokers Aon found 'loss of reputation' perceived as the second biggest of 17 listed threats to business, after 'business interruption' and ahead of more material threats like 'product liability/tamper/brand protection' [sic] and 'employee accidents' (Aon Corporation 2004).

Caution is necessary for several useful reasons. Much depends on how risks are defined and the gut responses of busy managers. Many if not all of Aon's listed risks – physical damage, crime and so on – damage corporate reputation, which makes 'reputation' the root of the matter and hoists its ranking. Nevertheless, reputation becomes a tangible factor precisely *because* it is an intangible asset, the collective expression of diverse realities.

Perceptions of the 'solid' threats are more volatile and vulnerable to trends in media coverage and individual high-profile incidents. The low position of 'other

133

crime' at 14 for instance, may change in next year's Aon survey – if indeed there is one, now that Aon itself hovers (in October 2004) on the brink of a reputation-damaging investigation into bribes and bid-rigging, charges already brought by the State of New York against the number one insurance brokerage Marsh & McLennan. Aon declared the allegations against its close rival were practices 'that would violate Aon policies and that, to the best of our knowledge, our employees have not engaged in' (Aon Press Releases 2004). Shares still fell over 30 per cent in four working days, before staging a recovery on a Friday. The following Monday, though, more damaging stories appeared, led by the *New York Times* which reported: 'investigators for the New York attorney general have discovered evidence at the Aon Corporation of deceptive and coercive practices, a person close to the inquiry said yesterday' ('Deceptive practices' 2004). 'Another person who had been briefed on the case', thought the New York Attorney General 'could bring a civil lawsuit against the company within two weeks' ('Deceptive practices' 2004; 'Aon may face civil suit' 2004).

Shifting media preoccupations with particular incidents like that, even when rare or industry-specific, may also lead survey respondents to change their perceptions of specific risks and to elevate generic risks that, like reputation, are hard to pin down and cannot be embodied in a single dramatic event, unlike terrorism (bottom of the list) or product tampering.

Two popular ways to build a 'crisis-proof' reputation are to incorporate it in the brand management process and to demonstrate good corporate citisenship, or Corporate Social Responsibility (CSR). Confusion clouds the relations between brands, CSR and reputation management. The latter must clarify its relation to the first two – brand management in particular – if it is to be useful in the new communication environment.

Rankin Frost and Cooke saw this when proposing a fourfold division of reputation into organisational identity, image, performance and reputation, a division they hoped would convert reputation from intangibility to manageability. The first three categories respectively described the view the company has of itself; those aspects of it that it wants communicated to audiences; and physically ensuring that this communication is effectively delivered at all points of stakeholder contact. The last category, reputation, referred to the combined effect of these features on stakeholders:

> The collective attitudes of all stakeholders at this stage form an organisation's full reputation. Given that it is rooted in the substance of an organisation, the reputation is relatively more stable than the image, which is abstract and transient.
>
> (Rankin Frost and Cooke 1999: 22–5)

Different target audiences meant the proposed model for reputation management should work alongside but not inside brand management, with both under a central coordinating control.

> Thus the effective management of brand and reputation needs a central function driving the organisation's strategy by identifying the organisational identity that will fulfil business objectives. By developing this strategy centrally, the organisation will ensure that each communication function will be expressing the same values to its specific stakeholder audiences.
>
> (Rankin Frost and Cooke 1999: 22–5)

Brand management scholars and professionals, however, are sequestering reputation's techniques, most notably CSR, for their own field as the growth of social expectations raise questions about how brands must respond. Maio views the brand's values as the 'touchstone for all corporate behaviors', and the brand management 'substructures and processes' as 'effective conduits for nurturing values-driven behaviors and measuring them' (Maio 2003: 235). Values-driven behaviour for brands is usually interpreted as CSR. Readers of the major UK industry publication *Marketing* were advised: 'Corporate social responsibility has to be a brand issue and not just a corporate affair. You can't manage a brand if you are not taking care of its personality and performance' ('Opinion: Marketing' 2003: 18).

'Reputation must be attached to the brand for competitive advantage to be gained', agreed participants at a UK Government-supported workshop on CSR (DTI, Forum 2003: 27). According to this argument the CSR adhesive helps reputation attach the brand to audience sentiment and *weltanschauung*. The British Government presently sells this with a Minister for Corporate Social Responsibility and a large website supported by the Department of Trade and Industry (DTI 2004). In fact, those curious about brands and CSR are spoiled for choice. There are articles to consult and events to attend, like the joint DTI and Forum for the Future sustainability workshop for civil servants, business and academics in May 2003, which cited telecoms multinational BT as 'proof positive of the CSR business case'. Statistically '99.95%' proof, in fact (DTI, Forum 2003: 27): 'Based on eighteen months tracking, BT have identified that CSR attitude accounts for at least 25% of the dimensions that drive BT's corporate reputation' (DTI, Forum 2003: 27).

CSR reinforces its case for protecting brands through nonprofits such as Forum for the Future or Copenhagen Centre in Denmark, through academic research and a cornucopia of case studies. These last include Ikea's energetic campaign to root out its global vulnerabilities and build bridges to activists ('The Teflon Shield' 2001: 26); the United Kingdom Co-op Bank's 12-year-old ethical policy forbidding investment in 'any government or business which fails to uphold basic human rights within its sphere of influence' and 'any business whose links to an oppressive regime are a continuing cause for concern' ('Our ethical policy statements' 2004). Less

135

predictably, clothing giant Benetton has pioneered edgy controversial tie-ins between the brand, design and dangerous interpretations of social issues, often by shocking posters and graphic, titillatingly ambiguous features about Aids, drugs, war, street violence and other plagues in Benetton's 'cultural quarterly' *Colors* (2004).

CSR is not restricted to western companies. The International Centre for Corporate Social Responsibility in Britain's Nottingham University found nearly three-quarters of India's top 50 corporations presented CSR policies and practices on their websites, and over 50 per cent in South Korea (Chambers *et al.*, 2003: 12). The same research team found that 90 per cent of Japanese firms produced dedicated CSR reports (12).

CSR does contribute a trust quotient to corporate reputation and it is important to stress the contribution that genuinely conceived and applied CSR can offer to companies struggling to differentiate themselves. At the same time it can be seen to throw up a shield or fence against the turbulent world of fully transparent business. It is notably unpersuasive in crisis and issues when tensions are already running high. Benetton owns around 900,000 hectares in Argentina, mainly for sheep-rearing (it is the world's biggest consumer of virgin wool). In 2002 a local family from the historically-oppressed and dispossessed Mapuche people took possession of 500 disputed hectares with official assent. Benetton's subsidiary evicted them, took their belongings, dismantled their home, and in May 2004 won a court case. The Argentinean media pounced on the cause which was taken up by activists and Nobel Peace Prize winner Adolfo Perez Esquivel, who told the Benetton brothers: 'Local people call your ranch "The Cage". Wired in and closed off, it has trapped the winds, the clouds, the stars, the sun and the moon. Life has disappeared, because everything has been reduced to its economic worth.' Benetton was locally re-branded as: 'United Colours of Land Grab'. This action, as the UK edition of *PR Week* commented 'floored' the company's 'touchy-feely and politically correct image' ('Hit or miss . . . Benetton' 2004: 52). When the story attracted attention in Europe, supporters of the evicted family demonstrated outside Benetton's biggest store in Rome. Luciano Benetton tried to restore reputational stability with CSR, offering 2,500 hectares (6,200 acres) to the Mapuche people. His gift of ancestral lands was rejected by a Mapuche spokesperson 'because they were theirs by right' ('Land "gift" from Benetton spurned' 2004), leaving the company in a dilemma that, temporarily at least, 'risks undermining Benetton's carefully constructed philanthropic image' ('Benetton accused' 2004).

The French energy firm Total faces probes and attacks on many fronts: into its activities in Myanmar (Burma), bribes to foreign government officials and money laundering ('Scandal returns' 2004: 27). Other problems include the fallout from a lengthy investigation into Elf Aquitaine's collaboration with the French intelligence service and yet more enormous payments to politicians, made before Total acquired the State-run oil firm in 1999. Total has chosen to respond through heavy applications of CSR. A Sustainable Development and Environment Department was created in 2002, and a Social Innovation and Diversity Department in 2003, a year which also produced a Total 'Corporate Social Responsibility Report' backing the 'Extractive Industries [Financial] Transparency Initiative' tabled by the G8 nations, 'as part of an action plan designed to combat corruption and enhance transparency' ('Sharing Our Energies' 2003: 4). Nevertheless, the Chairman and CEO conceded, with much truth in Total's case, that: 'Clearly, companies have yet to win the battle for legitimacy in the eyes of the general public, particularly in continental Europe' ('Sharing Our Energies' 2003: 3). This remark is broadly correct. Edelman's global trust survey discovered that 40 per cent of Europeans trust business 'to do what's right', but the percentages for Government, NGOs and the media were scarcely better at 31, 41 and 28 respectively: small comfort for corporations like Total which are the preferred public targets of the other three (Edelman 2004: 5).

The use of CSR to boost brand reputation in times of peace and of trouble is the legacy of a conviction that gathered steam in the 1980s and 1990s (but which had been applied decades earlier by public relations pioneers like Edward Bernays), that brands are not just consumer products. They can be lots of other things, countries or raw commodities – anything that marketers can successfully join to ideas and values in consumers' heads. Activist author Naomi Klein assails this concept, expressed in Virgin founder Richard Branson's desire to 'build brands not around products but around reputation'. In her influential polemic *No Logo: Taking Aim at the Brand Bullies*, Klein wryly noted that the idea presented 'an opportunity for seemingly limitless expansion. After all, if a brand was not a product, it could be anything!' (Klein 2000: 24).

Such cynicism is grounded in doubts about the sincerity of corporate commitment to CSR values when they are used to rescue a brand from well-deserved opprobrium. This strategy was evidently a temptation for Total. After a 48 per cent jump in first quarter profits in May 2003, Total used the good fiscal news and its CSR initiatives to further distance the brand from scandal by shortening its name from TotalFinaElf ('TotalFinaElf' 2003: 18). The well-known business watchers Don Tapscott and David Ticoll, though considerably more sympathetic to corporations than Naomi Klein, agree that the grip of Brand notions can be too strong, for instance: 'Many social and environmental reports are selective and self-serving sales pitches: they tout a company's purported contributions to employee health and safety or philanthropy, with no external assurance of these claims' (Tapscott and Ticoll 2003: 269). Total's report, it should be added here, is ethically audited by the UK-based GoodCorporation.

More evidence of the problems involved when branding priorities take the lead in times of trouble are vividly but not uniquely shown in the activities of Nigeria's Government. Nigerian executives at an African public relations conference in June 2004 heard a paper: 'Government and Reputation Management, The South African Experience'. A reporter for an online African investment news service mused:

> How come the South African brand was able to change the negative international perception to a positive one? Who was involved? With what strategy? What role did the media play? With what other impact? How come the country emerged as the first African country to host the world cup? What lessons are there to learn by Brand Nigeria builders?
>
> ('Brand Nigeria' 2004)

The job of re-imaging brand Nigeria belongs to the Nigerian Image Project, launched with fanfare by President Obasanjo and his Information Minister in July 2004 with \$4.61 million in Government funding, an invitation to the private sector to help, and an appeal to Nigerians aware of their country's shortcomings ('Nigerian president' 2004). One of the shortcomings was underlined shortly after the launch, when Berlin-based Transparency International rated Nigeria one of the three most corrupt countries in the world, with just 1.6 out of a possible 10 on their 'Corruption Perceptions Index', a score indicating 'rampant corruption' (Finland, the least corrupt, achieved 9.7) (Transparency International 2004).

Nevertheless: 'come, let's celebrate Nigeria' the Information Minister wrote in the inaugural edition of *Nigeria Monthly,* one of the Image Project's products (Chukwuemeka 2004: 6). In the private sector, a local academic and columnist appealed to the nation, and the media most of all:

> Even if the media do not tell the public what to think, they tell the public what to think about. The media set the agenda for public discourse. They are over time determinants of public perception. In the business of image-making or reputation management, perception is more important than reality.
>
> (Ajakaiye 2004)

This view joined a feeling that perception, mass participation, image and brand marketing notions must unite to generate a better reputation. At the 'Second Brand Nigeria Pre-Conference Summit' held five months before the project's launch, 'Dr. Chris Ogbechie of the Lagos Business School, said that the imperative of branding Nigeria should be to get the desired image, attract foreign investment, elicit informed pride in the citizenry and sharpen patriotism amongst Nigerians'. 'Helping the image of the country', a National Assembly Senator argued, 'should not be made a government affair because, as he puts it, "that would be the end of the project"' ('N/Assembly ready' 2004).

Non-government cyberspace responded, with some agreeing the project was one for branding to fix. 'Thank God, Obasanjo is coming alive', blogged a Nigerian in the USA working for the Governor of Georgia. 'Great countries are known for certain thing [sic]. For instance Georgia is known for its Peaches, making it a peach State. What will Nigeria be known for as a theme for this promotion?' [sic] (Ajayi 2004). Other émigrés were warier. The Information Minister, commented a

Nigerian blogger in London, 'deserves a chance with his team and also every help they can get especially from Nigerians in diaspora'. However:

> As I watched the ceremony on TV (yours truly was not invited) something kept telling me that we have all been down this road before, flashes of Idiagbon's War against indiscipline (WAI), Tony Momoh's Letters to my countrymen and Jerry Gana's MAMSER/NOA campaigns kept going through my mind. Is this another of those projects that government officials use to siphon public funds without any form of accountability and measured results? I remembered the Better life for women programme, the several state governors' wives pet projects, the people's bank scheme etc?
>
> (Nworah 2004)

In this ambitious project, the problems of treating reputation as a brand matter are obvious. Both a nation's and company's vulnerabilities are social, economic, political and global. They are above all complex. Reputation management cannot deal with them through the narrow aperture of a brand: its image visions, way of life promises, and necessary view of audiences as 'consumers'. Instead it must actively join in eliminating all-too solid barriers to a better reputation. In the case of Nigeria, Government-generated branding initiatives, publications and pronouncements can no longer succeed without addressing vast internal problems of corruption, internal instability and infrastructural decay, violence in the Niger Delta oil region and the single most persuasive encounter the global community has with that country. 'I can't think of Nigeria without recalling all the spam I've received over the years promoting one scam or another involving stolen Nigerian money', commented a branding consultant and blogger (Young 2004).

To those obstacles might be added the impact of local actions reported online and elsewhere by groups like the support network, Women Living Under Muslim Laws (http://www.wluml.org/english/about.shtml). Related issues at the time of writing include a north Nigerian Islamic Sharia Court's October 2004 judgement on 18-year-old Hajara Ibrahim, pregnant and sentenced to death by stoning for conceiving outside wedlock ('Hajara Ibrahim's family' 2004; 'Stoning sentence appeal 2004). Finally, Nigeria's reputation is shaped by prominent expatriates: 'Nigeria is a country that does not work. Schools, universities, roads, hospitals, water, the economy, security, life', the celebrated Nigerian author and United States resident Chinua Achebe lamented, declining to accept an honour from his homeland ('Who has the right to criticize?' 2004).

Despite the earlier claim that perception is more important than reality, it is clearly not: it must work with reality, especially when an all-too-transparent reality, communicated by credible stakeholders, carries a negative emotional charge audiences cannot discount. This suggests reputation management for exposed companies (or countries) should be elevated above feel-good CSR projects and brand preoccupations, involve itself with deep social and economic questions and use technology to win the trust, credibility, communication power, authenticity and nimbleness of other audiences. It is here that the future of the Government's Image Project will be settled.

FISSILE REPUTATION

Nigeria's challenges demonstrate that a 'branded' approach can fail for a reason briefly noted at the end of Chapter 4: reputation is becoming highly devolved. It is also highly fissile. Large parts of reputation, described by Rankin Frost and Cooke as the 'relatively stable' 'substance of an organisation' are losing stability and substance.

Reputation is devolved when significant corporate operations and intellectual capital are outsourced or offshored to consultants, subcontractors and part-time employees. That corporate-led devolution parallels a second, wider redistribution of reputation among non-profit organisations, online media and unaffiliated individuals. At the same time, other reputation ingredients – especially the potential causes of crisis – experience fission when audiences use technology to pick them apart. Flammable issues ignite smaller but potent points of debate and polemic, exploited by small numbers of people, seeking to strike pools of shared emotion among key audiences.

The splitting effect may produce emotive energy when attentive stakeholders find a sensitive subject; information technology taps that emotion with the help of talented participants, good communication strategies and some luck. 'You start a trickle of snow sliding as you ski. The trickle becomes a snowball', Werner Heisenberg says when explaining nuclear fission in *Copenhagen* (Frayn 1998: 33). Eventually, an issue or event experienced by many online communicators, generates sufficient emotion and reaction to produce Crisis, and: 'The thunder of the gathering avalanche is heard from all the surrounding mountains' (33).

The consequences for reputation are readily traceable. In April 2002 researchers from Stockholm University and the Swedish National Food Administration reported excessive levels of the cancer-causing chemical acrylamide in foods baked, grilled and fried under high temperatures including crisps, bread, chips and crispbreads. Unusually, the findings were announced at a large news conference before publication in a scientific journal because Swedish officials said the results were of 'special importance' ('High cancer risks' 2002).

The second report appeared in the *British Journal of Cancer* in January 2003 by researchers at Stockholm's Karolinska Institute and the Harvard School of Public Health in Boston, Massachusetts. Using a 1999 survey of 987 cancer patients and 538 healthy people, they reported 'no increased risk of cancer of the large bowel, bladder or kidney linked to food with high levels' of acrylamide ('Swedish, U.S. researchers dispute link' 2003).

In the 24 hours after the first announcement, potato crisp sales fell 50 per cent in Stockholm, but not chips and bread according to one Swedish daily newspaper ('Stockholm shops' 2002). Within days the news had attracted continuous global attention, researchers from Norway, Britain, Switzerland, Germany and the USA unearthed acrylamide in other products, the World Health Organisation announced an international conference of scientific experts to discuss global action and acrylamide's dangers grew to embrace 'damage to the nervous system, impotence, paralysis' ('WHO to hold meeting' 2002). The German consumer minister, an outspoken Green Party politician, advised the nation to eat less 'potato crisps, corn chips, fried potatoes, biscuits/cookies, crispy bread and most packaged breakfast cereals such as cornflakes' ('German official' 2002).

'They are the stalwarts of our breakfast table and the treats with which we fill our children's lunch boxes. Yet the breakfast cereals, breads, biscuits, chips and crisps that are part of our everyday diet – many of which have been marketed as particularly healthy food – could be killing us', the usually restrained United Kingdom's *Sunday Telegraph* declared under a headline: 'This isn't another food scare – this is really important' ('This isn't another' 2002).

The media had picked up the high temperature links and attached them to crisps, snacks and crispbread products, which became the focus of initial 'blame'. Barilla, a large Italian food group had acquired Wasabrod, a Swedish company and the world's biggest crispbread producer, selling 'around 60,000 tons of crispbread in 40 countries' (Wasabrod 2004). Further speculation meanwhile, began implicating pasta products, the core of all Barilla business worldwide.

Barilla's goal was to protect its reputation and its products. To do this, it had to be positioned as an authority in the debate swirling around the product, with comprehensive technical and research knowledge; and to partner with regulatory and political bodies to help the inquiry process – without drawing Barilla under the spotlight of attention as fronting the food industry in general, or in other words, becoming the scapegoat.

The company set up an international surveillance and monitoring network to deliver daily reports on activities and comments by regulators, politicians, ministers, interest groups and the media. It collated a technical white paper and a database on technical and scientific aspects of the issue; linked with third-party experts to provide independent support and managed and responded to the issue on a daily basis in the key markets of Australia, France, Germany, Sweden, Britain and the USA.

This communication-led reaction involved Barilla in the debate and helped it anticipate and handle new developments, without drawing negative media and public attention. Internal and external responses and communications were kept up to date and on track with day-to-day developments and, in spite of attempts to cite products made and marketed by Barilla and Wasabrod, there was no discernible drop in sales between the two announcements. The technical team at Barilla became recognised as experts on high temperature risks and its implications for food products.

The devolution of reputation in the global, connected economy is demonstrated by the small group of Swedish researchers who hooked – in a matter of hours – global media, national governments, international organisations (WHO and the UN Food and Agriculture Organisation) and other scientists with the power to destabilise Barilla's reputation among regulators, investors and consumers.

The fission of reputation is shown in its concentration around the science – obscure to all but a few specialists – of a single chemical that was successfully associated with a universal fear at a media event, and instantly released enough public energy to sidetrack a multinational company from its regular business. Barilla had to rapidly devote time, money and human resources to master a large new body of research, track opinion flow and execute a communication plan on a global scale.

Reputation management must adapt to instability. Sometimes companies originate and harness the communication avalanche themselves: we have seen that The Body Shop largely picks its own reputation-shaping issues thanks to inherent radicalism, apparent transparency, a careful choice of words and phrases and the judicious selection of five worthy 'activist' themes. Sometimes a company is trapped in the path of another's avalanche. Many serious reputation-shaping issues have descended on Shell but the company has decided to work at being a credible and trusted participant in all of them.

Both companies, one voluntarily and one initially less so, are committed to a considerable communication effort. In 'involuntary' situations devolution inside the company and among external audiences, and also issues fission, prevent reputation from subordinating itself to branding or CSR projects. To pick one instance, how many organisations are online and interested in influencing Shell's Nigerian operations? The most active include:

- Shell International, which recently appointed its first Nigerian Managing Director of Petroleum Development in Nigeria (Shell Petroleum and Exploration 2004), and which accommodates immoderate, moderate and often weird online critics in TellShell via several unmistakable discussion threads: 'Shell's misbehaviour in Nigeria', 'Bribery and corruption – when is a fee a bribe?' and 'Economic muscle and political influence'.
- Shell Nigeria, the largest producer of Nigeria's oil and gas, whose website is replete with CSR initiatives in the Niger Delta, 'People and the Environment' reporting and (in November 2004 at least) a perhaps inevitable scam alert.
- The Nigerian Government, whose Ministry of Petroleum page assures visitors: 'To ensure continuing and orderly development of the petroleum industry, a petroleum policy has been put in place' (Ministry of Petroleum

Resources 2004a). A further if unwelcome revelation, however, appears in the same page's links to the Nigeria National Petroleum Organisation and the Petroleum Equalisation (Management) Fund, which only take the curious to a sequence of commercial pop-ups (Ministry of Petroleum Resources 2004b).

- Transparency International, which observed that in Nigeria and several other countries 'public contracting in the oil sector is plagued by revenues vanishing into the pockets of western oil executives, middlemen and local officials' (Transparency International 2004).

- Human Rights Watch, which in April 2003 wrote to Ron van den Berg, then Managing Director of Shell Petroleum Development in Nigeria, and other oil firms, asking them to publicly oppose abuses by Government security forces in the unstable Niger Delta (Ganesan and Takirambudde 2003).

- The Nigerian Labour Congress, branding Shell an 'enemy of Nigerian people' [sic] for trying to stop oil workers joining a National Strike sparked by rising fuel prices ('NLC begins' 2004).

- Third World Traveler, a US run site claiming 5,000 website visitors a day and offering 'an alternative view to the corporate media'. Articles reproduced in its 'Oil Watch' section include: 'Drilling and Killing – Shell and Chevron in Nigeria', 'Shell Oil rules Nigeria' and 'Nigeria Deception – Shell' (Third World Traveler).

- Shellfacts.com, 'an honest effort to evaluate independently all available information on Shell's actions'; apparently run by a group of unnamed 'journalists, researchers and non profit agencies' who 'are dedicated to the protection of health and the environment'. The site features anti-Shell articles and excerpts from *Riding The Dragon*, a publication about Shell produced by the Environmental Defense Fund in Boston, with chapters titled 'Oh Canada: Sour gas, sick cattle and unhappy neighbors' and 'Nigeria: Lots of oil, brutal questions and a polluted country' (Shellfacts).

These eight entities are among those shaping Shell's reputation by concentrating on a single perceived vulnerability. They are private, non-profit and governmental; they are, large or small, staffed by people with diverse points of view and the ability to express them, officially or unofficially; they encourage external audiences to debate and discuss; they are a news resource for general and specialist media, for investors, activists, employees and regulators; they recycle and originate information and opinion.

Looking beyond Nigeria, many other e-fluentials have interested themselves in global and local threats to Shell's reputation. Turning inward again, the groups concentrating on Shell in Nigeria are influenced by others evaluating details of the company's environmental, political and community work in that particular country.

Inside these restless, adaptable and mobile communication structures, brand and CSR play their part, but crisis management before the information age was never just about brand protection and it is less so now, as the audiences whose perceptions shape reputation simultaneously grow, fragment and push companies deeper into alien social or political territory, far from everyday communication tasks.

The fragmentation of reputation-affecting issues is also the offshoot of a public demand for 'true' information that is seemingly insatiable. Between 80 and 100 per cent of survey respondents in each of six countries – the USA, United Kingdom, France, Germany, China and Brazil – agreed 'that they are more likely to believe something they see, read or hear from many different sources, rather than a single source' (Edelman 2004: 10). This fragmentation of sources is the offshoot of communication channels used by single issue groups. We see fragmentation more and more – particularly when health, safety and (junk) science is being played out in the public domain. Corporate managers, taking strategic 'wide angle' viewpoints, often find that transformation hard to comprehend – hence much of the miscommunication and consequent failures to influence or shape opinion.

Reputation management must fit into this rich, uneven, accessible and highly participatory landscape. It must be as 'authentic' as possible, diluting its assertions in frank conversation, managed transparency, credible spokespeople within particular communities, and in communication platforms that attract third parties and motivate 'real people' to act as unofficial reputation ambassadors online.

A topical analogy can be found in Robert Kagan's comparative study of *America and Europe in the New World Order* (2003). Kagan's hypothesis is that America sometimes feels compelled to act, coerce and enforce global security to guard civilisation against a Hobbesian state of nature where as Bertrand Russell explained: 'there is no property, no justice or injustice; there is only war' (Russell 1946: 535). Europe, under the European Union, has renounced this route, Kagan argues, and for exactly the same reason. To finally extricate herself from Hobbes's world of centuries of war on the continent and create a peaceful, prosperous alternative, the European Union is building a multi-state polity based on patience, negotiation, concession, compromise and a readiness to take the long view: a more Kantian construction in which individual interests must if necessary be sacrificed for the communal good.

This studiously 'powerless' approach is used by the European Union to tackle internal and external challenges. To bring about slow change and achieve harmony the European Union has lost the desire for superpower status and instead dissolves its diplomatic presence and considerable economic weight into a highly collaborative international landscape. America in 2004 felt it should take a more forceful course to contain threats to western civilisation – not all of which are imagined.

When it comes to reputation, many companies are at the junction separating these 'soft' and 'hard' expressions of power. In a less stable world where great threats blur with great opportunities, a corporation can assert itself by turning a deaf ear to critics, carefully constructing what it wants to say, inserting definitive messages into the public arena and going about its usual business. The alternative is for Business to decommission many of its traditional communication techniques, and cede some of its power to online communities in the wider world, and constructing a firmer reputation on shared and mutually agreed foundations. In this model, it must nurture reputation partly by communicating questions not answers, by offering an open-ended approach ahead of brand boosting, public relations messages or CSR claims. This model for reputation management requires:

- Willingness to talk naturally.
- Willingness to listen.
- Willingness to change.
- Willingness to tackle social issues particularly through engagement with key influencers.
- Willingness to risk speculation.
- Willingness to offer uncensored online space to others, as Shell or Microsoft are attempting to do, and a concurrent readiness to enter other groups' online spaces and freely engage with them.

CONTROL

The control problem remains. Inside the company, a person must exercise the 'central function' (Rankin Frost and Cooke 1999: 22–5) coordinating reputation management, branding and other communication tasks including human resources.

Twenty-first-century Reputation mirrors two assertions made by the nineteenth-century Prussian military thinker Carl von Clausewitz. First, his remark in *On War* that War is not a field of wheat, each stalk identical and ready to be mowed in the same way 'depending on the quality of the scythe'. It is rather 'like a stand of mature trees in which the axe has to be used judiciously according to the characteristics and development of each individual trunk' (Clausewitz 1832: 178). Clausewitz also advised the Prussian Crown Prince in *Principles of War*: 'War is a combination of many distinct engagements' (Clausewitz 1812: 1). For reputation management to succeed, judgement must be exercised engagement by engagement, target audience by target audience and communication tool by tool: 'For only a combination of successful engagements can lead to good results' (Clausewitz 1812: 1).

The diversity of tasks requires oversight, a holistic view of communication, or 'the comprehensive rather than the specialized approach' (Clausewitz 1832: 131). Reputation now lies in many hands: the Pentagon's Defense Science Board recommended in its Strategic Communication Report that performance ratings for United States diplomats 'should include mandatory comment on public diplomacy skills' (Office of the Under Secretary of State for Defense 2004: 75). The recommendation might also be applied to many senior and middle-ranking company executives with hitherto little interest and understanding of either corporate communication in general or reputation management in particular.

The numbers of people, issues, volatilities and technologies also suggests that oversight should be properly located in the senior group of crisis decision-makers described in Chapter 5 as Circle One. In that group a Chief Communication Officer (CCO) would in future define success by an ability to meet online corporate reputation needs in times of crisis and calm. These needs will include:

- Auditing internal and external issues affecting corporate reputation, both risks and opportunities.
- Understanding the connections between social challenges and corporate reputation.
- Defining particular 'tone' and technologies to be used for selected issues and audiences.
- Developing appropriate techniques to develop conversation, information distribution and transparency perceptions with key influencers, particularly those online.
- Preparing crisis plans and procedures with online response capabilities, including selection and training of appropriate online spokespersons for specific target audiences.
- Identifying and opening relations with e-fluentials defined by key regions, expertise or industry knowledge.
- Ensuring that brand vision, marketing, CSR, human resources and other corporate communication activities interlock with all reputation enhancement needs.

There must at root be an ability to see that communication is not about maintaining a technical toolset (the task of a Chief Information Officer), or just overseeing CSR projects or projecting brands (the task of a Brand Manager or Marketing Vice President).

The CCO manages these activities to ensure reputation management truly gets the strategic and tactical impetus Business and governments seem to agree it needs. In the information revolution, the function becomes vital to ambitious companies operating, perhaps for the first time, under conditions defined by high product, operational, political, social or regional uncertainties.

Above all, the chosen person must sense how to connect with the right audiences at the right moment and be given authority to do so. Clausewitz wrote of military leadership in words equally fitting to the CCO and the conditions necessitating the position's recreation:

We argue that a commander-in-chief must also be a statesman, but he must not cease to be a general. On the one hand, he is aware of the entire political situation; on the other, he knows exactly how much he can achieve with the means at his disposal.

(Clausewitz 1832: 130)

Conclusion: Carthago delenda est?

I am a feather for each wind that blows.
King Leontes (Shakespeare. *The Winter's*
Tale. Act 2 Scene 3 line 154: 1112)

Change in one field blows change into others. The wider the changes elsewhere, either immediately or over time, the more revolutionary or profound the originating event has proved to be. Technology is indeed changing the speed and potency of crises, but that is no more helpful than saying better guns and trains allowed armies to fire more accurately and move faster. On the eve of the Franco-Prussian War in 1870 technology had transformed battles, armies, society and society's response to communicated news and opinion. In 2004, information age technology changes everything that affects a crisis.

Everything about the crisis setting changes from now on: the possible vulnerabilities and society's view of those vulnerabilities, the choice and frequency of crisis-triggering events, the resilience of the corporate structure, the capacity for damage and the options for resolution. Everything about crisis communication is affected: numbers of participants, diversity of participants, the strategy, tools and content of the corporate communication response. Much of the planning and prevention process is altered: the crisis-fighting team, the management of threats and recognition by wise companies that communication's future does not exclusively lie in separate boxes marked 'human resources', 'marketing', 'investor relations' or 'public relations'.

These chapters have discussed those changes: the corporate imbalances created by malicious or objective employment of technology, by transparency, outsourced functions, sharing of inflammable information and opinion among vocal audiences, and their collective loss of patience at tardy or incomplete replies from their chosen corporate targets.

THE GEOPOLITICAL IMPACT OF INFORMATION

These changes herald the less equable, more intense, less rational, globally connected but fragile world. The tentative, uncertain reaction from Business is partly because this world contradicts intellectual expectations. It certainly contradicts Marx and Engels's prognosis for capitalism, shared by many of all political persuasions up to the present:

> National differences, and antagonisms between peoples, are daily more and more vanishing, owing to the development of the bourgeoisie, to freedom of commerce, to the world market, to uniformity in the mode of production and in the conditions of life corresponding thereto.
>
> (Marx and Engels 1848: 58)

Marx and Engels's thesis was that the ground was being cleared for the final revolution of the proletariat and the foundation of Communist society; but others were convinced that commerce would lead to a better world. Norman Angell, a British pacifist journalist, Labour Party activist and thinker, had an enormous impact on international business, academics, politics and popular opinion in the years before the Great War with his best-seller, *The Great Illusion* (1910). Angell held that commercial interdependence – or enlightened self-interest – meant that war would either be prevented or ended speedily, since the disruption to international credit would stop protagonists from sustaining themselves in the field. The Great War's actual appearance did not prevent Angell from winning the Nobel Peace prize with a second *Great Illusion*, published in 1933 – the year Hitler came to power.

Later, and further to the right, another Nobel Laureate made the same case in another influential bestseller. In *Free to Choose* Milton Friedman and Rose Friedman applied the idea to nations by comparing them to individuals: 'International free trade fosters harmonious relations among nations that differ in culture and institutions just as free trade at home fosters harmonious relations among individuals who differ in beliefs, attitudes and interests' (Friedman and Friedman 1979: 51). The World Trade Organisation (WTO) continues to enshrine the idea as a public relations message for website visitors. The first of ten listed benefits of the WTO claims: 'The system helps to keep the peace': 'Crudely put, sales people are usually reluctant to fight their customers. In other words, if trade flows smoothly and both sides enjoy a healthy commercial relationship, political conflict is less likely' (WTO 2004).

The events of this century, quite apart from those of more recent years, suggest that 'freedom of commerce' and 'the world market' have not yet succeeded in keeping world peace, and certainly not for Business. It may be that the theory fails –

149

becomes no more than a hope – because of continual failure to grasp communication's full impact on 'the Empire of Circumstance', so-called by eminent historian and scholar of international affairs Christopher Hill. We must remember, Hill recorded in his study of 'world opinion': 'Our environment is constituted of actors, actions, ideas and feelings, as well as the physical world. At the *a priori* level all these have equal status' (Hill 1996: 112).

Communication bridges between events and the physical world, through the creation and transmission of ideas, feelings, opinions and decisions. Unlike nuclear weapons or dangerous chemicals, its supply is largely uncontrolled and is actually encouraged by national governments and world authorities. But communication inflicts damage, as it becomes available to more and more people. As the power to communicate passes into the hands of millions and then billions, it will be difficult to exercise influence or control. Much will depend upon individual regulation and self-restraint.

One outcome of the collision between the Empire of Circumstance and the information revolution is more intervention in 'big picture' issues by groups and individuals who once were confined to local, discrete and anonymous activities against corporates. In these changed circumstances, a crisis does not even restrict itself to this issue or that problem but feeds off suspicion of a particular industry, sullies other companies, awakens large and latent discontents: health fears, anti-corporate attitudes, or anti-Americanism. A senior member of the United States Council of Foreign Relations and prominent Public Relations counsellor noted as much in the *Edelman 2004 Trust Barometer* in a reference to America's changing place in world opinion:

> The kind of anti-Americanism we're seeing today differs sharply from historic anti-Americanism. In the past, anti-American attitudes have been based on specific policies of the US government; today, these attitudes have become far more generalized, applying to almost all foreign policies, many of our domestic practices, as well as American culture, values and lifestyle.
>
> (Gelb 2004: 3)

Corporations are now regularly confronted by such generalisations, amounting to a crisis 'gaia', and this book has investigated how some of them are learning to respond. Those lessons must be applied to new and unfamiliar audiences armed with technology which can be used to engage or deliver information freely from all angles.

Businesses must embrace a global political vision of communication, or have it used against them. They might fittingly adopt Clausewitz's famous dictum on war.

> We see, therefore, that war is not merely an act of policy but a true political instrument, a continuation of political intercourse, carried on with other

means. What remains peculiar to war is simply the peculiar nature of its means . . . The political object is the goal, war is the means of reaching it, and means can never be considered in isolation from their purpose.

(Clausewitz 1832: 99)

Crisis participants have it in their power to echo, whenever they wish and to whoever they choose, Cato's famous demand to the Roman Senate: 'Carthago delenda est' – Carthage must be destroyed. Some will have the ruthlessness, passion, power and persistence, like Cato, to make that demand of a company until it is finally realised.

PERPETUAL PRESSURES

This is not to say that corporate destruction is inevitable – because it is not so. Nor is every critic bent on destroying corporate targets. However unless Business learns that survival and eventual success is aligned to the use of targeted communications, then the pressure upon corporate management is likely to be prolonged as different groups suffer impatience – and then lose trust in senior management and the company.

Communications needs to be considered a tangible asset, to be tapped when vulnerabilities are exposed and crises arise. Carefully managed communications, accurately delivered must then be deployed to deliver transparency. Outsourced, scattered organisations must learn to exist in this world:

> It's clear that companies cannot simply buy credibility through advertising, or from headquarters based in distant countries. Business needs to rebuild confidence by engaging media at a national level with local spokespeople and reach stakeholders through multiple channels because people are less likely to believe something until they see or read it several times.
>
> (Gelb 2004: 3)

This approach seems a step towards measured, monitored humanity, a world where even the spontaneous generation of relationships between people is smothered under surveys, bulleted recommendations and planned strategies. It should be remembered that we are talking about the world of work which – although it occupies a big part of many lives – is not among those spaces where 'natural' or 'organic' communication needs to occur: family, close friendships, the world of birth, finding a partner, and death. Work is a professional arena where the last ounces of advantages are leveraged in order to maintain a position or seize an opportunity. Professional relationships are preeminently based on finding and growing mutual value:

151

> As a general rule, articles of utility become commodities, only because they are the products of the labour of private individuals or groups of individuals who carry on their work independently of each other. The sum total of all these private individuals forms the aggregate labour of society.
>
> (Marx 1867: 72–3)

This has happened to communication and perception, commoditising because they are the sum total of individual communication activity, and because each has a value in times of danger. As a business discipline, then, communication demands renewed attention, and planning at new levels of detail. Spontaneity certainly has a place, must do so, but within carefully prescribed boundaries. The need in crisis is damage limitation, survival, reputation protection; winning advantages hangs on communicating accurately and effectively. To do that, communication must use technology to engage large numbers of people inside and outside the affected company in relationships perceived as 'authentic' and mutually satisfying.

Bunting, in her critical account of the new workplace, expresses the common concerns about the new world:

> Information Technology also increases the pressure on employees to perform, as companies themselves are subject to more exacting regulations and quality control. There is less room for shoddy work, for an absent-minded moment on the assembly line, because the technology enables tracking of products.
>
> (Bunting 2004: 38)

The pressure, so prevalent in corporate life, will not weaken when disaster comes. Detail is demanded, not just by the suffering company, but by the media, activists, investors, customers and all audiences whose opinions are counted. Globally available technology may not liberate the truth, but it will add to the emotional value of information in the issues, regions, and the cultures trying to derail a Business from its accustomed course.

Business sees the importance of orchestrating feelings and emotions when profits are at stake. Consultants conduct detailed empathy audits for customer call centres and propose ways to reinsert human qualities to what has been described by Bunting as 'a profoundly unbalanced human relationship' (Bunting 2004: 66). For the same reason Business sees the value of audience segmentation. 'The store wants to pick certain people out of the crowd. It wants to send a message – "You, yes, and you, but not you"'. Thus consumer behaviourist and retail consultant Paco Underhill, on Cartier's window display (Underhill 2004: 113). This selected messaging – this targeted communication – is an accepted driver of marketing and retail activities. Now communication technology straddles the globe, how can such attention to detail be reappraised, planned and practised in order to deliver crisis messages in the new information age?

152

It is not happening enough, because of a persistent view that communication technology is predominantly a technical matter. In the west, and America most of all, the 9/11 terror attacks caused some organisations to examine the role of technology in the management of crisis. However, this process was often seen as a matter of business continuity planning, with a focus on physical disaster and operational responses. A few months after 9/11, Gartner Research found organisations of all sizes, including 'large companies and government entities': 'Would be unable to quickly and smoothly execute basic business continuity measures' ('Businesses, Banks' 2001). Because of mobile phone overload and a four-hour 'dark' period when the agency shut networks to assess damage on 9/11, the United States Labor Department's Chief Information Officer reported, 'We couldn't talk to each other'. She concluded: 'One of the most important lessons to come out of that experience . . . is the need to plot a well-conceived communications strategy in advance.' This refers to the technical challenge of keeping channels open, but not a strategy to guide their content ('Wartime CIOs' 2002: 14).

There is a pressing need for fresh content. In his influential book *The Collapse of Complex Societies*, the scholar of ancient civilisations Joseph Tainter offers the following argument as one of four concepts explaining collapse: 'Information processing costs tend to increase over time as a more complex society requires ever more specialized, highly trained personnel, who must be educated at greater cost' (Tainter 1988: 195). We have explored the reasons behind this development in our own area and its impacts. Some reasons and impacts are known to both Society and Business but not applied to crisis communication; others are overlooked and applied nowhere at all. Companies must understand:

- The rise of communication as the one emotive and informational agent used to unite massive audiences, dispersed and often divided.
- The fragility of corporations whose reputation and record, like an overlong line of supply, runs across continents, cultures, subcontractors, part-timers and consultants. It is a situation 'when the lines of communication have begun to be overstretched' (Clausewitz 1832: 407) because of corporate expansion.
- The confused relationship between managing reputations and brands.
- The bottlenecks of the existing crisis management model in this environment.
- The problems these matters raise for 'rational', ordered communications and the challenges of creating 'climates of opinion'.
- The consequences of the information revolution for known corporate crises (health scares, recalls, boycotts, extortion, natural disasters, damaging rumours, rogue employees) and for generating new crises (cyber-terrorism, hacking and extraction of sensitive information, IT failures, hate sites and online hoaxes, loss of trust in a company because of flawed online communication).

153

The trends amount to radical compression of the crisis lifecycle, where the stages of crisis emergence, spread, ebb and recovery, squeeze into ever smaller slots. Companies sustain heavy damage because harmful, widespread and intense debate, rumour and speculation rapidly escalates beyond control. Such conditions contain volatility and uncertainty because there is little or no opportunity for reflection and less time to find and communicate with opinion-formers, to fend off disruptive protests and attacks while attempting to repair long-term damage to overall corporate reputation, sales, shares, morale and systems. There is in sum less time for a crisis team of senior executives, PR managers and company lawyers to analyse, plan and act as they keep pace with the speed, change and spread of events.

We have argued that the emerging, highly interactive crisis environment harms the ability of executives to coordinate a response led by one-way communication from a company to its audiences. Press statements, interviews, emails and news releases prepared by a crisis team and delivered by its spokesperson will not build consistent online relationships to satisfy customers, e-fluentials, investors, subcontractors, part-time employees and other stakeholders over continents and cultures, all accessing their own 'circles of cross-influence' ('PR must embrace' 2001: 3) for interactive opinion forming. The messages, actions and priorities of subcontractors of outsourced services and part-time workers split by time zones, regions, beliefs, countries or continents will be harder to harmonise or coordinate than with direct full-time on-site employees. Outsourced employees and services will be less inclined or able to display loyalty or empathy to a crisis-hit company, or to assist in creating effective messages. In addition, a company that is, in Charles Handy's words, 'not all there', by outsourcing formerly core functions, exposes itself and its brand name to the risks and issues of the overseas or domestic subcontractor.

We have asserted that crisis management is approaching a situation where communication activity not only drives and distorts crises but also becomes the crisis because of the decisions the participants can take by instantaneously uniting communications with concrete action. Vulnerable or crisis-hit companies can no longer treat emerging technology simply as a communication tool. The changes to stakeholder behaviour force company leaders to re-evaluate the role and meaning of communication. As far as crisis management is concerned, this re-evaluation should pursue several objectives:

- To tighten integration between communication needs and operational and management activity.
- To lay increased emphasis on anticipatory planning to pick up early warning signals of potential or emerging crises.
- To increase capabilities to conduct 360° anticipatory monitoring off- and online.
- To develop greater sensitivity to the impact of soft, emotional intangibles such as perceptions, emotions and trust.

154

- To identify key audiences and be ready and empowered to communicate with them in a timely and open fashion.

Future crisis planning must stress the 'pre-crisis' stage, and integrate crisis and issues management by continuous monitoring, early pick-up and rapid intervention when escalating issues emerge. This will demand joint issues management and monitoring programmes with outsourced employees and subcontractors and their local critics. Easy access to many points of view and of information, transparency expectations and any detected distrust of diverse online audiences further suggests that in the midst of a crisis, companies and their spokespeople must use a very different approach to language, content and style – less hedged in by legal caveats or corporate-speak, readier to accommodate alternative arguments, more styled to conversations.

A big obstacle to this, we claim (along with the problem of viewing cobra technology as a matter of technology and not communication) is fear of unmanaged messages and participating in or even encouraging diverse views within the uncontrolled world of the web. 'I'm still surprised at the large number of corporate websites who do not offer such an opportunity – or if they offer a feedback mechanism it is very limited and structured', TellShell's manager remarked in 1999 (Harris). Experience with censored and monitored company weblogs indicates that this lesson has still to be learned, yet technology's conversion of the internet into an arena for commerce brings crisis in its wake. Business cannot embrace the one and ignore the other. Future crises moving at speed and using communication technology to spread opinion and take action, force companies to pay more attention to once-overlooked audiences and sensitive issues, to engage with countries, peoples and cultures once unknown or left to overseas subcontractors, and to place more weight on the emotional, perceptual, interactive talents of their remaining full-time directly employed workforce.

In a breaking crisis the crisis team will, like the wider public, come under simultaneous pressures imposed by geographical dispersal of a large number of stakeholders, and the rapid concentration of stakeholders around online e-fluentials. We conclude that these factors, added to the compression of the crisis lifecycle, compel reorganisation of the crisis management team to accommodate these pressures. The reorganisation should include adding online communication expertise: company personnel authorised to protect the company's reputation by engaging in potentially continuous interaction online with third-party experts, key outsourced workers and subcontractors. This new organisation will prepare messages, identify participants and their online haunts; must create dialogue, distribute information and erect online forums that help present the company as a transparent, frank participant in the crisis. At the same time management must monitor, contain and instantly respond to damaging acts such as instant boycotts, rumours or cyber attacks.

155

PLANNED LIBERATION

It is a paradox, then, that all these plans to control communication are made to promote what might be viewed as an act of corporate liberation. Future managers will need to know more about communication, in order to use it more freely. They will use global technology to plan natural relationships inside their companies and externally with troubled stakeholders to be ready to empathise with selected critics, and, to a certain degree, encourage cooperative solutions. They must:

- Change the way they collate, analyse and exchange information in a crisis, before deciding what to say and through which channels to deliver key messages.
- Change the way to communicate with external audiences in a crisis and be ready to utilise an array of on- and offline conduits and techniques.

We have observed a few companies risking this pioneering step, Shell and Microsoft among them. Others will join in, often forced by a crisis or corrosive issue. The optimum relationship will be open, frank and attentive; the optimal participants will be those with the plan, confidence, belief and the technology to express themselves unofficially, from many points inside and outside of the company.

There is much for Business to do. Managers must strive to understand how their stakeholders experience technology. This means that, as much as possible, companies must mimic the tone and strategies of those who would criticise them. This is a scary proposition: the critics are comfortable with unfettered communication; less committed to accuracy and more committed to generating power from waves of public emotion. The best among them know how to talk to people – by leaving the impression they are talking *with* people. Activist groups and motivated individuals acting alone know how to make the information revolution a cold, alien place for targeted companies. These are talents that Business would be foolish to ignore, particularly when it wishes to cash in on its greatest assets: realism and expert knowledge, born of long experience and the ability to connect those assets to the everyday world.

The future will be dominated by new technology, while at the same time fraught with risk and dangers. But corporate managers must face changes that are already in train, realising they can shape the environment where crises will be escalated and driven. Success depends on imaginative, accurately targeted, rapidly delivered communications; on communicating to include the vulnerable company in the circle of cross influence – a trusted contributor to its own fate and to the aggressive deliberations, opinions and actions of worldwide communities.

LABADDIA: Not the end

Meat monoculture

It seemed to Megan as the global food scare entered early evening that she'd spoken to every lunatic on the planet in the last four hours, until they'd located one or two Chinese and Japanese e-fluentials – a term she had no knowledge of until that morning - to help them out in their own languages. But it was the phrase 'meat monoculture' above all that bothered her all day: it was easy, memorable and glib, and when she saw it spattered online in discussion fora and news sites, she realised it would be a tough soundbite to break – like 'passive smoking' or 'factory farming'.

It was clear that, despite the fact nobody knew much about their Asia Pacific subcontractors and suppliers, people – activists, investors, customers, distributors - were acting as if they understood everything, as if the worst had happened even when they didn't know what the worst could be, with the result that their actions made the worst happen.

David Corio had spent the day locked in a Frankfurt office, talking to investors.

Sarah Collins had spent the day in her office, talking to Labaddia representatives from twenty countries.

Jennifer Stone had been stuck on a train talking to employees and the media.

Megan had spent the day at her computer, talking to Corio, Collins and Jennifer Stone, intervening in discussion forums, correcting rumours, responding to allegations as they appeared – throwing buckets of water at a burning building.

Yet she surely had done some good. With Jennifer's help she'd inserted Labaddia people from five different countries into the online debate in their own languages, and helped correct some of the rising hysteria. At least that was what Jennifer, David Corio and Sarah Collins had told her during their periodic conference calls.

It was not over yet, but the first, massive tidal wave of information, speculation and accusation had perhaps been soaked up by Labaddia's intense, extemporised and immediate communication response. They had bought themselves time by talking with and to tech-empowered audiences, and not at them. They still did not know the identities of several of their biggest online critics. Megan supposed they never would know.

Yesterday, she had been helping Jennifer get started on the new crisis plan. The old crisis plan, assembled in the 1980s, the vanished pre-Information Revolution era of Mad Cow Disease, had been on her desk all day. Megan knew most of it by heart – the selection of team members, the set meeting times, lists of key official contacts, protocols for the preparation and distribution of corporate messages.

If they'd used the old plan today, she realised, it would have collapsed under the weight of communication. Its infrastructure and processes were designed for a different way of communicating: different technology, different content, different approach.

157

Today, they had gone from breaking news to a worldwide emergency in slightly over four hours. Today's crisis world was flatter, faster, potentially overpowering.

*

Jennifer Stone finally arrived at Kings Cross Station, two hours late. She trotted down the platform, with the lengthy apologies of the railway company echoing after her and around the cavernous roof.

Those announcements irritated her. What's the use of just saying sorry? Why did it happen so often? She wanted, along with every other passenger no doubt, to make them feel her pain. She wanted to know everything – the whole institutional chain of events leading to today's incompetence. Tomorrow, if there was time and if she had any energy left, she'd blast off an email – and get back yet another infuriating apology and perhaps a ticket voucher for next time.

More than anything, it was the powerlessness that infuriated her. There was nothing to do: unless, she suddenly realised, she took some leaves out of the book of the activists coordinating to target *her* company. Did she, she wondered, understand their powerlessness – or at least their ability to generate that impulsive, urgent, emotive charge globally among other audiences?

She thought that she did. In the course of her journey today she felt, at least, she had made a rudimentary, highly accidental start on the new corporate crisis plan.

Afterwords

Just watch people who have been conditioned to let themselves be enraptured and carried away: they do it all the time, in small matters as in great, over things which touch them and those which touch them not at all.

Michel de Montaigne (1533–92)
Montaigne, Michel de (c. 1592, 1993 edn)
'On restraining your will'. *The Complete Essays*
(M. A. Screech, trans.). London: Penguin: 1134

The odd thing is that so little seems to happen when no-one is watching. Do the newspapers make the world self-conscious? Do things happen simply because people are waiting for them to happen? I am afraid the full psychological effects of journalism upon world-temperament have yet to be studied. It is plain that a vast deal of our politics and statecraft is pure deference to the watching eye of the public which we call the Press; also a good deal of our art, and perhaps a certain proportion of our crime. Perhaps the world is one of those sensitive and obliging pots which boils when you look at it, and only simmers when you don't.

Robert Bell, Journalist, *Observer* article, first Sunday after Christmas, 1919
In Jones, Kennedy (1920) *Fleet Street & Downing Street*.
London: Hutchinson: 333

To give fine-sounding names to nasty things is to give jewellery to a drowning man. It cannot save him and he takes it with him as he sinks.

Peter Simple (aka Michael Wharton)
Simple, Peter (1963) *The Best of Peter Simple*. London: Johnson: 126

References

INTRODUCTION

Bergen, Peter L. (2002) *Holy War, Inc: Inside the Secret World of Osama bin Laden*. New York: Simon & Schuster.

Deutsch, David (2001) The Structure of the Multiverse. Unpublished Lecture. Oxford: The Clarendon Library, April.

Djerejian Committee (2003) 'Changing Minds, Winning Peace: A New Direction for US Public Diplomacy in the Arab and Muslim World.' Report of the Advisory Group on Public Diplomacy for the Arab and Muslim World submitted to Committee on Appropriations, US House of Representatives. Washington DC: Congress.

Edelman Worldwide (2004) 'Trust Barometer. An Annual Study of Opinion Formers in Key Global Markets.' New York: Edelman.

Gingrich, Newt (2003) 'Rogue state department.' *Foreign Policy*, July/August: 42–8.

Howard, Michael (1962) *The Franco-Prussian War*. New York: Macmillan.

Khan, Muqtedar (2003) 'Prospects for Muslim democracy.' *Middle East Policy*, Fall, 10(3): 79–89.

'Mass media can battle mass destruction.' (2002) *USA Today*. 19 March.

Moore, Simon (2004) 'Disaster's future: the prospects for corporate crisis management and communication.' *Business Horizons*, January–February, 47(1): 29–36.

9/11 Commission (2004) *Final Report of the National Commission on Terrorist Attacks Upon the United States*. Authorized edition with index. New York: Norton.

Office of Global Communication (2003). Home page. Available: http://www.whitehouse.gov/ogc/aboutogc.html# (accessed 4 August 2004).

Office of the Under Secretary of State for Defense (2004) Report of the Defense Science Board Task Force on Strategic Communication. September, Washington DC: Department of Defense.

Rees, Martin (2004) *Our Final Hour*. New York: Basic Books.

Schank, Roger C. (2002) 'Are we going to get smarter?', in John Brockman (ed.) *The Next Fifty Years*. New York: Vintage.

Seymour, Mike (2004) 'Fighting on all fronts.' *CEO Magazine*, September: 25–7.

Skidelsky, Robert (2003) 'Imbalance of power.' *Foreign Policy*, March/April: 46–55.

State Department (2003) Under Secretary for Public Diplomacy and Public Affairs. Available: http://www.state.gov/r/ (accessed 6 January 2004).

State Department Briefing (2003) 'Information Tools and the War on Terror Featuring Stuart Holliday, Coordinator, State Department International Information Programs.' 26 February. Available: http://www.state.gov/r/adcompd/19299.htm (accessed 5 June 2004).

'Unhip, Unhip Al Hurra. The Middle East hates its new TV station.' (2004) *Slate*. Posted Friday, Feb. 20, at 9:18 AM PT. Available: http://slate.msn.com/id/2095806/ (accessed 20 October 2004).

United States Advisory Commission on Public Diplomacy (2003) The New Diplomacy: Utilizing Innovative Communication Concepts That Recognize Resource Constraints. July. Available: http://www.state.gov/r/adcompd/rls/22818.htm

1 THE CHANGE

Anderson, G. (2004) 'Outsourcing America.' *The World & I*, Washington, January, 19(1): 38.

'Back to basics' (2001) *Edge*, October, 3(14): 39–41.

Benoit, William L. (1997) 'Image repair discourse and crisis communication.' *Public Relations Review*, 23(2): 177–87.

Brinson, Susan L. and Benoit, William L. (1996) 'Dow Corning's image repair strategies in the breast implant crisis.' *Communication Quarterly*, Winter, 44(1): 29–42.

'Business – IT costs – cut out or keep?' (2002) *Accountancy*, 22 January.

Cordes, David (2001) 'New technology will improve performance', in World of Science supplement. *USA Today*, New York. June.

Daruvala, T. (2003) 'When, where, how and other questions on going offshore.' McKinsey Consulting Report. 3 July. Available: www.mckinsey.com/knowledge/articles/going_offshore.asp (accessed 3 March 2004).

Drucker, Peter (1998) 'Peter Drucker takes the long view.' *Fortune*, 28 September: 162.

'EDS appoints Government IT security veteran as Chief of Homeland Security.' (2002) EDS news release, 29 January.

eMarketer (2002) 2002 eGlobal reports. Available www.emarketer.com/ereports/eglobal/welcome.html (accessed 4 May 2002).

'Fast-forward to 2010' (1999) in Trends Online. *PC Magazine online*. 27 January.

Fink, Steven (1986) *Crisis Management: Planning for the Inevitable*. New York: American Management Association.

Fishman, Donald (1999) 'ValuJet Flight 592: Crisis Communication Theory Blended and Extended.' *Communication Quarterly*, Fall, 47(4): 345.

Forrester Research (2001) 'Global online trade will climb to 18 per cent of sales.' *TextStrategy*, 26 December: 1–5.

Global Reach Market Research (2004) 'Global Internet Statistics (By Language).' Available: http://www.glreach.com/globstats/ (accessed 3 March 2004). Global Reach has been tracking non-English online populations since 1995.

'Government promotes IT outsourcing' (2002) *Computerworld* (Philippines), January 21.

Handy, Charles (1994) *The Empty Raincoat*. London: Random House.

Hickman, Jennifer R. and Crandall, William (1997) 'Before disaster hits: a multi-faceted approach to crisis management.' *Business Horizons*, March–April, 40(2): 75–80.

Hunt, Peter. Public Affairs Manager, Shell UK (1997) *Brent Spar: A Drop in the Ocean?* Business in the Community Occasional Paper 5. London: Shell.

ILO (2001) Overview. 'A Widening Digital Divide.' *World Employment Report: Life at Work in the Digital Economy*. Geneva: ILO. Available http://www.ilo.org/public/english/support/publ/wer/overview.htm (accessed 3 December 2004).

'In Brief: IBM outsourcing for banks in Japan.' (2000) *American Banker*, 17 November, 165(222).

InfoSys (2004) 'Financial highlights, 5–year overview.' Available: http://www.infosys.com/investor/pl2_print.htm (accessed 3 March 2004).

Internet World Stats (2004) 'Usage and population statistics.' Available http://www.internetworldstats.com (accessed 14 December 2004).

Kamer, Larry (1997) 'Crisis planning's most important implement: the drill.' *Communication World*. December, 15(1): 27–31.

'Kansas conference sheds light on future technology.' (2002) *Bank News*, March.

Lukaszweski, James B. (1997) 'Establishing individual and corporate crisis communication standards: the principles and protocols.' *Public Relations Quarterly*, Fall, 42(3): 7–15.

Marx, Karl and Engels, Frederick (1848; 1998 edn) *The Communist Manifesto: A Modern Edition*. London: Verso.

Molitor, G. (2001) '5 forces transforming communications.' *The Futurist*, September–October, 35(5): 32–5.

Moore, Gordon E. (1965) 'Cramming more components into integrated circuits.' *Electronics*, 19 April, 38(8).

Nua (2001) 'How many online? August.' Available: http://www.nua.ie/surveys/how_many_online/ (accessed 12 May 2002).

Nua (2002) 'How many online? September.' Available: www.nua.com/surveys/how_many_online/index.html (accessed 3 March 2004).

Office of the Under Secretary of State for Defense (2004) Report of the Defense Science Board Task Force on Strategic Communication. September, Washington DC: Department of Defense.

'Online shoppers buck talk of global downturn. 12% will shop more as a result of tragic events in USA.' (2001) WorldPay news release, 4 October.

'Outsourcing can save up to 20%.' (2001) *Business Times*, Kuala Lumpur, October.

'Outsourcing IT in insurance is gaining favor.' (2001) *National Underwriter Life & Health – Financial Services Edition*. 25 June.

Pauchant, Thierry and Mitroff, Ian I. (1992) *Transforming the Crisis-Prone Organization*. San Francisco: Jossey-Bass Management Series.

Pearson, Ian (2000) 'The power of direct action.' *Sphere*. BT's innovation and technology e-zine, 29 November. Available: www.bt.com/sphere/insights/pearson/powerofdirectaction.htm (accessed 3 March 2004).

Penrose, J. M. (2000) 'The role of perception in crisis planning.' *Public Relations Review*, Summer, 26(2): 155–71.

Peters, T. (2002) 'Tomorrow's orgs: itinerant potential machines.' *TomObservation*, 17 January. Available: http://www.tompeters.com/toms_world/observations.asp?id=89&date=1/1/2004 (accessed 1 March 2004).

Phillips, Nelson and Brown, John L. (1993) 'Analyzing communication in and around organizations: a critical hermeneutic approach.' *Academy of Management Journal*, December, 36(6): 1547–76.

Pines, Wayne (2000) 'Myths of crisis management.' *Public Relations Quarterly*, Fall, 45(3): 15.

PR Week (1995, UK edn) 'Shell puts more emphasis on PR.' *PR Week*, 22 September.

Seeger, Matthew (1986) 'The Challenger tragedy and search for legitimacy.' *Central States Speech Journal*, 37: 136–46.

Sellnow, Timothy L. and Seeger, Matthew (2001) 'Exploring the boundaries of crisis communication: the case of the 1997 Red River Valley flood.' *Communication Studies*, Summer, 52(2): 153–68.

Seymour, Mike and Moore, Simon (1999) *Effective Crisis Management: Worldwide Principles and Practice*. London: Thomson Learning.

Silva, M. and McGann, T. (1995) *Overdrive: Managing in Crisis-Filled Times*. New York: Wiley.

Sklarewitz, Norman (1991) 'Cruise company handles crisis by the book.' *Public Relations Journal*, May, 47(5): 34–7.

Slevin, J. (2000) *The Internet and Society*. Cambridge: Polity Press.

The St Paul (2001) 'St Paul Executive Discusses Strategies to Manage E-Commerce Risks, Impacts at Cyber Risk Conference.' The St Paul News release. Minnesota: The St Paul, 25 June.

'The St Paul Survey' (2001) *Cyberrisk Survey*. Minnesota: The St Paul.

Temkin, B. (2002) 'North America Will Lead Global eCommerce to $6.9 Trillion in 2004, According to Forrester.' Forrester news release. 20 April. Available: http://www.thetimesharebeat.com/archives/2000/fin/fnapr53.htm (accessed 3 March 2004).

'Why India is leading in IT outsourcing.' (2002) *Asia Pulse*, December.

WorldPay (2001) 'World wide web getting wider; WorldPay figures show new countries join eCommerce revolution; Residents in Bhutan, Benin and Cape Verde now shopping online.' M2 Presswire, August.

WorldPay (2004) 'About us. Worldwide.' Available: http://www.worldpay.co.uk/about/index.php?go=ab_worldwide (accessed 3 December 2004).

2 'COBRA TECHNOLOGY'

'ADL: Internet rumors about Microsoft Wingdings are false.' (2001) *US Newswire*, 21 September.

'Afghan women turn to internet to protest Taleban abuses.' (2000) *CNN Worldview*. 18:00 (EST). Saturday, 15 July. Transcript #00071508V18.

Ahold (2001) Annual Report. Available: http://ftp.pse.cz/Annual.rep/2001/AHOLD X12.pdf (accessed 10 December 2004).

Ahold (2002a) 'Employee and supplier diversity.' Ahold in Society – Social Issues. Available: http://www.ahold.com/aholdinsociety/foodtrends.asp (accessed 10 April 2002).

Ahold (2002b) 'Ahold leads the way with Global Food Safety Initiative.' Ahold in Society – Food Issues. Available: http://www.ahold.com/aholdinsociety/food trends.asp (accessed 10 April 2002).

Angell, Ian O. (1999) *Winners and Losers in the Information Age*. LSE Computer Security Research Centre, 26 November. Available: http://csrc.lse.ac.uk/people/AngellI/ (accessed 9 April 2002).

'Arabs fuel a boycott of US goods – impact is so far minor, but American executives fear long-term damage' (2002) *Wall Street Journal*, Eastern Edition. 19 April: A 11.

'Bank of China admits officials stole $915m.' (2002a) *The Straits Times*, Singapore. 17 March.

'Bank of China's mounting problems' (2002b) *New York Times*. (East Coast edition) 1 February: W 1.

'Beit Shemesh residents protest against non-kosher McDonald's.' (2001) *Jerusalem Post*. 12 February.

'Beyond digital . . .'(2000) *New Statesman*, 10 July: R20–R21.

Blinder, Alan S. (2000) 'Central Bank Policy: Why do we care? How do we build it?' *The American Economic Review,* December, 90(5): 1421–31.

'Boycott of US products begins in UAE.' (2002) *Itar-Tass News Wire.* 4 May.

Burson-Marsteller (2002) 'The e-fluentials. The power of online influencers: your company's newest stakeholder group.' New York: Burson-Marsteller.

Burson-Marsteller (2003) 'Corporate rumor mill moves from the water cooler to the web: 81 per cent of online influencers discuss and trade corporate rumors via the internet.' News Release. 26 June. New York: Burson-Marsteller.

'CalPERS adopts new model for investing in emerging markets.' (2002) CalPERS news release. Office of Public Affairs. 20 February. Available: http://www.calpers.ca.gov/whatsnew/press/2002/0220a.htm (accessed 8 April 2002). CalPERs's tough transparency recommendations for emerging markets coincided with a statement about Enron, which shows some of the costs associated with 'hidden activity'. 'We believe it is unrealistic to expect an investor, even one as large and active as CalPERS, to know facts and consequences which are hidden from view.'

CERT (2002) 'Overview of Attack Trends.' CERT Coordination Center. Pittsburgh: Carnegie-Mellon University. April.

CERT/CC (2004) 'CERT/CC statistics 1988–2004.' Available: http://www.cert.org/stats/#notes (accessed 10 December 2004).

'Countering cyber war.' (2001/2) *NATO Review,* Winter: 16.

'Cruel $12 billion hoax on Bhopal victims and BBC.' (2004) The Times online. 4 December. Available: http://www.timesonline.co.uk/article/0,,2-1387740,00.html (accessed 10 December 2004).

'Cyber terrorism: mass destruction or mass disruption?' (2002) *Canadian Underwriter.* February: 16–18.

DTI (Department of Trade and Industry) (2001) *Business and Society: Developing Corporate Social Responsibility in the UK.* London: DTI.

DTI (2002) *Business and Society: Corporate Social Responsibility Report 2002.* London: DTI.

'Dutch grocer to expand its reports' (2002) *New York Times,* 9 April.

Edelman (2002) Crisis Preparedness Survey. Unpublished presentation. London: Edelman.

'Fragile firms keep ear to Internet rumour mill.' (2002) *Asahi News Service,* 26 February.

'France pulls plug on Arab network.' (2004) BBC News online. 13 December. Available: http://news.bbc.co.uk/2/hi/europe/4093579.stm (accessed 13 December 2004).

'From "long boom" to days of doom and gloom.' (2000) *Javaworld,* 4 June.

Goyder, Mark (2000) 'Bridging the Divide.' Academy of Marketing Conference, 5 July: 4.

Harris, Clare E. (1999) 'Our experiences with the internet dialogue.' TellShell Post. From 'our values and commitments' discussion thread, under 'Engagement and Open Communication.' Available: http://www-forums.shell.com/ 16 November (accessed 12 April 2002).

Holland, John (2002) 'What is to come and how to predict it.' Chapter cited in *The Next Fifty Years.* Brockman, John (ed.). New York: Vintage, pp. 170–82.

'I hate you, and millions know it' (2000) *Business Review Weekly* (Australia), 7 July: 84.

'IBM unveils "BlueSpace": tech office of the future.' (2002) *NewsFactor Network,* 16 January.

'ICI confirms its 800m pounds deal after rumours cause sell-off.' (2002) *Euroweek*, 1 February: 26.

'If rumours were energy, Bill Gates would be envious.' (2002) *Africa News Service*, 22 March.

'India: breaking a silence.' (2001) *Businessline*, Islamabad, 3 September.

Innis, Harold (1950a) *Empire and Communications*. Oxford: Oxford University Press.

Innis, Harold (1950b) *The Bias of Communication*. Toronto: University of Toronto Press.

'Interactive PR: The Party Starts Now.' (2001) Unpublished report. Mainsail Interactive Services: 3. Available: http://www.prfirms.org/docs/mainsail_whitepaper.pdf (accessed 5 January 2002).

'Internet city pledges to take the offensive in cyber wars.' (2001) *Global News Wire: Gulf News*, 6 August.

'Internet rumors about tampons refuted.' (1999) *FDA Consumer*, March: 7.

'Interview. Dave Morris reveals his experiences of the trials of McLibel and how it feels to face Goliath.' (1996) McSpotlight website. 13 August. Avaliable: www.mcspotlight.org/people/interviews/morris97.html (accessed 2 April 2002).

'Is your crystal ball set on a 10-year cycle?'(1994) *Datamation*, 1 April: 84.

'Israeli organizations hit by e-mail viruses.' (2001) *Computer Weekly*, 22 March: 4.

Johnson, Paul (1991) *The Birth of the Modern: World Society 1815–1830*. London: Phoenix.

Kang, Liu Ming (2000) 'Corporate Governance in China: Issues and Prospects.' President's Speech. Bank of China, June. Available: http://www.bank-of-china.com (accessed 9 April 2002). See also 'Tightening the Rules for Healthier Development: Bank of China Spokesman' (2002) Bank of China. Public Announcement. Bank of China Website, 18 January.

Klein, Naomi (2000) *No Space, No Jobs, No Logo: Taking Aim at the Brand Bullies*. Canada: Knopf.

Kruk, L. B. and Lavenhar, P. (eds) (2000) *Technology Explosion: The Technological Explosion in the Workplace*. Holland, Michigan: Haworth.

'Management Week – Technology stops scandals.' (2002) *VNU NET*, 25 March: 34.

'Mass media can battle mass destruction.' (2002) *USA Today*, 19 March.

Mill, John Stuart (1848; 1998 edn) *Principles of Political Economy*. Oxford: Oxford University Press.

'Modem warfare' (1999) *The Guardian,* 13 January.

Moloney, Kevin (2002) *Rethinking Public Relations*. London: Routledge.

Moore, Simon (2004) 'Disaster's future: the prospects for corporate crisis management and communication.' *Business Horizons*, January–February, 47(1): 29–36.

'Networking new markets; Equipment maker sees hi-speed future.' (2000) *Bangkok Post*, 23 August.

'New technology, smarter patients augur vast change.' (2000) *American Medical News*, 13 March: 33.

'New way to work.' (2002) *Informationweek*, 28 January: 48–52.

'Not Ready For Real Time?' (2002) *Industry Week*, March: 32.

9/11 Commission (2004) *Final Report of The National Commission on Terrorist Attacks Upon the United States*. Authorized edition with index. New York: Norton.

'1901 – A New Century.' (1901) *The Melbourne Age*. Editorial. 1 January. Available: http://150.theage.com.au/view_bestofarticle.asp?straction=update&inttype=1&intid=410 (accessed 18 November 2004).

Office of the Under Secretary of State for Defense (2004) Report of the Defense Science Board Task Force on Strategic Communication. September, Washington DC: Department of Defense.

'Overview.' (2002) www.steelcase.com (accessed 25 April 2002).

'Overview of Attack Trends.' (2002) CERT Coordination Center. Pittsburgh: Carnegie-Mellon University. April.

Pearson, Ian (2000) 'The Power of Direct Action.' *Sphere*, BT's innovation and technology e-zine, 29 November. Available: http://www.bt.com/sphere/insights/pearson/ (accessed 18 January 2002).

'Permissible Equity Markets Investment Analysis and Recommendations.' (2002) Prepared for The California Public Employers Retirement System. Preliminary. January. Wilshire Associates, Santa Monica, California.

'PETA withdraws call for boycott of Safeway stores.' (2002) *Knight Ridder Tribune Business News*, 16 May.

'Protecting yourself against Cyberterrorism.' (2002) *Office Solutions*, February: 24.

'Q3 2004. The rise of Islamist hacking and criminal syndicates.' (2004) Mi2g news alert. 20 October. Available: http://www.mi2g.com/ (accessed 27 October 2004).

'Qatar: Al-Jazeera Director on New Media, changes, TV station projects.' (2002) *Global News Wire*. BBC Monitoring International Reports, 2 April.

'Quarterly reporting edges ever nearer.' (2002) *PR Week* (UK Edition), 5 April: 11.

'Ready to handle a crisis?' (2002) Edelman Public Relations Worldwide news release, 18 April.

'Rumormongers.' (1997) *Forbes*, 15 December: 54.

S11 (2001) '3 October 2001' S11 Homepage. Available: http://www.s11.org/ (accessed 12 April 2002); http://www.scoop.co.nz/features/s11.html (accessed 8 April 2005).

Seymour, Mike and Moore, Simon (1999) *Effective Crisis Management: Worldwide Principles and Practice*. London: Thomson Learning.

'Shock of the now.' (2001) *New Scientist*, 15 December: 54.

'Steelcase and IBM envisage tomorrow's workplace.' (2002) *Contract*, March: 22.

'Stock rigging show trial.' (2002) *South China Morning Post*, 7 June.

'Technology Journal – Health web sites usher in new era of patient activism – Users obtain information, share experiences.' (2001) *Asian Wall Street Journal*, 12 November: T6.

'Technology needs of aging boomers.' (1999) *Issues in Science and Technology*, Washington, Fall: 53–60.

'Technology timeline.' (2002) BTexact Technologies. White Paper. Reference: WP106. i1. 21 November 2001. Ipswich: 2002: 3. Available http://www.BTexact.com/ white_papers/downloads/WP106.pdf (accessed 26 April 2002).

'Technology visionaries scope the future.' (2001) *Computerworld*, 8 October: 54. Available: http://www.computerworld.com/managementtopics/management/story/ 0,10801,64491,00.html (accessed 10 December 2004).

'Telecoms companies losing 6,000 pounds a minute from downtime.' (2002) BT Wholesale news release, 7 May.

'The ads we can't avoid.' (2002) Dot.life. Sci/Tech. *BBC News online*, 11 June. Available: http://news.bbc.co.uk/hi/english/in_depth/sci_tech/2000/dot_life/newsid _1977000/1977830.stm (accessed 11 June 2002).

'The dangers of global cyber attacks.' (2001) *The Times*, 8 October.

'The era of blind investments is over.' (2002) *Business Week*, 11 March: 50.

'The future of cyber attacks analyzed by Computer Economics.' (2001) *M2 Presswire*, 27 December.

'The impact of the internet on public relations and business communication.' (2000) *Tactical Insights*. IMT Strategies: Connecticut.

'The new leadership challenge: managing in a changing world.' (2002) Speech by Peter R. Dolan, CEO Bristol-Myers Squibb to Economic Club of Detroit, 22 January. *Vital Speeches of the Day*, 1 March: 308–12.

'The new look of security.' (2002) *Insurance & Technology*, February: 28–32.

'The rise of corporate hate sites – lies, damned lies and extortion.' (2004) Mi2g news alert. 2 December. Available: http://www.mi2g.com/ (accessed 5 December 2004).

The Yes Men (2004) Website. Dow. 3 December. Available: http://www.theyesmen.org/hijinks/dow/ (accessed 10 December 2004).

'13,000 credit reports stolen by hackers.' (2002) *New York Times*, 17 May: Section C5.

'Trade finance: Untangle complexities with transparency' (2001) *The Asian Banker Journal*, 2 November.

'2004 e-crime survey shows significant increase in electronic crimes.' (2004) CERT news release and survey report. 25 May. Available: http://www.cert.org/about/ecrime.html (accessed 10 December 2004).

United Nations (2003) 'Norms on the responsibilities of transnational corporations and other business enterprises with regard to human rights.' Distr. GENERAL E/CN.4/Sub.2/2003/12/Rev.2. 26 August.

'Use your consumer power – don't buy Esso!' (2002) Last edited 2002–05–02. Available: www.greenpeace.org.uk (accessed 9 May 2002).

Van Dijk, J. (1991; 2000 edn) *The Network Society*. London: Sage.

Weissbrodt, David and Kruger, Muria (2003) 'Norms on the responsibilities of transnational corporations and other business enterprises with regard to human rights.' *The American Journal of International Law*, October, 97(4): 901–22.

'What can be done to limit damage of internet rumours?' (2001) *Marketing*, 31 May: 12.

'What lies ahead in the 21st century?' (2000) *USA Today*, World of Science Special, June: 16.

www.ethicalconsumer.org (accessed 14 September 2004).

'XML to speed financial data online.' (2000) *Information Week*, 17 April: 93. See also http://www.xbrl.org/Overview.htm (accessed 5 March 2001).

3 THE FUTURE FOR PUBLIC OPINION – 'AN IMITATION OF CLOSENESS'

'After Enron: The Ideal Corporation; Following the abuses of the '90s, executives are learning that trust, integrity, and fairness do matter – and are crucial to the bottom line.' (2002) *Business Week*, 26 August: 68.

'Already maxed out.' (2002) *Communications of the ACM*, July, 45(7): 12.

Andrews, W. (2001) 'Bohemian Communities in a Buttoned-Down World.' *Gartner Group Research Note*. 27 June.

Backer, L. (2001) 'The mediated transparent society.' *Corporate Reputation Review*, Autumn, 4(3): 235–51.

Chisick, H. (2002) 'Public opinion and political culture in France during the second half of the eighteenth century.' *English Historical Review*, February, 117(470): 48.

Churchill, Winston S. (1932) *Thoughts and Adventures*. London: Odhams.

'Cleansing salts for food labels.' (2002) *The Advertiser*, 13 March: 29.

Cooley, T. (1999) 'Interactive Communication – Public Relations on the Web.' *Public Relations Quarterly*, Summer, 44(2): 41.

'CropGen reports highlights absence of evidence on GM safety.' (2001) Soil Association news release, 7 December.

de Maistre, Josef (1797; 1994 edn) *Considerations on France*. Cambridge: Cambridge University Press.

Denning, Peter (2002) 'Internet time out: technology won't solve information overload. New commitment management practices will. (The Profession of IT).' *Communications of the ACM*, March, 45(3): 15–19.

'Do the right thing.' (2001) *BC Business*, 1 October: 33.

'Don't trust what you read on the web.' (2000) *Database and Network Journal*, December, 30(6): 7.

Drucker, Peter E. (1998) 'The next information revolution.' *Forbes*, 24 August.

'EU ruling on allergens hits food labelling.' (2004) *Marketing Week*. London, 4 November: 8.

'Food labelling creates storm in Germany.' (2004) *Canadian Grocer,* October: 27.

Fox, Robert (2002) 'A blessing and a curse.' (News Track). *Communications of the ACM*, February, 45(2): 9.

Freitag, Alan (1999) 'Dit dit dit – dash dash dash – Dit Dit Dit: SOS for PR Orthodoxy?' *Public Relations Quarterly*, Winter, 44(4): 36.

Grankvist, Gunne, Dahlstrand, Ulf and Biel, Anders (2004) 'The impact of environmental labelling on consumer preference: negative vs. positive labels.' *Journal of Consumer Policy*, June, 27(2): 213–30.

'Government to send food label falsifiers to prison.' (2002) *Japan Economic Newswire*, 12 April.

'Information overload.' (2002) *The Grocer*, 23 March: 42.

Jaffry, Shabbar, Pickering, Helen, Premachandra, Wattage, Whitmarsh, David, Frere, Julian, Roth, Eva and Nielsen, Max (2004) 'Consumer choices for quality and sustainability in seafood products.' *Food Policy*, June, 29(3): 215–28.

Kolsky, E. (2001) 'CEO Update: How to Retain Customers and Their Loyalty During Economic Downturns.' Gartner Advisory. *Inside Gartner*. 5 December.

Leamer, E. E. and Storper, M. (2001) 'The economic geography of the Internet age (impact of the internet on international business).' *Journal of International Business Studies*, Winter, 32(4): 641–66.

'Many consumers still baffled by basic nutritional labelling.' (2002) *The Grocer*, 26 January: 12.

'Micro-retailing 2002: Fragmentation of the mass market.' (2002) Verdict Research news release, 2 April.

Pew Internet and American Life (2004) 'Content creation online.' Survey report. 29 February. Washington DC: Pew Internet and American Life Project.

Potato Growers of Idaho (undated) Website. About Us. Available: http://www.potatogrowersofidaho.com (accessed 8 May 2002).

'Potato Poll. Dietary Fallacy.' (2002) *Potato Grower*. Available http://www.potatogrower.com/pollresults.cfm. (accessed 8 May 2002).

'PR must embrace "the paradox of transparency".' (2001) *The Holmes Report*, 12 March: 3.

'Public opinion swings towards GM foods.' (2001) CropGen news release. 3 April.

'Public perceptions influence biotech advances, Idaho Potato Growers learn.' (2002) *Knight Ridder Tribune Business News*, 4 February.

Schneiderman, B. (2000) 'Designing trust into online experiences.' *Communications of the ACM*, December, 43(12): 57–9.

TellShell (1999) Uncensored forums. Engagement and open communication thread. 23 April. Available: http://www.shell.com/home/royal-en/html/iwgen/tellshell/thread2/Thread.htm (accessed 29 October 2004).

'The e-fluentials.' (2000) Burson-Marsteller Report, New York: 3.

'The power of online influencers: your company's newest stakeholder group.' (2002) Burson-Marsteller Report, New York: 2.

'TV the most preferred medium in Europe. TV meets the web.' (2002). *M2 Communications Ltd/Van Dusseldorp & Partners*: Amsterdam, 15 February.

4 THE FRAGILE CORPORATION

'A vital part of the toolkit: logistics services.' (2002) *Financial Times*, 20 September: 5.

'Are Finance Directors burying their heads in the sand?' (2002) Orbys website, 28 August. Available: www.orbys.co.uk/press/press20020828.html (accessed 3 June 2003).

Ariss, Sonny, Nykodym, Nick and Cole-Laramore, Aimee A. (2002) 'Trust and technology in the virtual organization.' *SAM Advanced Management Journal*, Autumn, 67(4): 22–4.

'Backroom deals; Outsourcing to India.' (2002) *The Economist*, 22 February, 366 (8312).

'Bay, Wal-Mart win "Sweatshop" award.' (2002) *Toronto Star*, 19 December: C09.

Braue, David (2002) 'Home and away (telecommuting trend grows in Australia).' *The Bulletin with Newsweek*, 26 March, 120(6317): 62–4.

'British corporations heading to India for cheap labour.' (2003) *The Press Trust of India*. 14 February.

'BT employees highlight benefits and drawbacks of teleworking.' (2003) *Human Resource Management International Digest*. Bradford, 11(2): 17–21.

Campos, Guy (2000) 'Financial services firms risk outsourcing disaster.' (Government Activity), *Computer Weekly*, 15 June: 6.

Cap Gemini Ernst and Young UK (2003) 'New survey highlights communication issues that are hampering UK outsourcing projects.' Cap Gemini Ernst and Young UK news release (PR1455), 28 May. Available: http://www.uk.cgey.com/news/pr2003/pr1455.shtml (accessed 7 August 2003).

Carr, Nicholas (2003) 'IT doesn't matter.' *Harvard Business Review*, May, 81(5): 41–9, 128.

Carr, Nicholas (2004) *Does IT Matter? Information Technology and the Corrosion of Competitive Advantage*. Cambridge, MA: Harvard Business School Press.

'Controversy over bank move.' (2003) *New Straits Times*, Malaysia. 8 June: 1.

'Data laws push firms to check suppliers' vetting procedures.' (2003) *Computer Weekly*, 23 March: 6.

Dimensioni (2004) 'Business Process Outsourcing (BPO).' Available http://www.dimensioni.net/web-services/BPO-outsourcing.html (accessed 10 December 2004).

'Down and out in white-collar America.' (2003) *Fortune*, 9 June.

Drucker, Peter (1986) 'The changed world economy.' *Foreign Affairs*, Spring, 64(4): 768–91.

'EDS "Not Prejudiced" by Standard Bank cancellation.' (2002) *Africa News*, 11 July.

'5 keys to getting top value from your contractors.' (2003) *Customer Interface*, January: 10.

'Focus on converged communication solutions pays off: Tata Telecom's 2002–03 PAT shows 18% growth.' (2003) Tata Telecom news release. India: Mumbai, 21 May.

Foster, Tom (1999) '4PLs: The next generation for supply chain outsourcing?' *Logistics Management & Distribution Report*, 30 April, 38(4): 35–6.

Fowler, Julia (2003) 'Offshore deals or employees: you decide.' *Computer Weekly*, 6 May: 33.

'GE champions India's world class services.' (2003) *Financial Times*, 3 June: 11.

'Global chip sales growth forecast cut to 10% this year; Industry group cites Sars, Iraq war, low IT spending.' (2003) *The Business Times Singapore*, 13 June.

IPOA (2004a) Website homepage. Available: http://www.ipoaonline.org (accessed 9 December 2004).

IPOA (2004b) Mission. 'IPOA's mission is to end wars.' Available: http://www.ipoaonline.org/background/mission.htm (accessed 9 December 2004).

Kistner, Toni (2004) 'Mixed messages of telework's future.' *Network World*. Framingham, MA, 2 August, 21(31): 28.

'Letting go but not giving up.' (2003) *Financial Mail*, South Africa. 14 February: 42.

Miller, Jim (2001) 'Managing the risks in outsourcing.' *Biopharm*, June, 25(6): 82.

Nasscom (2003) Why India: Competitive Costs. Available: http://www.nasscom.org/artdisplay.asp?cat_id=31 (accessed 2 November 2004).

'Nike Statement Regarding Indonesia Report.' (2002) Nike news release. 7 March. Nikebiz.com, Beaverton, Oregon. Available: http://www.nike.com/nikebiz/news/pressrelease.jhtml?year=2002&month=03&letter=c (accessed 5 October 2002).

OECD (2003) *OECD Employment Outlook 2003. Towards More and Better Jobs.* OECD.

'Offshore outsourcing will destroy livelihoods.' (2003) Letter. *Computer Weekly*, 24 June: 32.

'Opinion: Outsourcing offers route to efficiency but not a short cut.' (2003) *Marketing*, 6 March: 17.

'Outsourcing is inevitable, but all is not lost.' (2003) Letter. *Computer Weekly*, 24 June: 32.

'Outsourcing the dirty work; the military and its reliance on hired guns.' (2003) *The American Prospect*, May: 17.

'Peak season hangs in the balance.' (2003) *South China Morning Post*, 27 June: 8.

'Philippine Leader aims to lure more outsourcing.' (2003) *Boston Globe*, 22 May.

Quah, D. T. (1997) 'Weightless economy packs a heavy punch.' *Independent on Sunday*, 18 May: 4.

Riabokon, Volodymyr (2002) 'Outsourcing Risk Management.' *Energy-Markets.com*. Available: http://www.energy-markets.com/reports/RISKColumn.pdf (accessed 3 May 2003). See also company White Paper (2002) 'Outsourcing Risk Management Applications for Utility companies.' Lohika Systems Inc., San Mateo, CA. January.

Schwartz, Nelson D. (2003) 'The Pentagon's Private Army.' *Fortune*, 17 March, 147(5): 100.

'6 ways to effectively manage your software development risk.' (undated) Thomas Parackal, CEO, Stylus/Indiaweb, Bangalore India. Available: http://www.indiawebdevelopers.com/client_care/riskmanagement.asp (accessed 23 June 2003).

'Software company tries to survive terrorism investigation.' (2002) *Associated Press*. 31 December.

'Standard Bank opts for in-house strategy.' (2002) Standard Bank news release. July, 2002. Available: http://www.standardbank.co.za/site/about/aboutPressHistory51. html (accessed 5 October 2002).

'Study: Outsourced HR Growing.' (2002) *eWeek*, 18 July.

'Support Indian bank workers' fight for justice.' (2002) Available: http://www.unifi. org.uk/international/circulars/IndianBanks110302.htm (accessed 5 December 2003).

Swaminathan, J. M. (2003) 'SARS exposes risk of global supply chains.' *Journal of Commerce*, 9 June: 38.

'Tactical outsourcing: a smart play in uncertain times.' (2001) *Communications News*, December, 38(12): 50–1.

Taylor, Robert (2002) 'Britain's world of work: myths and realities.' Economic and Social Research Council Report. UK: ESRC.

'Teleworking.' (2003) *Labour Market Trends*. London: September, 111(9): 433.

'Telework connection. Benefits to the environment.' Undated. Available: http://www. telework-connection.com/environment-benefits.htm (accessed 7 June 2003).

'The man who invented management.' (2001) *Weekly Toyo-keizai*. Interview with Atsuo Ueda. 16 June. Online. Available: http://www.iot.ac.jp/manu/ueda/ (accessed 30 November 2004).

The Outsourcing Institute (1998) 'Top Ten Outsourcing Survey.' Available: http:// www.outsourcing.com/content.asp?page=01i/articles/intelligence/oi_top_ten_ survey.html&nonav=true (accessed 14 April 2002).

Theroux, Paul (2000) *Fresh Air Fiend*. Boston: Houghton Mifflin.

'Top 100 contracts suggest a bright future for the Outsourcing Services Market, IDC says.' (2003) IDC news release. Framingham, MA, 9 June. Available: http://www. prnewswire.com/news/ (accessed 23 June 2003).

Verton, Dan (2003) 'Ptech workers tell the story behind the search.' *Computerworld*, 17 January. Available: http://www.computerworld.com/securitytopics/security/ story/0,10801,77682,00.html (accessed 2 August 2003).

Washtech (2002) Available: http://www.washtech.org/reports/ (accessed 3 May 2002).

'Where's your contractor's work force?' (2002) *eWeek*, 13 May.

5 DESCENT INTO THE MAELSTROM: THE UNEXPECTED CRISIS

Berlin, Isaiah (1959; 1992 edn) *The Crooked Timber of Humanity*. New York: Vintage.

Bernays, Edward (1928; 2005 edn) *Propaganda*. New York: Ig.

Broch, Hermann (1930; 1986 edn) *The Sleepwalkers*. London: Quartet.

IMT (2000) 'The impact of the internet on public relations and business communication.' *Tactical Insights*. Connecticut: IMT Strategies.

James, William (1901–2; 1994 edn) *The Varieties of Religious Experience*. Being the Gifford Lectures on Natural Religion Delivered at Edinburgh. New York: Modern Library.

Le Bon, Gustave (1895; 2002 edn) *The Crowd: A Study of the Popular Mind*. UK: Dover.

6 LEARNING CONVERSATIONAL TRANSPARENCY

Bellini, James (1999) 'Emotions will rule in 2025: Futurist.' *The Age*. Melbourne, 13 October: Business Section 1.

Bin Laden: 'Goal is to bankrupt US.' (2004) CNN.com World. November 1. Available: http://www.cnn.com/2004/WORLD/meast/11/01/binladen.tape/index.html (accessed 2 November 2004).

Brady, Peter J. (1994) 'How likeability and effectiveness ratings of college professors by their students are affected by course demands and professors' attitudes.' *Psychological Reports*, June, 74(3): 907–14.

Bunting, Madeline (2004) *Willing Slaves: How the Overwork Culture is Ruining Our Lives*. London: HarperCollins.

Burson-Marsteller (2003) 'Burson-Marsteller Launches New Analytic Tool To Gauge Web-Based Crisis Communication. Burson-Marsteller's Prepare Helps Organizations Put Their Web Sites To Work In Times Of Crisis.' e-Fluentials news release. New York, 23 April.

Burson-Marsteller (2004) 'Crisis and Issues Management.' Company website. Available: http://www.bm.com/pages/functional/crisis (accessed 16 September 2004).

'Can we still be sure of Shell?' (2004) BBC News online, 5 February. Available: http://news.bbc.co.uk/1/hi/business/3461145.stm (accessed 15 May 2004).

'Cefic aims to recapture "Trust".' (2004) *Chemical Week*, 13 October, 166(33): 19.

Center for Public Integrity (2003) 'Winning Contractors. US contractors reap the windfalls of post-war reconstruction.' 30 October. Available: www.publicintegrity.com/wow/report.aspx?aid=65 (accessed 20 November 2004).

Channel 9 (2004) 'The 9 guys – who we are.' Seattle. Available: http://channel9.msdn.com/ShowPost.aspx?PostID=74 (accessed 27 October 2004).

Channel 9 (2004) 'Channel 9 Doctrine.' Seattle. Available: http://channel9.msdn.com/ShowPost.aspx?PostID=110 (accessed 27 October 2004).

Channel 9 (2004) 'Video introduction to who we are.' Seattle. Available: http://channel9.msdn.com/ShowPost.aspx?PostID=74 (accessed 27 October 2004).

'ChevronTexaco response to reclassification of Shell Reserves.' (2004) ChevronTexaco Press release. 9 January.

Derakhshan, Hossein (2004) Available: http://www.hoder.com/weblog/ (accessed 27 November 2004).

Erdem, Tulin and Swait, Joffre (2004) 'Brand credibility, brand consideration, and choice.' *Journal of Consumer Research*, June, 31(1): 191–9.

EU (2004) Chemical Legislation in the EU. Available: http://www.eurunion.org/legislat/chemical.htm (accessed 14 December 2004).

Fernando, Angelo (2004) 'Big Blogger Is Watching You! Reputation Management in an Opinionated, Hyperlinked World.' *Communication World*, San Francisco: July/August, 21(4): 10–11.

'Firm's Iraq deals greater than Cheney has said; Affiliates had $73 million in contracts.' (2001) *Washington Post*, 23 June: A01.

Frayn, Michael (1998) *Copenhagen*. New York: Anchor.

Freemantle, David (1999) 'Recruit people who customers like – not ones who just fit the description.' (Workforce Extra). *Workforce*, January, 78(1): E8–12.

Gates, Bill (2004) 'Remarks by Bill Gates, Chairman and Chief Software Architect, Microsoft Corporation.' Microsoft CEO Summit 2004, Redmond, Washington.

20 May. Available: http://www.microsoft.com/billgates/speeches/2004/05–20CEO Summit.asp (accessed 17 October 2004).

Gillmor, Dan (2004) 'Executive blogging for fun and profit.' *Computerworld*, 2 August, 38(31): 14–15.

'GOP to play Bush's likability card; Speakers will tout his man-of-the-people style, but critics say his policies belie the image.' (2004) *Christian Science Monitor*, Boston, MA, 31 August: 1.

Halliburton (2003) 'Halliburton provides update on fuel delivery mission in Iraq.' Halliburton News Release, October 21.

Halliburton (2004a) Current Iraq Situation. Press statements. May *passim*.

Halliburton (2004b) FAQs. Available: www.halliburton.com/news/faq.jsp (accessed 2 November 2004).

Halliburton (2004c) Homepage. Available: www.halliburton.com (accessed 2 November 2004).

Henry L. Stimson Center (2002) 'Compliance through science: US pharmaceutical industry experts on a strengthened bioweapons nonproliferation regime. A collaborative research report of experts from the US pharmaceutical and biotechnology industries.' Report No. 48. September. Washington: Stimson Center.

Hill and Knowlton (2004) Corporate website. Practices – marketing. Available: http://www.hillandknowlton.com/us/index/practices (accessed 30 September, 2004).

'Inside story: profits of war.' (2004) *Guardian*, 22 July: Features, p. 16.

Kahle, Lynn R. and Homer, Pamela M. (1985) 'Physical attractiveness of the celebrity endorser: a social adaptation perspective.' *The Journal of Consumer Research*, 11(4), March: 954–61.

'Kerry and the "likability" index; Campaign stresses his "softer" side to offset an aloof image.' (2004) *Christian Science Monitor*, Boston, MA, 27 July: 01.

Kiss, Jemima (2004) 'Labour chair takes to the blog.' *Dot Journalism: online news for online journalists*. Posted: 30 September. Available: http://www.journalism.co.uk/news/story1083.shtml (accessed 30 September 2004).

Knobel, Lance (2004) 'Conversations not messages.' Unpublished paper. London: Edelman.

Leather, Phil, McKechnie, Sally and Amirkhanian, Manon (1994) 'The importance of likeability as a measure of television advertising effectiveness.' *International Journal of Advertising*, Summer, 13(3): 265–81.

Mitchell, Ronald B. (1998) 'Sources of transparency: Information systems in international regimes.' *International Studies Quarterly*, 42: 109–30.

9/11 Commission (2004) *Final Report of the National Commission on Terrorist Attacks Upon the United States*. Authorized edition with index. New York: Norton.

Ochman, B. L. (2004) 'PR people not getting blogging.' 29 October. Available: http://www.whatsnextblog.com/archives/2004/10/pr_people_not_g.asp (accessed 9 December 2004).

O'Neill, Onora (2002) 'Trust and Transparency.' Reith Lecture 4. Available: http://www.bbc.co.uk/radio4/reith2002/lecture4.shtml (accessed 10 November 2004).

Ortega y Gasset, Jose (1930; 1957 edn) *The Revolt of the Masses*, New York, Norton.

'Oxburgh: Shell Chairman apologizes to investors.' (2004) *Forbes*, 29 July. Available: http://www.forbes.com/facesinthenews/2004/06/29/0629autofacescan03.html (accessed 2 November 2004).

Pew Internet and American Life (2004) 'Content creation online.' Survey report. 29 February. Washington DC: Pew Internet and American Life Project.

Philip Morris International (2004) Corporate website. *Homepage.* Available: www.philipmorrisinternational.com. (accessed 15 September 2004).

Philip Morris USA (2004) Corporate website. *Mission and Values.* Available: www.philipmorrisusa.com (accessed 15 September 2004).

Phillips, Nelson and Brown, John L. (1993) 'Analyzing communication in and around organizations: a critical hermeneutic approach.' *Academy of Management Journal,* December, 36(6): 1547–76.

Rees, Martin (2004) *Our Final Hour.* New York: Basic Books.

Rubel, Steve (2004) 'CEO bloggers should be conversational executive officers.' 27 October. Available: http://www.micropersuasion.com/2004/10/ceo_bloggers_sh.html (accessed 9 December 2004).

Sewell, Graham (1998) 'The discipline of teams: the control of team-based industrial work through electronic and peer surveillance.' *Administrative Science Quarterly,* Special Issue: Critical Perspectives on Organizational Control. June, 43(2): 397–428.

Shell (2004a) 'Proved reserve recategorisation following internal review: No material effect on financial statements.' Shell news release, 9 January.

Shell (2004b) 'Message to staff from Sir Philip Watts on the recategorisation of proved hydrocarbon reserves.' 16 January.

Shell (2004c) 'Royal Dutch/Shell group of companies management changes.' Shell news release. 3 March.

'Shell auditors told of problems with overstated reserves two years ago.' (2004) *The Independent,* 16 July: 39.

'Shell needs to open up to fresh thinking.' (2004) *Financial Times,* 6 February: 20.

Shell UK (2004a) 'New Academy for Corporate Social Responsibility was launched last night.' Shell news release, 6 July.

Shell UK (2004b) Corporate website. *Issues.* Available: www.shell.com (accessed 28 September 2004).

Simple, Peter (a.k.a. Michael Wharton) (1969) *More of Peter Simple.* London: Johnson.

Tapscott, Donald (2002) 'It's a blue world.' *Intelligent Enterprise,* 16 April: 18, 21.

Tapscott, Donald and Ticoll, David (2003) *The Naked Corporation: How the Age of Transparency will Revolutionize Business.* Toronto: Viking Canada.

Tapscott, Donald and Ticoll, David (2004) 'The best-seller that isn't (yet).' *Across the Board.* New York. July/August, 41(4): 9.

'The "likability" issue takes center stage.' (2004) *Boston Globe* (third edition), 13 June: H.12.

'The struggle for Iraq; reconstruction; Bush got $500,000 from companies that got contracts, study finds.' (2003) *The New York Times,* 31 October: Section A, Col. 1, p. 8.

'Transparency demands for a new EU chemicals policy.' (2002) Joint statement by environmental and animal protection groups. 15 April. Brussels. Available: http://www.foe.co.uk/resource/briefings/transparent_eu_chemicals.pdf (accessed 5 April 2003).

Tripp, Carolyn, Jensen, Thomas D. and Carlson, Les (1994) 'The effects of multiple product endorsements by celebrities on consumers' attitudes and intentions.' *The Journal of Consumer Research,* March, 20(4): 535–47.

'Ultimatum for Shell chief after oil reserve bombshell.' (2004) *Sunday Times,* 11 January: Business, p. 1.

'Underclass of workers created in Iraq.' (2004) *Washington Post,* 1 July: A01.

UPI report (2001) 'Halliburton Iraq ties more than Cheney said.' *NewsMax,* 25 June. Available: www.newsmax.com/archives/articles/2001/6/24/80648.shtml (accessed 27 June 2002).

Von Furstenberg, George M. (2001) 'Hopes and delusions of transparency.' *North American Journal of Economics and Finance,* Greenwich: March, 12(1): 105.

What's the key to landing a job? Your best asset is likability.' (2004) *Knight Ridder Tribune Business News.* Washington: 7 July: 1.

7 DEVOLUTION AND FISSION: THE FUTURE FOR REPUTATION MANAGEMENT

Ajakaiye, Alaba (2004) 'Rewriting Nigeria's History.' *Vanguard,* Nigeria. 7 October.

Ajayi, Femi (2004) 'The Nigeria Image Project – the way to go!' *Nigeriaworld,* 16 August. Available: *http://nigeriaworld.com/columnist/ajayi/081604.html* (accessed 14 October 2004).

Aon Corporation (2003) 'Greatest threats to business.' The Aon European Risk Management and Insurance Survey. (Chicago) Available: http://www.aon.com/about/publications/issues/uk_2003_survey/2003_uk_greatest_threats.jsp (accessed 15 October 2004).

'Aon may face civil suit.' (2004) *CNNmoney. CNN Website.* 25 October. Available: http://money.cnn.com/2004/10/25/news/fortune500/aon.reut/index.htm (accessed 25 October 2004).

Aon Press Releases (2004) Statement of Aon Corporation On New York Attorney General Complaint Against Marsh & McLennan. Chicago, IL – October 14 – (Aon Corporation NYSE: AOC). Available: http://www.aon.com/about/news/press_release/pr_007FC4E6.jsp (accessed 20 October 2004).

'Benetton accused of land grabbing in Patagonia.' (2004) ANSA English Media Service. 14 July.

'Brand Nigeria: Lessons from Proudly S. Africa Campaign.' (2004) *Liquid Africa,* 8 June.

'Business: Shell advert seeks "our man in Iraq".' (2004) *Guardian* (London) Final Edition. 11 August: Guardian City, 16.

Chambers, Eleanor, Chapple, Wendy, Moon, Jeremy and Sullivan, Michael (2003) 'CSR in Asia: a seven country study of CSR website reporting.' *ICCSR Research Paper Series,* No 09–2003. ISSN – 1479–5124. UK: Nottingham University.

Chukwuemeka, Chikelu (2004) Publisher's Pitch. *Nigeria Monthly,* June, 1(1). Available: http://www.nigeria.gov.ng/ (accessed 13 October 2004).

Clausewitz, Carl von (1812; 1942 edn) *Principles of War.* Pennsylvania: Telegraph Press.

Clausewitz, Carl von. (1832; 1993 edn) *On War.* New York: Everyman's Library.

Colors (2004) Benetton. Available: http://www.colorsmagazine.com/issues/colors62/index.php (accessed 10 November 2004).

Copenhagen Centre (2004) http://www.copenhagencentre.org/sw204.asp Denmark. (accessed 7 November 2004).

'Deceptive practices are found at Aon, too.' (2004) *New York Times,* 25 October. Available: www.nytimes.com (accessed 25 October 2004).

DTI (2004) www.societyandbusiness.gov.uk (accessed 3 November 2004).

DTI; Forum for the Future (2003) *Sustainability and Business Competitiveness*. London: Forum for the Future. December. Available: www.societyandbusiness.gov.uk.

Edelman (2004) *2004 Trust Barometer: An Annual Study of Opinion Formers in Key Global Markets*, New York: Edelman.

Frayn, Michael (1998) *Copenhagen*. New York: Anchor.

Ganesan, Arvind and Takirambudde, Peter (2003) Letter to Shell Petroleum Development Company of Nigeria. Human Rights Watch. 7 April. Available: http://www.hrw.org/press/2003/04/nigeria040703shell.htm. (accessed 1 November 2004).

'German official issues crisp warning on fried foods.' (2002) *Deutsche Presse-Agentur*, 13 November.

'Hajara Ibrahim's family appeals against death sentence.' (2004) *The Vanguard*, Nigeria, 25 October.

'High cancer risks from fried potatoes, other staples: report.' (2002) *Agence France Presse*, 24 April.

'Hit or miss . . . Benetton.' (2004) *PR Week*, 9 July: 52.

Kagan, Robert (2003) *Of Paradise and Power: America and Europe in the New World Order*, New York: Knopf.

Klein, Naomi (2000) *No Space, No Jobs, No Logo: Taking Aim at the Brand Bullies*, Canada: Knopf.

'Land "gift" from Benetton spurned.' (2004) BBC News online. 10 November. Available: http://news.bbc.co.uk/2/hi/americas/3999201.stm (accessed 10 November 2004).

Maio, Elsie (2003) 'Managing brand in the new stakeholder environment.' *Journal of Business Ethics*, May: 235–47.

Ministry of Petroleum Resources. (2004a) Major Policy Thrusts. Available: http://www.nigeria.gov.ng/ministries/petroleum.htm (accessed 20 November 2004).

Ministry of Petroleum Resources (2004b) Functions and Responsibilities. Available: http://www.nigeria.gov.ng/ministries/petroleum.htm (accessed 20 November 2004).

'N/Assembly ready to assist in branding Nigeria.' (2004) *Vanguard*, Nigeria, 27 February.

'Nigerian president launches "Image Project" to change nation's bad image.' (2004) *Xinhua News Agency*, 14 July.

'NLC Begins Indefinite Strike Nov 16.' (2004) Nigerian Labour Congress news release. 1 November. Available: http://www.nlcng.org/november2004/strikestartsnovember16.htm (accessed 1 November 2004).

Nworah, Uche (2004) Diasporas and the Nigerian Image Project. Weblog, 6 September. Available: http://www.nigeriavillagesquare1.com/Articles/Nworah/2004/09/uche-Diasporas.html (accessed 13 October 2004).

Office of the Under Secretary of State for Defense (2004) Report of the Defense Science Board Task Force on Strategic Communication. September, Washington DC: Department of Defense.

'Opinion: Marketing Society – Brands are now judged on what they do, not say.' (2003) *Marketing*, 11 December: 18.

'Our ethical policy statements: Human Rights.' (2004) The Co-op Bank, UK. Available: http://www.co-operativebank.co.uk (accessed 19 October 2004).

Rankin Frost, Alison and Cooke, Chris (1999) 'Brand vs. reputation: managing an intangible asset.' *Communication World*, February–March, 16(3), 22–5.

Russell, Bertrand (1946, 2nd edn 1991) *History of Western Philosophy*. London: Routledge.

'Scandal returns to haunt Total Oil & Gas.' (2004) *Financial Times,* 4 October, London Edition 1, Companies International: 27.

Shakespeare, William (c. 1611; 1988 edn) *Othello,* in Stanley Wells and Gary Taylor (eds) *The Oxford Shakespeare. The Complete Works. Compact Edition*. Oxford: Oxford University Press.

'Sharing Our Energies' (2003) Corporate Social Responsibility Report. Total, France. Available: http://www.total.com/en/home_page/ (accessed 19 October 2004).

Shell Production and Exploration (2004) 'Shell appoints first Nigerian to head SPDC as Finlayson becomes EP Africa CEO.' Shell news release. 20 July. Available: http:/ /www.shell.com/home/Framework?siteId=eandp-en&FC2=&FC3=/eandp-en/html/ iwgen/news_and_library/press_releases/2004/spdc_first_nigerian_ceo_19072004. html (accessed 29 October 2004).

Shellfacts. Available: http://www.shellfacts.com/background.html (accessed 2 November 2004).

'Stockholm shops report reduction in sales of crisps.' (2002) *Nordic Business Report,* 26 April.

'Stoning sentence appeal.' (2004) *The Sun,* 27 October. Available: http://www. thesun.co.uk/article/0,,2-2004500524,,00.html (accessed 27 October 2004).

'Swedish, U.S. researchers dispute link between acrylamide and some types of cancers.' (2003) *The Associated Press,* 29 January.

Tapscott, Don and Ticoll, David (2003) *The Naked Corporation: How the Age of Transparency Will Revolutionize Business*. Canada: Viking.

'The Teflon Shield.' (2001) 'TRENCH WAR: With activists on the march, multi-nationals are desperate to deflect the brand-bashing attacks of the anti-global protesters. Here's how the prototypical Teflon multinational does it.' *Newsweek International*, 12 March.

Third World Traveler. Oil Watch. Available: http://www.thirdworldtraveler.com/ Oil_watch/Oil_watch.html (accessed 2 November 2004).

'''This isn't another food scare − this is really important.'' High levels of acrylamide found in some popular foods, including those promoted as being good for your health − such as cereals and crispbread − have sparked an urgent investigation into their link to cancer, reports Lorraine Fraser.' (2002) *Sunday Telegraph,* 30 June: 16.

Transparency International Corruption Perceptions Index (2004) Press release and Index. 20 October. Available: http://www.transparency.org/pressreleases_archive/ 2004/2004.10.20.cpi.en.html (accessed 21 October 2004).

'TotalFinaElf shortening name to Total.' (2003) *The Independent,* 7 May.

Wasabrod (2004) Website. Facts about Wasabrod. Available: http://www.wasa.com/ Wasa/smpage.fwx?page=2&main=about (accessed 8 November 2004).

'Who has the right to criticize?' (2004) BBC News online. 21 October. Available: http:/ /news.bbc.co.uk/1/hi/world/africa/3764370.stm (accessed 22 October 2004).

'WHO to hold meeting from June 25 on cancer-causing acrylamide in food.' (2002) *Agence France Presse,* 21 June.

Young, Dave (2004) Branding Nigeria. Branding Blog, 27 February. Available: http:// www.brandingblog.com/2004/02/branding_nigeri.html (accessed 21 October 2004).

CONCLUSION: CARTHAGO DELENDA EST?

Angell, Norman (1910) *The Great Illusion; A Study of the Relation of Military Power in Nations to Their Economic and Social Advantage*. London: W. Heinemann.

Bunting, Madeleine (2004) *Willing Slaves: How the Overwork Culture is Ruining Our Lives*. London: HarperCollins.

'Businesses, Banks Need to Be Better Prepared for Disasters.' (2002) *Electronic Commerce News*, 1 April.

Clausewitz, Carl von (1832; 1993 edn) *On War*. New York: Everyman's Library.

Friedman, Milton and Friedman, Rose (1979; 1990 edn) *Free to Choose*. San Diego: Harcourt Brace.

Gelb, Leslie H. (2004) A matter of trust. *Edelman 2004 Trust Barometer*. New York: Edelman.

Harris, Clare E. (1999) Our experiences with the internet dialogue. Email, 16 November. TellShell Forum. 'Our values and commitments' discussion thread, in 'engagement and open communication.' Available: http://www-forums.shell.com/ (accessed: 2 September 2003).

Hill, Christopher (1996) 'World opinion and the empire of circumstance.' *International Affairs (Royal Institute of International Affairs 1944–)*, January, 72(1): 109–31.

Marx, Karl (1867; 1887 edn) *Das Kapital*. Volume 1. Frederick Engels (ed.) 1975 reprinting. New York: International Publishers.

Marx, Karl and Engels, Frederick (1848; 1998 edn) *The Communist Manifesto: A Modern Edition*. London: Verso.

'PR must embrace "the paradox of transparency".' (2001) *The Holmes Report*, 12 March: 3.

Shakespeare, William (*c.* 1611; 1988 edn) *The Winter's Tale*, in Stanley Wells and Gary Taylor (eds) *The Oxford Shakespeare. The Complete Works. Compact Edition*. Oxford: Oxford University Press.

Tainter, Joseph (1988) *The Collapse of Complex Societies*. Cambridge: Cambridge University Press.

Underhill, Paco (2004) *Call of the Mall*. New York: Simon & Schuster.

'Wartime CIOs alter security strategies.' (2002) *Computerworld*, 8 April: 14.

WTO (2004) The Ten Benefits. WTO website. Available: http://www.wto.org/english/ thewto_e/whatis_e/10ben_e/10b01_e.htm (accessed 19 November 2004).

Bibliography

BOOKS

Clausewitz, Carl von (1812; 1942 edn) *Principles of War*. Pennsylvania: Telegraph Press.

Clausewitz, Carl von (1832; 1993 edn) *On War*. New York: Everyman's Library.

Innis, Harold (1950) *Empire and Communications*. Oxford: Oxford University Press.

Klein, Naomi (2000) *No Space, No Jobs, No Logo: Taking Aim at the Brand Bullies*. Canada: Knopf.

Le Bon, Gustave (1895, 2002 edn) *The Crowd: A Study of the Popular Mind*. UK: Dover.

Moloney, Kevin (2002) *Rethinking Public Relations*. London: Routledge.

Rees, Martin (2004) *Our Final Hour*. New York: Basic Books.

Regester, Mike and Larkin, Judy (2001) *Risk Issues and Crisis Management*. London: Kogan Page.

Seymour, Mike and Moore, Simon (1999) *Effective Crisis Management: Worldwide Principles and Practice*. London: Thomson Learning.

Silva, M. and McGann, T. (1995) *Overdrive: Managing in Crisis-Filled Times*. New York: Wiley.

Slevin, J. (2000) *The Internet and Society*. Cambridge: Polity Press.

Tainter, Joseph (1988) *The Collapse of Complex Societies*, Cambridge: Cambridge University Press.

Tapscott, Donald and Ticoll, David (2003) *The Naked Corporation: How the Age of Transparency will Revolutionize Business*. Toronto: Viking Canada.

Van Dijk, J. (1991; 2000 edn) *The Network Society*. London: Sage.

ARTICLES

Ariss, Sonny, Nykodym, Nick and Cole-Laramore, Aimee A. (2002) 'Trust and technology in the virtual organization.' *SAM Advanced Management Journal*, Autumn, 67(4): 22–4.

'Businesses, Banks Need to Be Better Prepared for Disasters.' (2002) *Electronic Commerce News*, 1 April.

Carr, Nicholas (2003) 'IT doesn't matter.' *Harvard Business Review*, May, 81(5): 41–9, 128.

Chambers, Eleanor, Chapple, Wendy, Moon, Jeremy and Sullivan, Michael (2003) 'CSR in Asia: A seven country study of CSR website reporting.' *ICCSR Research Paper Series*. No 09-2003. ISSN – 1479-5124. UK: Nottingham University.

179

Cockburn, Tom and McKie, David (2004) 'Imaging uncertainty: creative tales of corporate and global futures.' *Global Business and Economics Review,* June, 6(1): 92–106.

Drucker, Peter (1986) 'The changed world economy.' *Foreign Affairs,* Spring, 64(4): 768–91.

Erdem, Tulin and Swait, Joffre (2004) 'Brand credibility, brand consideration, and choice.' *Journal of Consumer Research,* June, 31(1): 191–9.

Hill, Christopher (1996) 'World opinion and the empire of circumstance.' *International Affairs (Royal Institute of International Affairs 1944–),* January, 72(1): 109–31.

Maio, Elsie (2003) 'Managing brand in the new stakeholder environment.' *Journal of Business Ethics,* May: 235–47.

Moore, Simon (2004) 'Disaster's future: the prospects for corporate crisis management and communication.' *Business Horizons,* January–February, 47(1): 29–36.

Pearson, Ian (2000) 'The power of direct action'. *Sphere,* BT's innovation and technology e-zine, 29 November. Available: http://www.bt.com/sphere/insights/pearson/ (accessed 18 January 2002).

Penrose, J. M. (2000) 'The role of perception in crisis planning.' *Public Relations Review,* Summer, 26(2): 155–71.

Phillips, Nelson and Brown, John L. (1993) 'Analyzing communication in and around organizations: a critical hermeneutic approach.' *Academy of Management Journal,* December, 36(6): 1547–76.

Pines, Wayne (2000) 'Myths of crisis management.' *Public Relations Quarterly,* Fall, 45(3): 15.

Rankin Frost, Alison and Cooke, Chris (1999) 'Brand vs. reputation: managing an intangible asset.' *Communication World,* February–March, 16(3), 22–5.

Tapscott, Donald (2002) 'It's a blue world.' *Intelligent Enterprise,* 16 April: 18, 21.

'The Teflon Shield.' (2001) 'TRENCH WAR: With activists on the march, multinationals are desperate to deflect the brand-bashing attacks of the anti-global protesters. Here's how the prototypical Teflon multinational does it.' *Newsweek International,* 12 March.

Von Furstenberg, George M. (2001) 'Hopes and delusions of transparency.' *North American Journal of Economics and Finance,* Greenwich: March, 12(1): 105.

REPORTS, SPEECHES

Aon Corporation (2003) 'Greatest threats to business.' The Aon European Risk Management and Insurance Survey (Chicago). Available: http://www.aon.com/about/publications/issues/uk_2003_survey/2003_uk_greatest_threats.jsp (accessed 15 October 2004).

Colors (2004) Benetton. Available: http://www.colorsmagazine.com/issues/colors62/index.php (accessed 10 November 2004).

Edelman (2004) *2004 Edelman Trust Barometer.* New York: Edelman.

Gates, Bill (2004) 'Remarks by Bill Gates, Chairman and Chief Software Architect, Microsoft Corporation'. Microsoft CEO Summit 2004, Redmond, Washington. 20 May. Available: http://www.microsoft.com/billgates/speeches/2004/05-20CEO Summit.asp (accessed 17 October 2004).

'Interactive PR: The party starts now' (2001) Unpublished report. Mainsail Interactive Services: 3. Available: http://www.prfirms.org/docs/mainsail_whitepaper.pdf. (accessed 5 January 2002).

Kang, Liu Ming (2000) 'Corporate governance in China: issues and prospects.' President's Speech. Bank of China, June. Available http://www.bank-of-china.com (accessed 9 April 2002).

OECD (2003) *OECD Employment Outlook 2003. Towards More and Better Jobs.* OECD.

Office of the Under Secretary of State for Defense (2004) Report of the Defense Science Board Task Force on Strategic Communication. September, Washington DC: Department of Defense.

'Permissible equity markets investment analysis and recommendations.' (2002) Prepared for The California Public Employers Retirement System. Preliminary. January. Wilshire Associates, Santa Monica, California.

Pew Internet and American Life (2004) 'Content creation online'. Survey report. 29 February. Washington DC: Pew Internet and American Life Project.

'Sharing Our Energies.' (2003) Corporate Social Responsibility Report. Total, France. Available: http://www.total.com/en/home_page/ (accessed 19 October 2004).

'The impact of the internet on public relations and business communication.' (2000) *Tactical Insights.* IMT Strategies. Connecticut.

'Transparency demands for a new EU chemicals policy.' (2002) Joint statement by environmental and animal protection groups. 15 April. Brussels. Available: http://www.foe.co.uk/resource/briefings/transparent_eu_chemicals.pdf (accessed 5 April 2003).

UN (2003) 'Norms on the responsibilities of transnational corporations and other business enterprises with regard to human rights.' Distr. GENERAL E/CN.4/Sub.2/2003/12/Rev.2. 26 August.

WEBSITES

CERT Coordination Center. Available: www.cert.org (accessed 5 December 2004).

Channel 9 (2004) 'The 9 guys – who we are.' Seattle. Available: http://channel9.msdn.com/ShowPost.aspx?PostID=74 (accessed 27 October 2004).

Dowethics – an anti-Dow site not connected to the company in any way, but a representative example of what some call a 'hate site': www.dowethics.com.

DTI (2004) www.societyandbusiness.gov.uk (accessed 3 November 2004).

IPOA (2004) Website homepage. Available: http://www.ipoaonline.org (accessed 9 December 2004).

Mi2G digital risk specialists. Available: http://www.mi2g.com/ (accessed 5 December 2004).

Philip Morris USA (2004) Corporate website. *Mission and Values.* Available: www.philipmorrisusa.com (accessed 15 September 2004).

Rubel, Steve (2004) 'CEO bloggers should be conversational executive Officers.' 27 October. Available: http://www.micropersuasion.com/2004/10/ceo_bloggers_sh.html (accessed 9 December 2004).

The Yes Men (2004) Website. Dow. 3 December. Available: http://www.theyesmen.org/hijinks/dow/ (accessed 10 December 2004).

Index

183